T0251302

Best Practices
in Business
Technology
Management

Best Practices
in Business
Technology
Management

Stephen J. Andriole

CRC Press
Taylor & Francis Group
Boca Raton   London   New York

CRC Press is an imprint of the
Taylor & Francis Group, an **informa** business
AN AUERBACH BOOK

Auerbach Publications
Taylor & Francis Group
6000 Broken Sound Parkway NW, Suite 300
Boca Raton, FL 33487-2742

© 2009 by Taylor & Francis Group, LLC
Auerbach is an imprint of Taylor & Francis Group, an Informa business

No claim to original U.S. Government works
Printed in the United States of America on acid-free paper
10 9 8 7 6 5 4 3 2 1

International Standard Book Number-13: 978-1-4200-6333-2 (Hardcover)

Library of Congress Cataloging-in-Publication Data

Andriole, Stephen J.
  Best practices in business technology management / Stephen J. Andriole.
    p. cm.
  Includes bibliographical references and index.
  ISBN 978-1-4200-6333-2
  1. Information technology--Management. I. Title.

HD30.2.A535 2008
658.5'14--dc22   2008010920

Visit the Taylor & Francis Web site at
http://www.taylorandfrancis.com

and the Auerbach Web site at
http://www.auerbach-publications.com

Contents

Preface

Best practices are often confusing, redundant, and subject to all varieties of interpretation. At the same time, they're often useful, the way maps are useful to first-time travelers. Even experienced travelers consult good maps from time to time, just as those responsible for the acquisition, deployment, and support of information technology (IT) sometimes need insight into what makes practical sense.

Practical is the key word. The best practices discussed here are not theoretical or untested. They are the result of trench warfare, of real applications, not ideas about what might work or what might make sense. They represent the discussions one might overhear among veteran technology professionals who have solved a lot of problems over the years.

The discussions are organized in six chapters:

- Chapter 1: Perspectives
- Chapter 2: Organization
- Chapter 3: People
- Chapter 4: Acquisition and Measurement
- Chapter 5: Operational Effectiveness
- Chapter 6: Strategic Effectiveness

Chapter 1, Perspectives, provides insight into the field, the way decisions are made, trends, alignment, optimization, processes, and timing, among other areas. Chapter 1 includes:

- The 5 × 7 Business Technology Strategy
- Revisiting the "IT Doesn't Matter" Argument
- Ten Things IT Should Tell Management
- Ten "New Rules" for IT
- Ten Questions for Everyone
- Still Too Many Dollars
- Preparing for the Tsunami
- IT's All about Processes

- Does Any of This Sound Familiar?
- Markets, Pills, and Timing
- That Was Then, This Is Now
- Trends That (Really) Matter
- What They're Doing
- Business Technology Trends to Worry About
- Collaborate/Integrate: What to Do about Business Technology
- Strategy, Anyone?

The essence of Chapter 1 is attitude, insights, and what it means to leverage technology on to business models and processes to yield cost management profitable growth. There's a fair amount of yelling in Chapter 1. Several sections provide an opportunity to yell at management, vendors, and the bean counters who throttle technology at every turn. Pay special attention to the fourth section ("Ten 'New Rules' for IT") and the ninth section ("Does Any of This Sound Familiar"). If you're cynical or skeptical, they will ring true.

Chapter 1's bookends discuss strategy—business strategy—and how technology needs a coherent, specific business strategy to optimize its contribution to success. Without a clear business strategy, even the most talented technology strategist will find it tough not to under- or overspend on IT.

Chapter 2, Organization, is exceedingly practical. It begins with a mission: alignment (also known as convergence or optimization). It then turns to self-imagery: cost centers versus profit centers. The "Just Enough Organization" section is the *Cliff Notes* of organizational structure. The chapter also addresses corporate culture ("Grading Industry Cultures"), the whole context of the business technology relationship ("The Whole Context and Nothing but the (Whole) Context"), and another identity self-assessment ("What Kind of Technology Center Are You, Really?").

The 21 sections in Chapter 2 are:

- Five Flavors of Alignment
- Cost versus Profit Centers
- Should Boards of Directors Govern Technology?
- Just Enough Organization
- Tuning Up the Business Technology Organization
- Would You Survive an Alignment Audit?
- You Report to Who?
- Who's Minding the Technology Store?—Time to Promote the Gurus
- Five Hours to Influence
- Grading Industry Cultures
- Whatever Happened to Mentoring, Meritocracies, and Sabbaticals?
- Has Anyone Been to Nordstrom's?
- Do You Have a CTMO?

- Another Audit
- The Whole Context and Nothing but the (Whole) Context
- What Kind of Technology Center Are You, Really?
- Who's in Control?
- Discipline
- Making Money with IT: Three Ideas for Revenue Generation
- A Little Exercise Goes a Long Way: Internal Focus Group Problem Solving
- Of PMOs, VMOs, and XMOs: Why So Many Management Offices?

Chapter 3, People, is a little scary, as it deliberately unveils some of the worst aspects of people in the business and the realities of Dilbert-like management. Chapter 3 includes:

- Time for New Skills: People Readiness for the Second Digital Revolution
- Feel My Pain
- IT Begins in the Classroom
- Decision-Making Discipline: An Executive Course on Multicriteria Selection Methods
- Theory versus Practice: Who Owns IT Education and Training?
- Tweaking Business Technology Leadership: What Academia Can Learn from Executive Education
- How's the Team Doing? An Unbalanced Scorecard
- Three Brands for the Millennium
- Can We Handle the Truth?
- The Real Truth
- Do You Speak Business?
- Leadership, Likability, and Life
- Politics, Culture, and You
- Consultants in the Hen House

Chapter 3 also discusses education, training, and professional development, along with leadership, likability, and corporate politics. There's a fair amount of truth-telling in this part of the book as well.

The real takeaway here is that we live in a professional world populated by lots of crazy people who, when forced to spend large amounts of time in cramped spaces, get crazier. The other takeaway is that it's really hard to find (and keep) good (qualified and sane) people.

Chapter 4 focuses on the Acquisition and Measurement of technology. The 19 sections discuss a range of topics including how to measure technology impact, how and when to in-source, co-source, and outsource, how to assess technology readiness, how to squeeze vendors, how to pay for technology, how to sell (and manage) tough technology projects, and how to turn vendors into bona fide partners. This chapter includes:

- Many Happy Returns
- Sourcing, Sourcing Everywhere
- Concepts to Clusters: The Real Technology Chasm
- Vendors, Vendors Everywhere … Who's the Fairest of Them All?
- Three Reasons More Outsourcing Is Inevitable
- Squeezing Willing—and Not-So-Willing—Vendors
- Guerilla Budgeting
- Dissenting Opinions about Outsourcing
- Selling Tough Projects
- What's Your Core IT Competency? Really?
- Who Pays for All This Stuff?
- Who's Measuring All This Stuff?
- Security Solutions Outsourcing: It's Time
- Project Management—Yes, Again …
- What to Do? Triangulating on Requirements
- Sourcing the Sources: Who Does What Today? Who Wins Tomorrow?
- Strategy, Applications, and Architecture Sourcing: Where There Are Still Competitive Advantages
- Advanced Vendor Management: A Graduate Course in the Optimization of Vendor Relationships
- Project Management Rigor (or Rigor Mortis)

The focus is on Operational Effectiveness in Chapter 5. The 18 sections in this chapter emphasize the decisions we should make to improve operational effectiveness, decisions like the selection of thin versus fat clients, to assess open source software, to pilot software-as-a-service, and decisions about which applications, communications, and infrastructure technology should command priority investments. This chapter includes:

- Thin Is Beautiful
- Vinfrastructure
- Another Look at Open Source Software
- Commodities: Where Premiums Meet Payments
- Who Needs PCs?
- Where Does Software Come From?
- Everyone to the Woodshed
- What You Need to Know about Pervasive Analytical Computing
- Ten Things You Can Do Tomorrow to Improve Biz/IT Convergence
- Killer Apps
- Communications
- Data's Still King
- Don't Forget the Plumbing
- Standards Now or (Lots of) Cash Later

- Should You Buy or Rent?
- Don't Crack the Box
- Data → Information → Decision Making: Platforms → Analysis → Real-Time Management
- Open Source Software Redux

The coup de grace is the discussion of Strategic Effectiveness in Chapter 6. Just 13 sections deliver the message that strategic technology is the antidote to the "IT doesn't matter" syndrome. This chapter includes:

- Appropriate CRM
- Web 2.0 and the Enterprise
- Thinking about Web 2.0: The Right Questions for the Right Impact
- The Reality of New
- It's the Data, Stupid
- They Know What We Like—And Where We Are!
- Back to the Future: Herding 3,000 Cats through a Worm Hole
- The Consumer's Internet: Thin Clients and Fat Hosts for Everyone
- Commercializing Information Technology: A Four-Step Methodology
- Business Intelligence in the Early 21st Century: Models and Mining for Dynamic Real-Time Business Optimization
- Master Data Management for Business Intelligence and Customer Analytics
- Strategies and Tactics around "New": Time for a Reality Check
- Profiling Your Strategic Technology Alliances

Chapter 6 of the book focuses on how technology can add strategic advantage to your company. The best practices here focus on business intelligence, customer analytics, commercialization, innovation, strategic alliances, and—among other technologies—Web 2.0.

The book tries to be a tour de force of business technology management. It's the result of decades of work in the field—some successful and some not so successful—but always instructive. It is not an academic treatise on the theory of what constitutes a best practice or a deep longitudinal analysis of best practice trends. It is full of insights that represent what successful companies have done—and continue to do—to optimize the business technology relationship.

Acknowledgments

I need to thank all of my personal and professional mentors. As I think about the length of my education and training—which goes back nearly 35 years—two things become clear: I could not possibly list all of my mentors and even if I wanted to I'm sure I'd forget a large number of them. So thanks to all of those friends and colleagues who over the years have influenced how I see things, solve problems, and prioritize life's challenges.

I would, however, like to specifically thank the Labrecque family for the endowed chair—the Thomas G. Labrecque chair—that I hold at Villanova University School of Business, which supports applied research in business technology optimization. Without this kind of support it would be difficult if not impossible to compile volumes such as this.

About the Author

Career Summary

Stephen J. Andriole, PhD, has focused on the development, application, and management of information technology and analytical methodology to all varieties of problems in his career. These problems have been in government and industry: Dr. Andriole has addressed them from academia, government, his own consulting companies, a global insurance and financial services company, from the perspective of a public operating company, and from the perspective of a private equity venture capitalist. The focus of his career has been on technology innovation, the optimization of technology and technology acquisition, deployment, and support of best practices. He is currently the Thomas G. Labrecque Professor of Business Technology at Villanova University in the Villanova School of Business.

Government

Dr. Andriole's government experience began at Decisions & Designs, Inc., a company that designed and developed interactive computer-based resource allocation, forecasting, and decision-making systems for the federal government. It was at Decisions & Designs that Dr. Andriole implemented an interactive system for monitoring the interactions among nations, a system that was originally funded by the Defense Advanced Research Projects Agency (DARPA) as part of Dr. Andriole's PhD dissertation research, and whose output was eventually published in President Reagan's daily briefing book.

Dr. Andriole was the director of the Cybernetics Technology Office of DARPA, where he managed a $25M program of research and development that led to a number of important scientific and technological advances in the broad-based information, decision, and computing sciences. While at DARPA, Dr. Andriole supported the development of spatial data management and multimedia systems, decision support systems, computer-aided simulation and training systems, and intelligent technology-based command and control systems. Dr. Andriole's research program at DARPA seeded the MIT Architecture Machine Group, which evolved into the internationally known Media Lab. The program also contributed to the development of the ARPANET (which became today's Internet), interactive training simulations, such as SIMNET, and a whole host of artificial intelligence-based advances. Dr. Andriole has consulted with the National Academy of Sciences, the National Science Foundation, and various offices and agencies of the U.S. Department of Defense.

Industry

Dr. Andriole's career in industry has taken several forms. He's been a senior vice president and chief technology officer at a Fortune 50 company, a senior vice president and CTO at a public operating and venture capital company, a principal at a private equity venture fund, and an entrepreneur where he's been a founder, cofounder, and CEO of several technology consulting companies.

Dr. Andriole was CTO and senior vice president of Safeguard Scientifics, Inc., where he was responsible for identifying technology trends, translating that insight into the Safeguard investment strategy, and leveraging trends analyses with the Safeguard partner companies to help them develop business and marketing strategies. Dr. Andriole was also a principal at TL Ventures, one of the Philadelphia region's largest private equity funds. While at Safeguard, Dr. Andriole worked closely with many companies at all stages of their development; he was also the primary Wall Street contact for Safeguard, frequently interacting with the analysts who covered SFE. He also participated directly in raising nearly $1B for Safeguard and its partner companies. At their peak, the value of Safeguard and its partner companies exceeded $100B.

Dr. Andriole was CTO and senior vice president for Technology Strategy at CIGNA Corporation, a $20B global insurance and financial services company, where he was responsible for the enterprise information architecture, computing standards, the technology research and development program, data security, as well as the overall alignment of enterprise information technology investments with CIGNA's multiple lines of business.

As an entrepreneur, Dr. Andriole founded International Information Systems (IIS), Inc., which designed interactive systems for a variety of corporate and government clients. IIS specialized in requirements analysis and prototyping, the design of user-computer interfaces, and software systems evaluation. IIS also performed technology investment risk assessments for government and industry. He is also the founder of TechVestCo, a new economy consulting consortium that identifies and leverages technology trends to help clients optimize business technology investments. He recently cofounded Ascendigm, LLC, a company that specializes in the development and commercialization of computing and communications technology, as well as consulting around technology optimization. He is a cofounder of the Musser Consulting Group, LLC, and a cofounder of Radnor Technology Partners, a strategic consulting organization.

Academia

Dr. Andriole is formerly a (tenured, full) professor of Information Systems and Electrical and Computer Engineering at Drexel University in Philadelphia, Pennsylvania, where he conducted applied research in information and software systems engineering, principally through the Center for Multidisciplinary Information Systems Engineering, which he founded and directed. The center generated more than $5M in external funding, from industry, the federal government, and foundations. While at Drexel, and as part of the Center's R&D program, Dr. Andriole—with support from the Alfred P. Sloan Foundation—designed and implemented the nation's first totally online master's program in information systems. This program continues today with some significant repeat industrial customers, including CIGNA and MetLife, as well as a large number of independent students. The program was featured in the nationally broadcasted PBS special *net.learning*.

Dr. Andriole was a (tenured, full) professor and chairman of the Department of Information Systems and Systems Engineering at George Mason University; he was awarded an endowed chair from the university becoming the university's first George Mason Institute Professor of Information Technology. The ISSE department was home to 30 full-time and part-time professors and had an annual external sponsored research budget of $3M. Several research centers were established in the department during this time including the Center for Computer Security and the Center for Software Engineering.

General

Dr. Andriole is a prolific author and speaker. Some of his 30 books include *Corporate Crisis Management* (Petrocelli Books, Inc., 1984), *Interactive Computer-Based Systems Design and Development* (Petrocelli Books, Inc., 1983), *Microcomputer Decision Support Systems* (QED Information Sciences, Inc., 1985), *Applications in Artificial Intelligence* (Petrocelli Books, Inc., 1986), *Information System Design Principles for the 90s* (AFCEA International Press, 1990), the *Sourcebook of Applied Artificial Intelligence* (McGraw-Hill, 1992), a (co-authored with Len Adelman) book on user interface technology for Lawrence Erlbaum Associates, Inc. entitled *Cognitive Systems Engineering* (1995), and a book for McGraw-Hill entitled *Managing Systems Requirements: Methods, Tools & Cases* (1996). He has recently published articles in the *Communications of the AIS*, *Communications of the ACM*, the *Journal of Cases in*

Information Technology, the *Journal of Information Technology Education, INFORMS, IEEE Software,* and the *Cutter IT Journal.* Overall, he has published more than 500 articles, monographs, reports, and book chapters. He is also a monthly columnist for *Datamation Magazine* on business technology convergence. His most recent book—*The 2nd Digital Revolution: Candid Conversations about Business Technology Convergence* —outlines a new approach to optimizing the interrelationships among business, technology, and management (IGI Publishing Group, 2005). Another book, *Technology Due Diligence*, will be published in 2008 also by IGI Publishing. This book looks at the technology acquisition due diligence process as it's practiced by industrial R&D executives and venture investors. Dr. Andriole is also developing a book on corporate strategy and management with the working title—*Random Acts of Business*—which will juxtapose popular business wisdom with experiences observed in five industry sectors.

Dr. Andriole is listed in numerous directories of *Who's Who*, is the recipient of the U.S. Department of Defense Meritorious Civilian Service Award, and is a Charter Member of the U.S. Senior Executive Service (SES). He served on the Industrial Advisory Board of the ABET (the Accreditation Board for Engineering and Technology), as a member of LaSalle University's Advisory Board on Computer Information Science, and a member of the Industry Advisory Board of the First Industrial Realty Trust Corporation. He received the Information Technology Exhibitions and Conferences (ITEC) Lifetime Achievement Award for Excellence in Information Technology in 1999 and an Honorary Doctorate from LaSalle University in October 2000 for his accomplishments in information technology. Dr. Andriole is a director of Epitome Systems, Radnor Technology Partners, LiquidHub, TechVestCo, the Musser Foundation, and NPower. He is a member of the advisory boards of Gestalt and Vivat and serves as the chairperson of the Technology Advisory Board of Prudential Fox Roach/Trident.

Dr. Andriole received his BA from LaSalle University in 1971 and his master's and doctorate degrees from the University of Maryland in 1973 and 1974. His master's and doctoral work was supported by a National Defense Education Act Fellowship. His PhD dissertation was funded by DARPA.

Chapter 1

Perspectives

The 5 × 7 Business Technology Strategy

Our consulting practice in business technology strategy often repeats itself. Not in terms of the same recommendations to different companies but in terms of the big questions that need to be asked of all organizations as they try to optimize their technology investments.

We've developed a repeatable template that can be used to assess business technology strategies. The 5 × 7 matrix (Figure 1.1) summarizes the assessment areas according to:

- The issues
- The current situation
- Proposed recommendations
- An execution strategy
- Expected impact

The big issues include:

- Operational versus strategic technology
- Technology image building and messaging
- People skill sets
- Data, applications, and communications technology
- Security and disaster recovery
- Sourcing and funding
- Measurement

Issue	Current	Recommendations	Execution	Impact
Operational versus Strategic Technology				
Technology Image-Building & Messaging				
Skill Sets				
Data, Applications & Communications				
Security & Disaster Recovery				
Sourcing & Funding				
Measurement				

Figure 1.1   The 5 × 7 business technology strategy assessment matrix.

Operational and Strategic Technology Recommendations

- In our experience, companies should segment their technologies into operational and strategic layers (as suggested in Figure 1.2) and adjust their acquisition, deployment, and support procedures accordingly. They should also segment the professionals who tend to perform these tasks, and consider formalizing the operational/strategic distinction as corporate policy.
- Companies should consider formally reorganizing themselves according to the organizational structure in Figure 1.3.
- The governance around all this should assign responsibility and authority across lines of business and the enterprise.

Rationale

- Most companies' operational technology teams cannot easily support the strategic technology mission; operational technology delivery should not be mixed with more strategic technology initiatives primarily because it dilutes delivery focus.
- Future profitable growth in most companies is tied to strategic product and service development, not operational efficiency (which, of course, must remain excellent, but has finite efficiency limits); lines of business have a better feel for where the business is going and the highest return technology-based products and services.

Figure 1.2   Strategic versus operational technology.

Figure 1.3   Strategic versus operational technology.

- As operational technology becomes increasingly commoditized, there's less need to invest organizational or management resources to it; operational technology should not become a distraction to strategic technology-based innovation.
- The segmentation allows companies to focus on new products and services as well as customer service; segmentation also permits operational technology to address delivery without the added pressure of (a) unresolved governance issues and (b) actually stepping up strategically, which its skill sets will not easily permit it to do.

Technology Image Building and Messaging Recommendations

■ Companies whose products and services are in any way, shape, or form driven by technology should engage in technology image building and messaging campaigns—at least enough to put a technology stake in the ground—and especially one that speaks directly to what their competition is advertising it's doing with technology.

■ Web sites should become more technology branded. Ownership of the Web site should be decentralized. The general recommendation is to decentralize content ownership across sales and marketing *and* the lines of business, and to bring sites in-house for agile updating and support (that is, not to out-source the hosting of the site).

■ All of these recommendations might be accelerated through the creation of technology advisory boards (TABs) comprising internal and external business technology professionals in the vertical industries in play. TABs generate buzz and are generally cheap to form and run; they can also really help a company optimize its technology investments as the resident "honest brokers."

■ Companies should also develop internal technology marketing campaigns to make sure that their internal technology customers understand what investments have been made, what delivery models are in place, and what results are being achieved.

Rationale

■ Technology "buzz" activities are inexpensive (white papers, press releases, downloadable product and service brochures, etc. can be created quickly and cheaply).

■ Decentralizing Web site content management to include sales and marketing *and* the lines of business is consistent with the decentralization of strategic technology product and service development.

■ Hosting sites internally facilitates easy and rapid updating and the eventual integration with existing applications and databases as sites become more and more transaction based.

■ It's important for internal communications channels regarding the provisioning of technology to be wide and deep.

People and Skill Sets Recommendations

■ Companies should continuously *and objectively* assess the operational and strategic skill sets of their technology teams to determine where gaps may exist (TABs can help here).

- Nearly all of the operational technology delivery teams we've seen over the years need to improve their skills in internal consulting, project management, program management, and internal communications, among related skills; internal customer service surveys should be regularly administered to determine which skills need the most attention.
- Strategic technologists should be recruited by the lines of business and compensated according to industry standard salaries; they should be incentivized differently from operational personnel.
- Additional skill sets that are often necessary at the operational level include application integration, application/data/communications architecture, digital security, and disaster recovery.

Rationale

- It is very difficult to transition primarily maintenance-oriented teams into strategic teams.
- The skills really necessary to improve the image and performance of operational technology delivery teams are not innovative or strategic but consulting skills, which are teachable and trainable (though by no means guaranteed to improve every aspect of the business–technology relationship).
- Investments in additional technology personnel should generally be at the strategic level, not the operational level; in fact, over time, as more and more operational technology becomes commoditized, operational costs should actually decline (through head count reduction and improving hardware and software price/performance ratios).

Data, Applications, and Communications Recommendations

- Companies should select a primary data and applications vendor and define its operational governance around that vendor; this direction should be maintained and declared as the company standard data, applications, and communications architecture.
- Lines of business should be consulted regarding the general direction and then expected to comply with the architectural implications of a company's architectural directions; although this can be a give-and-take process, ultimately a standardized infrastructure and architecture must emerge from these discussions.
- When strategic applications are designed and developed by lines of business, support requirements should be determined before development begins (as one of the strategic/operational governance rules).
- Most companies will benefit from a migration to multiprotocol label switching (MPLS) communications architectures, especially if the business strategy

calls for more digital technology and increased communication among the company's employees, customers, and suppliers; IP (Internet Protocol) ubiquity will eventually become real so all decisions regarding communications should be made with reference to bona fide pervasive computing.

■ All companies—in spite of continuing security issues—should prepare for, and integrate, a more widespread use of wireless communications.

Rationale

■ Moving toward a primary vendor is an industry best practice, especially given all of the vendor consolidation that has occurred over the past few years; a primary vendor also makes it easier to integrate and support applications.

■ Rules need to be explicit about the definition and support of data, applications, and communications architectures.

■ The exploitation of the newer (MPLS and virtual private LAN services [VPLS]) communications architectures for additional service offerings makes sense especially given how communications costs continue to fall as more and more communications capacity becomes commoditized.

Security and Disaster Recovery Recommendations

■ All companies should assess the cells in the matrix of Figure 1.4. Companies should identify their major digital threats today and likely threats in the near-term future, especially if the nature and volume of Web-based transaction processing is likely to increase.

■ Companies should coordinate closely with their lines of business regarding security and new security requirements that the lines of business may need satisfied—on top of the standard infrastructure security requirements.

■ Disaster recovery should receive special attention and funding with assessments made regarding acceptable levels of downtime versus cost.

Rationale

■ If digital technology is going to become more and more important—which it is—then digital security will become more important.

Acquisition and Funding Recommendations

■ Companies should assess on a regular basis the cost/benefit of outsourcing their operational technology (infrastructure and support); given the trends toward the commoditization of infrastructure and support, it will likely be cost-effective to outsource nearly all operational technology in a few short years.

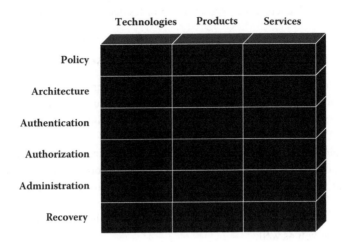

Figure 1.4 The digital security matrix.

- Metrics should be developed to track opportunities over time to determine if and when significant cost savings can result from operational technology outsourcing.

Rationale

- The trends toward infrastructure outsourcing are clear: there will come a time when the cost/performance ratio will tilt toward alternative outsourcing solutions.

Measurement Recommendations

- Companies should identify the assets, processes, and outcomes they need to track and report either for performance measurement or public company reporting—or both—reasons.
- Companies should develop dashboards for operational and strategic technology, which should provide transparent reporting on strategic and operational technology performance and projects.

Rationale

■ As technology becomes more important, the discipline of tracking and reporting all digital assets, processes, and outcomes needs to improve.

The 5 × 7 Business Technology Strategy Assessments

Our assessments seek to fill every cell in the matrix in Figure 1.1. Taken together, the content of the cells represents an assessment of the current situation as well as a "to be" strategy with specific recommendations and insights into the impact each recommendation—if implemented properly—will have.

Too simple? Well, there are all kinds of strategic assessment and planning methods, tools, and concepts out there that are often much more elaborate than our 5 × 7 matrix, but we think the matrix touches on the major issues facing a great many companies in the early twenty-first century.

The application of the matrix has become one of our best practices. I suspect it would work for you as well.

Revisiting the "IT Doesn't Matter" Argument

There were inklings of concern in the early 1990s, but they all disappeared when the Internet intoxicated everyone. But since 2000, there've been a series of challenges about the value of information technology, about whether or not information technology (IT) is still really important. Paul Strassmann (www.strassmann. com), for example, has argued for years that investments in technology do not predict profitability or growth. Longitudinal research reported by Joyce, Nohria, and Roberson in *What (Really) Works* (Harper Business, 2004) reports "no correlation between a company's investment in technology and its total return to shareholders." All of these—and other—arguments were made in Nickolas Carr's famous piece in the *Harvard Business Review* with the provocative title: "IT Doesn't Matter" (May 2003). Carr is convinced that technology's strategic impact has run its course, that the technology playing field is now level.

Well, it's been a few years now since the Carr culmination: what do we think? Should we believe that computing and communications technology are frauds, that they bring very little to the competitive table, that the over $1 trillion a year U.S. companies spend on hardware, software, and technology services is somehow misspent?

Arguments that IT no longer matters are flawed. In fact, we're confusing several healthy trends with what some see as declining influence. For example, there's no question that personal computers (PCs), laptops, and routers are commodities; even some services—like legacy systems maintenance and data center management—have become nearly fully commoditized. Are PCs, personal digital assistants (PDAs), and servers "strategic"? Of course not. But if we botch the acquisition of these devices, or fail to adhere to sound management practices like standardization, they become tactical liabilities. Far from being irrelevant, they're actually tactically necessary and potentially dangerous.

Another misinterpreted trend is the increase in discipline used to acquire, deploy, and manage technology. We're much more sophisticated about the use of business cases, total cost of ownership (TCO) models, return on investment calculations, and project management best practices than we were a decade ago. Put another way, the acquisition and management of technology has become routine, no longer the high-profile, ad hoc process it once was. Does this mean that it's no longer important? I'd argue that our ability to more skillfully acquire and manage IT is an indicator of maturity, not unimportance.

Another trend that seems to confuse the technology-doesn't-matter crowd is our willingness to outsource technology. Companies are reevaluating their sourcing strategies and have lengthened the list of potential candidates for partial and full outsourcing. Some of these include help desk support, programming, and application maintenance. If we extend this trend, it's likely that we'll see a lot more hosting of even large applications—like enterprise resource planning (ERP) applications—that companies will increasingly rent (to avoid implementation and support problems). But does this trend spell the end of IT? Hardly. Outsourcing trends dovetail perfectly with commoditization trends. Companies have correctly discovered that they don't need to develop core competencies in maintaining PCs or supporting Microsoft Office—and why should they? This kind of support should be left to specialists who can offer economies of scale, reliability, and cost-effectiveness.

The real story here is not commoditization, discipline, or outsourcing, but the separation of technology into operational and strategic layers. Operational technology is what's becoming commoditized; strategic technology is alive and well—and still very much a competitive differentiator. It's even possible to argue that because operational technology has been commoditized, we're finally ready to strategically leverage technology. In other words, the era of strategic computing has only just begun.

Operational technology enables current and emerging business models and processes in well-defined, predictable ways. Hardware price/performance ratios are perhaps the most obvious example of this trend, but there are others as well including what we're willing to pay for programming services (here and abroad). We now expect companies to excel in the acquisition, deployment, and management of operational technology. We expect them to know what they're doing here—recognizing that mistakes can be extremely costly and even threaten a company's position in the marketplace. Far from being irrelevant, given the size of our technology budgets and our growing dependency on technology, it's essential that we get the operational layer right. Many companies are very good at it; some companies are horrible. There's huge opportunity—and risk—here; try telling a chief executive officer (CEO) that a botched $100M ERP project doesn't matter.

Strategic technology on the other hand is the result of creative business technology thinking where, for example, a Wal-Mart streamlines its supply chain, a Starbucks offers wireless access to the Web to its retail customers (to keep them inside their stores spending money), and a Vanguard leverages its Web site to dramatically improve customer service. There's no limit to how strategic the business technology relationship can be. Again, the exploitation of strategic technology—like customer relationship management (CRM) and its personalization and customization cousins—is dependent on solid operational technology. The same is true of wireless communications, automation, and dynamic pricing. You mean to tell me that the ability to change wholesale and retail prices in real time is not strategic?

Strategic technology is liberated by operational technology. How much time did we spend putting out operational brushfires in the 1980s and 1990s? Was there any time left to think strategically? A lot of basic hardware and software just didn't work that well back then, but now technology's reliable and cheap—and now there's finally time to strategically leverage technology—so long as the distinction between operational and strategic technology is well understood. Marching orders? Solid operational technology that enables creative strategic technology. If we get this relationship right, technology can contribute directly to efficiency, profitability, and growth.

There's a solid argument that can be made for technology's new—larger—strategic role in the process by which companies profitably grow. Business process modeling (BPM) is one of the new levers—powered by technology—that can redesign critical processes and whole business models. More importantly, new processes and models can be designed to improve efficiencies, market penetration, customer service, and whatever strategic goals management decides to pursue. Supply chain planning and management, rules-based pricing, whole customer management, and real-time business intelligence (BI) are just a few ideas that are decidedly strategic when customized to specific companies and vertical industries. You see, this is one of the traps of the "IT doesn't matter argument." Of course there will be, for example, consolidation in the BI industry, and all companies will have access to the three or four major BI platforms. This commoditization trend will, according to the IT-doesn't-matter crowd, level the playing field for all BI users; however, the real leverage comes not from the standard BI platforms but from the creative customization and implementation of the platforms. This customization and implementation creativity is absolutely strategic, not operational (though, again, there will be an operational/support prerequisite to success).

We are entering a new strategic era in the business technology relationship. The distance between business processes and technology enablers is gone. It is impossible to think about new business processes or models without simultaneously thinking about technology, and vice versa. The idea that one could develop new products, enhance customer service, or expand into new markets without technology is silly. The major change over the past five years is the separation of technology into operational and strategic pieces. Operational technology is commoditized;

strategic technology is still highly variable: some companies will get it right and some will miss huge opportunities. It's also likely that the strategic importance of IT will grow—not shrink—over time. Competitive advantage will accrue to those who invest in creative thinking about the synergism between business models and technology, as well as those who can anticipate the trajectory of emerging technology—and exploit new technology to innovate business models and processes. New product development, dramatically improved customer service, and real-time process management are only a few of the areas that will benefit from the creative application of current and especially emerging technology.

The failure to see the distinction between strategic and operational technology has distorted perceptions about the business value of IT. Operational technology will continue to become commoditized and, barring stupid acquisition, deployment, and support practices, will not provide competitive advantage. But competitive battles will be fought with a variety of technology weapons. The companies that design, develop, and creatively deploy these weapons will gain strategic advantage; those that don't will suffer strategically.

Make no mistake: IT still matters. In fact, IT matters more now than it ever did. If IT were a basket of stocks (which it is), I'd short the operational ones and go very long on the strategic ones. It's really that simple.

Ten Things IT Should Tell Management

The *Wall Street Journal* published "Ten Things Your IT Department Won't Tell You" (July 30, 2007) that lists some things you might do to get around your chief information officer's (CIO) policies and procedures, things like how to download forbidden software or get your e-mail from lots of places when your corporate messaging server doesn't want to cooperate. I thought this was a silly article. It was like I was reading about how 12-year-olds plot to confuse their parents to get more access to video games. After complaining to some friends about the whole premise of the article, one of them challenged me to turn the message around. "So, big shot, what would you tell 'management' about technology?"

Here's what I'd say:

1. "First of all—'management'—technology is an asset that needs to be nurtured—like a brand or a customer service reputation. If you don't invest in the asset, its value will fall—just like any asset. Just ask Dell or Mercedes what happens when service and quality—respectively—suffers."

2. "And while we're talking about all this, remember that although operational technology has definitely commoditized, there are still strategic technology investments we need to be very careful about making. It's possible to make some major mistakes in the acquisition of all kinds of technology, so let's get some serious discipline in the technology acquisition process—and, please,

don't listen too closely about killer apps at cocktail parties. Everyone knows that alcohol and technology don't mix."

3. "Don't forget that technology is still complex, even though industry standards have helped improve integration and interoperability. Listen, while there are fewer moving parts, the way we deploy them still makes the technology world tough to manage—and our vendors don't always help us."

4. "Please stop making exceptions to the governance process. If you want to save money and keep us agile, then do not allow all the flowers to bloom; instead, publish the standards and then stick with them. Every time you let someone off the hook, you make our life more complicated—and expensive."

5. "Make the company's business strategy as transparent as possible (unless you really don't like talking about your own strategy). The more the technocrats know about the business strategy, the more efficient they will be acquiring and deploying technology."

6. "Please make us account for our technology investments. Please make us link them to the business strategy and the impact each investment has on operational or strategic success. In spite of what you may think, we like ROI (return on investment) thinking. Hold us—*and everyone*—to it."

7. "Stop underestimating the impact the Web will have on business. I am really tired of our thinking that the Web is just another channel. The Web is not an evolutionary channel. It's definitely a revolutionary one that changes dramatically every year. Please allow us to pay close attention to new Web technologies and Web-based business models. By the way, why aren't we crowdsourcing our R&D (research and development)?"

8. "Listen to my whining about the lack of a discretionary budget. I need some money to try new things. I need to fail fast and fail cheap, but without a discretionary budget I can't do either."

9. "Please don't acquire any companies until I've looked at their technology. Never assume that our technologies will 'seamlessly integrate.' Never assume that there are automatic technology gains that will result from a merger or acquisition. Nothing is farther from the truth."

10. "Invest in the right people with the right skills at the right price. Reward major contributors and prune out the losers. There's nothing else you can do to excite the troops more. They need to believe that hard work will be rewarded—and that lousy work will be punished."

What would you say to "management" about technology? It might make sense to think about what you'd say if given the opportunity. You never know when you might be invited to rant. Such rants should become part of the IT "road show" that you dust off whenever you get even the slightest opportunity to sing your praises.

Ten "New Rules" for IT

For those of you familiar with Bill Maher's "New Rules" on his HBO series *Real Time*, you might appreciate some new IT rules. (For those who don't know the show you might still appreciate the perspective represented by the following rules— *which should be followed at all times!*)

Here we go:

1. CIOs should come from the business not the technology ranks: technology-rooted CIOs will never really understand the importance of business as *the* technology driver. When prospective CIOs start talking about network latency and virtualization, it's time to get the hook out; go with the pro talking about up-selling and cross-selling every time.

2. Business technology professionals should be grown in BT farms, the way we grow shrimp, salmon, and lobster. These pros, like the fish, will be tastier and freer of the toxins they may have picked up in data centers (which are known disease breeders).

3. Vendors are designed to be squeezed. Can anyone justify the margins that software or services vendors get? Please, if someone's going to get 50+ percent margins on their products and services they deserve to have someone hold them upside down and shake the cash out of their pockets.

4. Software is designed to be rented. Who—in 2008 and beyond—in their right mind would embark on a five-year, $500 million implementation project? Only crack addicts would smoke this story. Even Microsoft, the mother of all enterprise software vendors, gets this.

5. Get over the lack of privacy. It's been gone for years, and most Americans would sell their personal data for $50 a year, so long as you promised them a free Diet Coke. The fact is that privacy—like everything else in the world—is for sale at the right price.

6. Hardware, software, and services contract risk should be shared. Which professionals (besides lawyers) get to screw up and still get paid? The rule from now on is that performance should predict payment: no performance, no money.

7. Digital security is adequate. Yes, data will be stolen and transactions hacked, but by and large the Web is secure enough to support all kinds of business-to-business (B2B) and business-to-consumer (B2C) transaction processing.

8. Colleges and universities need to revamp their business technology degree programs from the ground up—moving them at least to the late-twentieth century. This would include rethinking degree programs in computer science, computer engineering, and management information systems, among other programs that deal with digital technology and how it supports business models and processes. The new rule is simple: if it's not relevant, it doesn't go into the curriculum.

9. By 2010 the Wintel conspiracy will officially end and only thin clients will be permitted in 30 of the 50 states. The last 20 states will ban fat clients and bloatware no later than 2015.
10. Meritocracies will replace consensus-by-brothers-in-law/cronies/ex-girl-friends/ex-boyfriends/idiot sons and daughters/golf buddies—at least in this (if not a parallel) universe.

Ten Questions for Everyone

It's amazing to me that many of the companies I work with cannot answer the following questions. Can you?

1. **How much money do you spend annually on all flavors of technology and technology support services?** It's important to know the total and the relative allocations across the obvious categories—hardware, software, communications, support, consultants, and so forth—but also across categories of special importance to your company and your industry, like privacy and security in the financial services industry and supply chain planning and management in the manufacturing and distribution industries.
2. **What percentage of your gross revenues do you spend on technology (again, broadly defined)?** The numbers here are important to determine if you're a tactician obsessed with managing costs or if you're a strategist seeking competitive advantage from your technology investments. Companies that spend 4 percent or less of their gross revenue on total technology investments per year tend to be operationally and tactically focused, that is, on managing technology as a cost center. If the people in your organization wax poetic about how they look to technology for strategic advantage but spend less than 4 percent of gross revenue on technology, they need a wake-up call. Companies that spend more than 4 percent—and upwards of 10 percent—of their gross revenue on technology are genuine strategic technology investors.
3. **How much do you spend on technology per employee?** The numbers here actually range from $2K all the way up to $40K per employee per year. Obviously the high end is insane—unless there are very special circumstances (none of which come to mind here). The key here again is spending segmentation: how do the annual expenditures break down per employee per year? Does it go for hardware, break-and-fix, access to communications networks, cellular phones, security, or consulting?
4. **What are your direct competitors spending on technology?** If your competitors are spending twice what you are, it could mean several things. Perhaps you are spending too little, or perhaps they are spending too much. A little competitive intelligence here is worth its weight in gold. Not only do you need to know what they are spending, but you also need to know how

they are spending their technology dollars. The same segmentation you use to profile your own spending should be used to profile your direct competitors' spending.

5. **What is the average spend (as a percentage of gross revenues) on technology in your industry?** Your competitive intelligence efforts will expose your direct competitors' spending but you still need to benchmark your (and your competitors') spending against the whole industry. You may discover—as with your direct competitors' technology profiling—that you are spending way less than the industry average—or way more. Or, you're spending way differently from the industry. For example, you may be spending more on communications than the industry or way more on enterprise applications. Discrepancies should be carefully analyzed.

6. **What is the history of your technology spending?** Are you trending toward becoming a strategic technology investor or a cost-obsessed bean counter? Are you spending more and more every year on consultants (while your internal budget remains the same or also increases)? What's getting cheaper? If you extrapolate out a few years, what will your spending look like? Are you comfortable with the trends? Or do they represent a series of yellow and red flags?

7. **What is the breakdown between "operational" and "strategic" technology?** This one is very important—and dovetails with technology spending as a percentage of gross revenues data you also need to collect and analyze. Operational technology is all that technology that relates to infrastructure including communications networks, back-office applications, and internal communications and other applications, such as e-mail, workflow, groupware, and the like. Strategic technology touches customers, suppliers, and partners. The ratio here is telling: if all of your technology investments are operational, then you are clearly a tactical technology investor and probably missing some strategic opportunities for leveraging technology on to new and merging business models and processes. The trends here are important: are you becoming more operational or more strategic?

8. **How much of the technology budget is discretionary versus nondiscretionary?** Is there any freedom in your budget? If the boss came in and asked for $500K for a strategic project would you be able to find the money? Or $100K for a tactical one? Is most of the annual technology budget already accounted for, or is there some room for special projects, pilots, and so forth?

9. **What is the TCO of your major spending categories (hardware, enterprise software, security, communications)?** This is real trench data. It's important to know the total cost of applications, PDAs, cell phones, and such, to better understand where the money goes. Hard and soft costs should figure into all these calculations.

10. **How do you measure return on your technology investments (ROI)?** If you don't measure ROI—with explicit operational *and* business metrics— then it will be impossible to get a feel for the impact that your technology spending is having at your company. If there's no dominant methodology, then you should—along with the financial professionals at your company— develop one.

Once you get the answers to these ten questions, put them in a dashboard for everyone to see—unless, of course, the answers are—well—not what you think everyone should hear. You make the call.

Still Too Many Dollars

In spite of how far we've come and how elegant and powerful much of our information technology really is, and in spite of bear market prices, I must admit that we still spend too much money on business technology—way too much. Let's look at what's going on—and how we might get more bang for the buck.

*Way Too Pricey**

Let's start with some grim news. According to recent benchmarking research:

■ On average, U.S. companies spend more than $8,000 per year per employee on computing and communications technology and support; on the high end there are companies that actually spend more than $20,000 per year per employee on technology.

---

* There's a lot of "evidence" about over spending. The Gartner Group publishes lots of TCO and RO) analyses (www.gartner.com), as does the Standish Group (www.standishgroup.com); both generally report that we often pay more than we should for hardware, software, and services. NIST (www.nist.gov) published a report that software bugs cost users and vendors almost $60B annually. The *Nestle vs. SAP* case is widely known (see Ben Worthen, "Nestle's ERP Odyssey," *CIO Magazine,* May 15, 2002), as are other failed enterprise projects (see Kim Girard's report on the *"Department 56 vs. Arthur Andersen*—'Blame Game,'" *Baseline Magazine,* March 2002). Litigation sometimes results from implementation problems. See PricewaterhouseCoopers, "Patterns in IT Litigation: Systems Failure (1976–2000)." Also see Meredith Levinson, "Let's Stop Wasting $78 Billion a Year," *CIO Magazine,* October 15, 2001, and Charles C. Mann, "Why Software Is So Bad," *Technology Review,* July/August 2002. Paul Strassmann's work is relevant here. See www.strassmann.com for tons of insight and data. While there are any number of horror stories out there, there are also some huge success stories, not to mention the everyday success of word processors, presentation packages, databases, and e-mail. Finally, regarding CRM, see Michelle Schneider, "CRM: What It's Worth," *The Net Economy,* February 5, 2001, and Rich Cirillo and Dana Silverstein, "Can CRM Be Saved?" *VARBusiness,* February 4, 2002.

- *CIO Magazine* reported that companies waste $78 billion a year on failed software projects.
- PricewaterhouseCoopers reported that over the past 25 years the number of failed technology projects that resulted in litigation has grown dramatically, with 48 percent resulting from warranty breaches, 13 percent from fraud, 11 percent from breach of contract, 9 percent from negligence, and 7 percent from misrepresentation, among other problems.
- The National Institute of Standards and Technology (NIST) found that software bugs cost the U.S. economy almost $60 billion a year.

How can we waste so much cash?

Hype, Misalignment, and Bad Biz/IT Management

Unfortunately, hype still too often degrades to disenchantment. Let's look at a short list of overhyped "killer apps": ERP, network and systems management, eBusiness, sales force automation, and the most recent disappointment, CRM. Do you know what these applications cost—and what impact they've had on your business? Questions about technology's contribution to business ride on answers to questions about business' clarity regarding technology's enabling role. Although we've had problems, this stuff can work—especially if it's matched with the right business requirements. But when the match is wrong, technology investments become insatiable sink holes.

Most technology investment decisions are made with less than perfect information. More often than not, there are as many intangible variables as tangible ones. Keep in mind that the Gartner Group (and other research organizations) report that over 75 percent of all major technology projects fail.

The numbers are staggering. So how is it that we still invest more than a trillion dollars a year in technology products and services when so much of it doesn't work? One answer is that investment criteria were relaxed or nonexistent during the mid- and late 1990s: how many companies really scrubbed their eBusiness investments? But as I've said repeatedly, even though lots of technology is misapplied or out-and-out wasted, we're at a point where it's possible not only to avoid major mistakes but also to integrate technology and business in ways that were impossible five years ago.

Depending on your title, you see technology differently. Some see it as the aforementioned sink hole; others see it as a way to differentiate your company from its competitors, your edge. Some see it as a sandbox. Others see it as a necessary evil. If you're a chief marketing officer, you should probably understand how software vendors "manage" versions to optimize their revenue streams (just as you do with your products and services). But if you're a chief financial officer (CFO), you may not fully understand how middleware works or why it's so important to your company, or how consultants identify problems that only they can solve. Are you surprised when it takes several years to install an application? Or when you hear about outsourcing lawsuits? All of these alternative views of technology are expensive to maintain.

I'd argue that our understanding of technology is unfinished. We've been conditioned to think about technology as a silo—and we've managed it accordingly. Most companies still have "systems divisions" or "technology groups," when they should do whatever they can do tear the silos down and rebuild integrated business technology organizations and processes. We're evolving—not revolutionizing—the relationship between business and technology. We don't do nearly enough due diligence concerning technology investments, don't know how to measure ROI, and still make major technology decisions on the basis of incomplete and highly politicized information, and for some reason still resist the development of clear business models.

One-Third Off?

I sometimes tell my consulting clients that I can reduce their technology budgets by 33 percent. After they regain consciousness, I explain how it's possible. There's so much low-hanging fruit, I tell them; for example: you've got several—or more—database platforms (with too many platforms and data warehouses that you have to maintain), too many data centers (that can be consolidated), little or no standards (and therefore lots of expensive variation), poor human resource management (resulting in too many people doing the wrong things), suboptimal vendor management (resulting in too many uncoordinated procurements), and incomplete metrics (making it difficult if not impossible to know where you are—or where you're going). At this point, they usually nod. I tell them that they shouldn't feel too bad, that I can't even make a dent in the second 33 percent.

Preparing for the Tsunami

There are a number of things likely to come true in 2008. How should we prepare for them?

Fewer Vendors—and Choices

Forecast

Consolidation will continue except the pace will increase. This trend is fueled by the desire of larger software and services companies to move downstream in the market where they can sell their wares to small- and medium-sized businesses (SMBs). The larger companies will acquire vendors that service these markets. They will also acquire companies that are essentially innovation incubators. Technology buyers will have fewer choices, but the ones they end up with will offer more integrated (hardware/software/services) solutions than past vendors have offered.

Preparations

Consolidation requires all of us to select the right vendors. Although this does not mean that we need to select only acquiring vendors, it does mean that we need to select vendors whose products and services are likely to persist regardless of the outcome of a merger or acquisition. How can we know which ones will persist and which will perish? The answer lies in market share. Products and services with relatively few customers will fall through the cracks of most mergers and acquisitions (unless the technology is stunning), but when there are lots of customers involved, mergers and acquisitions (M&A) transactions tend to return to the sources of revenue, to the accretive side of the M&A equation.

It also makes sense to track mainstream standards and architectures—to avoid being out of sync with discernible trends. Acquire and deploy the products and services that are consistent with prevailing standards and architectures. Finally, be careful about early decisions here: can you say HD and Blu-Ray?

Make Money or Else

Forecast

The real leverage going forward is the role technology will play in generating profit: in 2008 and beyond there will be clear and consistent pressure placed on technology organizations to become profit centers versus their long-term roles as cost centers.

Preparations

The clear suggestion here is first to assess the profit-making potential of your technology organization. Some organizations will have no prospects for making money; others will have great potential. Organizations with excess capacity, with an unusually talented core of architects or professionals with deep business savvy, for example, could easily make money in their vertical industries, but organizations struggling to keep the lights are unlikely to balance their own books, let alone turn a profit.

The next step is to identify the business solutions most likely to result in increased revenue and profitability for your company. Technology-enabled solutions that lead to more customers, up-selling, cross-selling, and cost controls will make money for the company. It's time to develop and unleash your internal consultants to find the leverage to profitable growth.

Finally, you need to market your technology organizations as good guys, that is, professionals who can help the business grow. Everyone needs to understand just how committed the technology organization is to its new role as a profit center.

Devices Don't Matter

Forecast

Over time, it won't matter how we get to networks but how we get there securely and ubiquitously. We buy one brand instead of another because we get a better deal, not because we think there are significant performance or reliability differences. Standards are making everything easier to connect. Interoperability is a major trend in the industry due largely to consolidation and the standardization that consolidation enables. Soon it won't matter what device is used to access networks, data, and all forms of media. Think iPod, Zune, and other MP3 players. Sure there are proprietary flavors here, but the content is standardized and therefore portable— and accessible to all these (and other) devices. This trend continues aggressively in 2008.

Preparations

Convergence is the watchword: whenever you can decrease the number of devices in your company it's a good thing.

It's also a good idea to start piloting some of the newer access architectures such as thin client computing. PC tablets, smart phones, and new generation PDAs also fall into this category (as does the Apple iPhone).

But remember that standardization is still important as you move toward converged devices or experiment with newer access devices that could end up in your company.

There's also a software component to new access devices. Do you really need the bloatware that sits—idly—on your PC or laptop? While we all think about skinnying down hardware, we should also spend some time thinking about how much software we really need.

Software Is a Service

Forecast

There are major trends here that will definitely exceed their expected impact. The first is the rent versus buy/install/support trend. Only organizations that believe they absolutely positively have to own their data and applications will persist with the buy/install/support process. Just about everyone else will rent applications over the Web. The software-as-a-service model will enable the renting trend, because not only will we be able to rent standard application packages, but we'll also be able to customize applications via new architectures and standards designed to provide flexibility to clients over the Web.

Preparations

If you haven't rented any applications yet, you need to start—if only in an experimental way. It's important to determine the impact that renting versus installing applications might have on your organization not just in terms of cost but also productivity. There's a larger philosophy that also needs to be explored: are you a renting kind of organization or do you need to control the software that you use? Would you embark on a multiyear ERP project at this stage of the game? Or would you consider renting the same application? It's time to learn as much as you can about new software acquisition models.

Open Source—Regardless of What They Think

Forecast

This will be the year when we all change the way we think about open source software (OSS). Instead of positioning OSS as competition to proprietary software, we will begin to see it as an augmentation to it; within a few years it will begin to replace significant stacks of proprietary software. We will see the increased adoption of open source desktop software (to compete with MS Office) and even Linux on the desktop. We will see the widespread adoption of open source CRM and database applications; many companies—especially smaller ones—will move toward holistic OSS solutions. In response to this trend, the major proprietary software vendors may decide to dramatically reduce their prices to avert the increased adoption of open source solutions. It remains to be seen if they fight with this tactic, but 2008 is probably the year when they have to make some tough decisions.

Preparations

You really must take a look at StarOffice and OpenOffice, among other OSS applications. SugarCRM is an interesting alternative to proprietary CRM applications. Because you're probably already running Linux and Apache, you have some experience with OSS. Derive cost and performance metrics from this experience. Develop business cases for open source alternatives; do not dismiss OSS simply because it's "different"—especially if yours is an SMB. If you're considering renting software, then it makes even more sense to look at an open source alternative as you won't have to support it or force its compatibility with your proprietary software.

Business Process Modeling for the Rest of Us

Forecast

CIOs, COOs (chief operating officers), and CEOs plan to play with business process/performance management (BPM) this year. They want to determine the value the new perspective and tools might provide to improving business models and processes, especially in terms of efficiencies. They are not looking to "reinvent" or "reengineer" their companies with BPM technology; rather, they want to mend them, improve them, extend them—cost-effectively. As more and more companies try to fine-tune their operations, they will extend the efficiency mission business processes that directly support the business models that contribute the most to growth and profitability: 2008 will be the year for major BPM pilots. Let's hope that they are well conceived and executed.

Preparations

It's time to buy, rent, or activate an existing BPM application at your company. I suggest that you first determine if activation makes sense because many of us already have access to a BPM module through our larger ERP platforms. There are lots of off-the-shelf packages as well. It also makes sense to invest in process modeling training and internal consulting, because BPM activities should become core to your company. I'd suggest working with some consultants in your industry to initially learn the BPM capabilities of the software application you will be using. Then I'd determine if I need further help or if it might make more sense to develop an internal BPM competency center. Regardless of the route you take, the destination should be clear: a deeper understanding of your business processes and models and the ability to optimize alternative processes and whole new business models. BPM expertise should become a high priority at your company, as it's impossible to improve processes and models we don't understand.

Wired and Wireless Communications

Forecast

There's a major push to make everyone mobile. The industry will continue to ramp up its wired and wireless communications capabilities in 2008 and beyond. This also appears to be the year when we'll remove most of the glitches in Voice-over-Internet Protocol (VoIP) services. The revolution in communications technology will change the way we conduct business. Continuous transaction processing is enabled by ubiquitous (wired and wireless) communications; 2008 will continue trends that began several years ago, trends that will continue indefinitely.

Preparations

Wired and wireless communications is a moving target. An internal center of excellence or even a smaller competency center—linked to BPM projects—could yield significant benefits. There are trade-offs among wired, Wi-Fi, and WiMax communications technology. Understanding them and the role they should play at your company is crucial to cost-effective implementations. VoIP pilots should also be undertaken—but not in a vacuum. VoIP technology relates closely to others—like unified messaging and communications, IP video, and an assortment of Web 2.0 technologies. All of these should be explored holistically.

Data Ins and Outs

Forecast

CIOs, COOs, and CEOs are planning to widen and deepen their investments in business intelligence in 2008. There is also interest in increasing investments in competitor intelligence. Of special note is the interest in customer analytics. Personalization and customization are the objectives of customer analytics: the more companies know about their customers, the more they can customize and personalize their products and services. CIOs are also interested in Web analytics, as there's pressure to increase eBusiness, to expand the digital channel. Business intelligence, competitor intelligence, customer analytics, and Web analytics are all part of growing strategies to leverage data, information, and knowledge to fuel growth and profitability—where technology needs to go.

Preparations

If ever there was a high-priority investment area, business intelligence and analytics is it. If you haven't already invested heavily here, you should strongly consider doing so. There are so many ways to leverage data and information that it hardly deserves special mention. But many companies underexploit their data architectures. One very specific recommendation is to invest in your master data. In fact, master data management should be a focus of the majority of companies in the Cutter family. More than that, a corporate data strategy should guide investments in database management platforms, data warehouses, data marts, and—underlying it all—master data management. Once the data strategy is implemented, then pursue the analytics it will enable.

Secure—But Not Quite as Private

Forecast

All of the CIOs I talk to will spend more on security in 2008 than they spent in 2006 (a continuation of a trend started in 2002). The growing identity theft problem has stimulated additional investments in data security and network security; there remains considerable concern about wireless security, a concern that is still affecting the desire for more and more broadband wireless communications. Privacy is taking a back seat to security partly because of the Patriot Act and partly because individuals appear more interested in deals than discretion.

Preparations

The first thing to do is conduct a security/privacy audit. This should involve your regular corporate auditors, the board of directors' audit committee, and the internal controls professionals responsible for both physical and digital security. The results of this audit should determine what you do next. If the audit is clean, then continue your best efforts to stay abreast of both threats and countermeasure technology. If the results are bad, then you have a series of decisions to make about sourcing, technology, and governance. If you believe that your culture is just not "security ready," then you might consider outsourcing all your physical and digital security. Regardless of how you source the gaps, you will need unambiguous security governance. Be harsh here: take no prisoners; accept no breeches or violations. If you're a public company, redouble your security efforts—and budgets.

Organization

Forecast

The segmentation of technology into "strategic" and "operational" technology is driving significant organizational changes. Many CIOs are interested in reorganizing their teams into layers of responsibility that fine-tune technology management roles. Many CIOs are appointing deputies with specific responsibilities for applications, data management, security, infrastructure, and strategy, among other duties. Many are experimenting with offices of the CIO and technology directorates as mechanisms to distribute responsibility across their teams. As more functions are outsourced, there's also increased interest in professional vendor management, which is manifest in the increasing number of vendor management offices (VMOs) we're seeing.

Preparations

Step back and objectively assess your organizational structure and effectiveness. Is it working? Given the new emphasis on the business value of technology it makes sense to deploy business technology liaisons in your company. These "translators" are crucial to success. You need people who can translate—and prioritize—business requirements into technology solutions. These people also need to possess healthy amounts of soft skills. If you don't have such people, then grow them organically or recruit them into your organization. You should also determine what the pieces of your organization should look like. Do you need a CIO/deputy CIO structure? Do you need a VMO? What about a project management office (PMO)?

You also need to make sure you have the right people doing the right things. This is perhaps the hardest task you have. Organizations—as all of you know all too well—are only as good as their people.

The ultimate task is to organize technology in ways that support business goals while maintaining a cost-effective computing and communications infrastructure. This means that politics, friends, and other distractions should play little or no role in how you optimize your business technology organization. Yes, a very tall order.

Summary

All these recommendations should help us prepare for the changes occurring in the business technology relationship. Consider them carefully. Some of them will work for you and some will not. The trick is to find the suite of suggestions that will take business technology to the next level in your company.

IT's All about Processes

Little by little we've been moving toward a major distinction between strategic and operational technology, with the latter the source of much debate (because everyone knows that it no longer matters). Yes, Nick Carr has had an impact on how we think about business technology, but to some extent his "IT Doesn't Matter" mantra was already fairly well known to—and practiced by—many CIOs and chief technology officers (CTOs) long before the publication of his now too-famous article in the *Harvard Business Review*. Of course, PCs, servers, and even enterprise applications are commodities. We knew this years ago when we stopped seriously worrying about Dell or IBM, versus HP PCs and laptops. But what is persistently new is the role that technology plays in mapping and reengineering business processes—which are not commodities.

If "technology" now "works" and there's little competitive advantage in the deployment of PCs, laptops, networks, servers, or data centers, where do we find differentiation? The answer lies in business processes and business models. Technology can help here. Although I was one of the early skeptics about BPM concepts and software, I am now tilting toward BPM as the source of real business technology impact. What I like most is the assumption within the larger BPM framework that business and technology are inseparable. Ten years ago this is what many of us thought would happen, though at the time everyone was still obsessed (as many still are) with business technology "alignment."

BPM is initially about descriptive mapping where business technologists identify how existing business processes make (or lose) money for the company. After the descriptive phase, the real work begins to reengineer the processes to increase efficiency and thereby enable them to contribute more directly to profitable growth. This is the hard part. Not only must we be creatively prescriptive, but we must think about BPM tools as hypothesis generators and testers where alternative processes are modeled, simulated, and assessed. This is where business processes meet business models and the overall business strategy. If the processes consistently yield greater efficiencies (and by implication contribute to revenue growth and profitability), when taken together they should (better) support your company's business strategy.

It's at this point where some companies hit a wall. What if the newly engineered business processes don't support the company's business models or overall business strategy? What if the processes themselves indicate that major organizational changes are necessary to optimize processes, models, and strategy? What if the description of business processes exposes some ill-conceived—and somewhat embarrassing—processes?

Corporate cultures define the boundaries of the processes that can be described, prescribed, and implemented. In other words, unless your culture will yield to objective analyses and logic, you should not expect too much from BPM exercises. On the other hand, if the culture is flexible enough to acknowledge some of the inefficiencies that BPM modeling will expose, then by all means proceed with mapping your processes and simulating alternative ones.

Is this any different from CRM, SFA, or even ITIL or COBIT infrastructure management applications? Not at all. Cultures always define process possibilities regardless of the domain. How many CRM projects failed because the corporate culture was not customer friendly? How many infrastructure management initiatives failed because of poor governance? BPM is no different: the culture must be receptive to the changes that the application suggests. If your culture is open to changes in its manufacturing, sales, distribution, customer service, and B2B processes, then the current crop of BPM applications can really help get processes, models, and even whole strategies to the next level.

Does Any of This Sound Familiar?

Here's a conversation that may or may not touch some nerves out there. Let me know if it hits home.

The participants include a whole hoard of "chiefs": a chief executive officer (CEO), a chief operating officer (COO), a chief financial officer (CFO), a chief marketing officer (CMO), a chief security officer (CSO), a chief learning officer (CLO), a general counsel, and a "facilitator"—me. The venue was stimulated by loud complaints from the lines of business about technology problems in a large enterprise. I was called in to moderate.

The CEO ...

"Basically we think you've screwed up the relationship between business and technology, and now because of all of the screw-ups, we have to rethink it—again ... so much for the 'business technology alignment' process."

The CFO ...

"Sounds like 're-thinking' will cost money ... will the outcome of all this require me to write more checks? I remember everyone talking about Y2K and eBusiness the same way ... what's different here? Alignment costs money ..."

The CIO ...

"Yeah, and what about all the good stuff we do day in and day out? Does anyone get any credit for this? The lines of business are clueless about what we do all day and have never given us clear guidance about what to buy—and not buy ... all they want is everything to work all of the time and cost less each year ..."

The CEO ...

"OK, you deserve some credit ... feel better? But I have to tell you that there's still a price on your head ... there are a lot of people in the trenches that want you gone ... I get calls every day about systems that crash ... not to mention what your team costs all of us ..."

The CTO ...

"There's no justice ... you want five 9s for no pain ... our infrastructures and architectures are obsolete because you bastards won't spend any money on the basics ..."

The COO ...

"What the hell is an 'architecture'?" "What are 'five 9s'?"

The CSO ...

"All of this makes sense, I guess, but we still have holes in our infrastructure and environment ... we can get hacked anytime ... we need to spend a lot more money here ... I've been telling you this for years ..."

The CMO ...

"Is there a reason why I should be here? I don't hear anything really new ... you've been talking about all this for at least a couple of decades and nothing really changes ... if there's no new message here or something I can really spin, then I have some other things to do ..."

The General Counsel ...

"Me too ..."

The CEO ...

"Everyone, just sit down ..."

The Facilitator ...

"Great group we have here ... you've all missed the point. Here's what's we need to do ... first, forget about Y2K, the dot.com bubble, and the great deals you got on unproven technology and service models ... second, strip away the hype and remember that vendors and consultants are not necessarily our friends, at least not yet ... next, rethink your business models and the best that technology can offer, especially as they involve collaboration and integration ..."

The CFO ...

"I like this ... finally, a hammer ..."

The CEO ...

"I like it too, but it's a hell of a lot more than a hammer ... it sounds like a way to finally get all this stuff to work together ... good timing, by the way, because I'm tired of dealing with the 'relationship' the same old way ... and the board of directors is actually starting to understand this stuff ..."

The CLO ...

"Did someone give them 'The Idiot's Guide to Technology'?"

The Facilitator ...

"Cute ... let's continue with a conversation about what collaboration and integration really mean ... one step at a time—but I guarantee all of you that this will work—at least a whole lot better than things work now ... stay with me ..."

The COO ...

"Not so fast ... summarize all this in English ..."

The Facilitator ...

"Fine ... for several decades the relationship between business and technology evolved as silos ... there were people responsible for business, technology, and the management of all this stuff ... we tried to 'align' these activities but by and large we failed ... we developed business strategies and then turned to technology to make it all work, underemphasizing the role of technology—just as, by the way, business planners underappreciated what technology could really do for business ... our management consisted of a set of 'worst practices' that we repeated for decades ... and to make matters worse, we confused ourselves about how all this should be organized ... the net effect is probably the worst track record in the history of business ..."

The COO ...

"Maybe I really didn't want it summarized ..."

The Facilitator ...

"It gets better ... all of this was exacerbated by the perfect storm ... our temporary insanity over Y2K, eBusiness, and how cheap the venture capitalists were selling 'killer apps' ..."

The COO ...

"Give it to me straight ... the whole truth and nothing but the truth ..."

The CEO ...

"The *truth*? You can't handle the truth ..."

The CIO ...

"Let's get to the good stuff ... so what else are you telling us?"

The Facilitator ...

"The future is about business technology convergence ... the silos have to come down ... we have to recognize that business, technology, and management are inseparable and that this inseparability has huge implications for how we develop business technology strategies, how we buy stuff, how we make it work together, and—essentially—how we kick the competition's ass ..."

The CEO ...

"So we have some work to do ... before we spend any more money on gear!"

The CFO ...

"Hallelujah! I've died and gone to heaven ..."

The Facilitator ...

"Not quite yet ... now we need to drill down on all these ideas ..."

The COO ...

"I thought this was going to be easier ..."

The CFO ...

"But we're not spending any more money, right?"

Markets, Pills, and Timing

Let's talk about timing. Or about that job we didn't take that would have turned out great, or the project we should have skipped that turned out so horribly, or the plan that we should have implemented a year ago.

Let's talk about business technology timing. Let's also talk about vitamin pills and painkillers, and let's talk about buying and selling technology and the really big drivers of technology decision making.

So here's the deal: capital markets drive spending which in turn determines the market for vitamin pills and painkillers. As Figure 1.5 suggests, both drivers are on a continuum.

Bear markets kill technology (and other) spending. Bull markets cause us to lose our heads and buy just about everything we see. Vendors of course hate bear markets—but buyers should love them. Painkillers include those investments that reduce costs and increase efficiency. They're usually made at gunpoint: someone decides that an investment has to be made before some huge technology problem arises. It's usually the CIO who holds the gun to the CFO's head.

Vitamin pills—those to-die-for applications that will completely transform your business—are the elixirs of bull markets. Vendors love bull markets because the normal business-case-before-we-buy discipline flies out the window propelled by unbridled optimism about business technology success. Bull markets breed silver bullets; bear markets take silver bullets for the team.

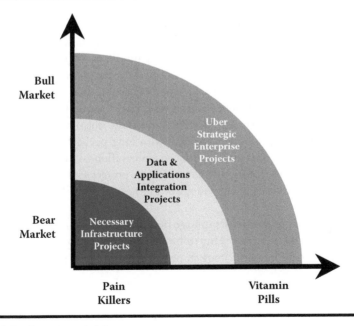

Figure 1.5 Investment drivers.

Why Should You Care?

Why is it so important to understand where we are, where we're going, and the competitive advantages each place provides?

Let's first pretend that we're buyers inside a company that spends serious money on business technology every year. Let's assume that we're in a bear market where capital spending is generally—and specifically in technology—way down. First, don't even think about proposing huge "strategic" enterprise projects. This of course is not to argue that they might be necessary and even prudent, but when competition for funds is fierce, it only makes sense to fight battles you can win. Second, work your vendors to a price unheard of during bull markets. Will they "cooperate"? Absolutely. They have to make their revenue numbers—which supersede earnings in bear markets. Third, take a hard look at your infrastructure with an eye to what it must do when the market turns. In bear markets, we expect relatively little from our computing and communications environments, but as the market transitions from bear to bull, expectations will rise. Can your infrastructure handle the transition? When times are tough, it's time to tune-up the infrastructure, assess its vulnerabilities, and get it into good enough shape to scale in anticipation of the transactions it will need to support. Any outsourcing deals you do in bear markets should be shared risk deals, where the vendors only get paid if they perform well, not if they just "perform."

Now let's pretend you're a vendor. First, you need to embrace TCO and ROI calculations. You need to champion tough business cases and pilot applications. You need to offer incentives to your buyers to open their checkbooks; you need to stay close to them during all phases of the work. In short, you need to hustle. But unlike the hustling you do during bull markets, bear market hustling must be quantitative. In bear markets vendors must sell painkillers, but in bull markets they sell vitamin pills. The trick of course is to morph the same products or services from painkillers to vitamin pills as the capital markets swing. But this is tougher than it sounds. Some products just don't morph well. CRM applications are optimistic, enthusiastic applications that assume more and more customers that have to be handled just right. They're often expensive with long payback periods. But some other investments—like data and applications integration—can be sold offensively and defensively, as investments that can help you protect and optimize what you have as well as tools that can help you grow. Pretty cool, huh? In this case, timing is flexible.

When times are good, vendors splurge because their customers splurge. If you sell stuff in a bull market, you want to be on commission. But if you start your career as a salesperson in a bear market, negotiate a high base salary.

Do You Know What Time It Is?

Regardless of where you sit, you need good timing. And you need to know what to do with it. It's essential that we all understand market context, that we understand what's expected of us and what's realistic. Capital markets fundamentally change the buying and selling climate; capital markets determine the popularity of pain-killers versus vitamin pills.

How sensitive are you to context? What changes have you made to how you buy or sell business technology since capital technology markets weakened? Can you morph your product and service pitches? The rules of the game change as markets swing. You can increase the chances of a successful sale or a productive deployment if you know exactly what market you're in and what each market wants to buy and deploy.

Timing is still everything.

That Was Then, This Is Now

I was at a meeting recently and someone asked "what happened in the late 1990s … what the hell was everyone thinking and why did we all lose our minds?" Just in case anyone's forgotten, we overspent on technology, deployed questionable killer apps, and generally suspended the use of due diligence, business cases, TCO analyses, and ROI requirements.

It was a great question. Here's an answer—and some thoughts about what we may have missed while we were intoxicated.

The Perfect Storm

Three storms collided in the period 1995 to 2000, storms that most of us misinterpreted as the launching of the new digital economy. It was, as George Clooney discovered in the movie of the same name—the perfect storm.

- Our absolute need to make our computing and communications technology Year 2000 compliant triggered a ton of spending to remediate old code, buy new PCs, and install huge ERP applications, among other applications and gear.
- The eBusiness frenzy got to just about everyone; companies spent uncontrollably on Internet projects that sometimes made sense, but sometimes didn't. Just like Y2K budget lines, excessive eBusiness spending was "protected."
- Capital was essentially free during this period. Bad business models from start-ups solving Y2K and eBusiness problems were financed by (professional and amateur) private equity venture capitalists who shoveled cash out the door as quickly as they could find sometimes good but mostly goofy business

models; stuff was cheap back in those days largely because the companies' (nonexistent) revenues were subsidized by venture funding that was playing the new economy momentum for everything it was worth. This distorted the companies, the technologies, and the business models. On the other side of the cost-of-capital equation was the ease with which public and private companies could raise money based on bloated valuations; who wouldn't raise money at 100 times earnings—or with no revenues? Unfortunately, the corporate wealth effect drove companies to do technology deals that didn't make too much sense, deals that were interpreted as validation of the new economy and its fledgling technologies.

All of this contributed to a massive misinterpretation of events that made too many of us believe that the world had indeed changed, that the "old economy" had collapsed under the weight of the "new economy." We were off and running. Or so we thought.

The net effect of all this was one of the deepest retrenchments of capital technology spending we've ever seen. Way, way overdone.

The Glass Is Half Full

But there's another way to look at the perfect storm. Although many eBusiness models failed (at least in the short term), the storm got everybody thinking hard about how to exploit a new communications and transaction channel. We also averted any major Y2K catastrophes; and finally, the bear market scared most of the amateur venture capitalists off the playing field (to the chagrin of their investors still searching for returns on their investments).

But it's also important to understand the period from 1995 to 2000 as the period that built the foundation upon which serious technology integration and interoperability now rests. Many of us missed a new generation of integration/ interoperability technologies that enable new collaborative business models. What began in the form of published applications programming interfaces (APIs) evolved to generic enterprise application integration (EAI) tools, and now we're making significant progress in *über* glue: Web Services.

Computing and communications technology is actually starting to work; the stuff is coming together in ways we couldn't imagine ten years ago and had trouble describing even five years ago. Business models are morphing toward collaboration, supply chain integration, personalization, and customization, among other connectivity-based processes. There's a rhythm to these trends: collaborative business models moving nicely with integration technology.

The inertia of old business technology management practices is still, however, driving too many of our technology investment decisions, still driving us toward piecemeal applications, ill-conceived sourcing and staffing strategies, crazy organizational strategies, and metrics that measure the wrong things.

It's time for a second look. Shake off the hangover and look at the collaboration and integration possibilities around you. The frenzy of the mid- to late 1990s shouldn't paralyze us. Isn't it amazing how we overreact—and then overreact? The pendulum never seems to adjust to reality. Just as we lost our minds in the 1990s and did some really stupid things, now we're not doing any smart things, which of course is stupid. When will we get it right? Let's just hope that in five or ten years when the frenzy returns (over god knows what)—we'll recognize it for what it is.

What do you think? Will we be smarter next time?

Trends That (Really) Matter

What do we *really* need to know?

Do we need to know every specific feature the next release of Microsoft Office will have? Do we really need to know exactly what the next version of the SAP ERP platform will look like? Or is it the macro trends that influence what we buy, deploy, support, decommission, and optimize that matter most? I've been working with some colleagues about the short list of trends that matter. One of the participants in the project calls this list the "if-we-only-had-perfect-information-about-these-trends-life-would-be-perfect" list.

1. **Regulatory Trends**—Will the government regulate eBusiness? Will it tax Internet transactions? Will it legislate the end of spam? Will it define and uphold privacy rights? Will it develop policies around intellectual property? Will it regulate outsourcing? I'd love to have the answers to all of these questions. If the government actually discovers the digital world and decides to respond to its requirements, then things could change dramatically for those of us who make our livings around business technology. But if the government stays in digital denial, we can expect lots of problems and occasional chaos.

2. **Interoperability Trends**—Will everything work together? Will Web services become ubiquitous? Will we be able to (remember the phrase?) plug-and-play? This Holy Grail has eluded us for decades, but for the first time that I can remember, prospects for integration and interoperability are—if not excellent—at least good. The way the open versus proprietary trends play out will determine just how connected data, applications, and communications become. I'd love to know how it will all shake out.

3. **Supply Chain Trends**—Will Wal-Mart connect the world? Will Dell take collaboration and integration to the next level? Will demand forecasting, dynamic pricing, and inventory management marry radio frequency identification (RFID) to enable real-time management? Will business become

continuous? Although enormous progress has been made in supply chain planning and management, there's still a long way to go to bridge the supply chain haves and have-nots. How will it play out? If we knew how the world was going to connect and collaborate, we could make business technology decisions that prepare us for supply chain optimization.

4. **Architecture Trends**—Will thin clients make a comeback—and then rule the world? Will fat clients get even fatter? Will super servers graze on super server farms? What will data standards look like? Security standards? Wireless communications standards? As the industry consolidates, architectures will also consolidate. But what will they look like? Perfect information here could save the industry billions of dollars every year. As it is, we have to hedge our technology bets—and hedging can be expensive.

5. **Sourcing Trends**—Will it make sense to outsource? Will technology "utilities" finally emerge? Will companies be able to pay by the drink? Will shared risk contracting become pervasive? Will we develop best practices around sourcing for infrastructure services, database management, applications, and communications? Will robust sourcing TCO and ROI models emerge? Information about how the industry organizes its providers and users would provide critical strategic information about what and how to source technology products and services.

6. **Infrastructure Trends**—Will the Internet collapse? Will security breaches become routine? Will viruses continue to invade our computing and communications infrastructures? Will they become intelligent and self-healing? Will we upgrade them on a scheduled basis? While we tend to think more creatively about customer-facing applications, the need for secure, reliable, and scalable infrastructures will continue to grow. There's a growing chorus about the vulnerability of our networks—particularly the Internet. Are they alarmists, or is there something to really worry about? It would be great to actually know.

7. **Disruptive Technology Trends**—There are always lists of "emerging" technologies, technologies that lots of us think will "disrupt" business models and processes. I'd love to know that the real list looks like in 2010. Will wireless communications technology revolutionize B2C and B2B transaction processing? Will VoIP enable most of our data and voice communications? Will intelligent systems technology penetrate our infrastructures and applications portfolios? I'd sure like to see the list that will define the next decade.

Perfect information is impossible to acquire. So what should we do with lists like the one above? First, I think it's the effort—not the list—that matters. What would your list look like? If you can identify the major drivers of business technology change, you should be able to steer your business technology investments. Perfect information exercises are intended to reduce uncertainty about macro trends.

Although uncertainty cannot be eliminated, it can be "managed." Try it; pick five, seven, or ten things you'd really like to know—and then think about their trajectories—and your business technology strategy.

What They're Doing

I recently spent some time with some CIOs of Fortune 500 companies and asked them what they planned to do this year (and next). A few of them just started laughing, a few of them nodded their heads (I guess indicating that they indeed *did* plan to do something), and a few others actually perked up. After a few minutes, they all chimed in. Perhaps the most startling thing about their responses was the operational and practical nature of their plans; though there's some bona fide "strategy" embedded in their responses as well.

Here are the plans organized around some areas we're all familiar with:

- Strategy
- Applications
- Communications
- Data
- Infrastructure
- Security
- Organization
- Management

Strategy

The CIOs plan to play with BPM this year. They want to determine the value the new perspective and tools might provide to improving business models and processes, especially in terms of efficiencies. They are not looking to "reinvent" or "reengineer" their companies with BPM technology; rather, they want to mend them, improve them, extend them—cost-effectively.

Applications

The big story here is about optimization. Many CIOs feel that they've spent a ton of money on enterprise applications (like ERP, CRM, and network and systems management applications), and it's now time to reap the benefits of these huge investments. Benefits realization is the story for 2005: there's very little appetite for installing new systems as most of the CIOs want to exploit what they have.

They also plan to start looking at the applications that make things connect: application integration tools (especially Web services–based tools), wireless applications, synchronization tools, and collaboration tools (including distributed meeting tools and, of course, supply chain planning and management applications).

Communications

Wireless, wireless, wireless. There's a major push to make everyone mobile. The expectations about wireless technology-driven cost savings—which include reduced real estate and office expenses—are huge. Let's hope the industry can deliver.

This also appears to be the year when just about everyone will pilot some VoIP technologies. But there's still disappointment about the cost-effectiveness of voice recognition technology.

Data

If you own stock in data-mining companies and companies that have larger offerings in business intelligence, hold on to it. All the CIOs we interviewed were planning to widen and deepen their investments in business intelligence. Perhaps surprisingly, there was also interest in increasing investments in competitor intelligence. There was concern among the CIOs about the management of whole new data streams, especially the ones that will be generated by the deployment of RFID tags, as well as the middleware necessary to make back office applications talk with active RFID tags. Data storage is also on their minds, as more and more data is collected and mined.

Of special note was the interest expressed in customer analytics. It seems that all want to know more about their customers than they used to. Applications and tools that enable customer profiling are more popular than ever. Personalization and customization are the objective of customer analytics: the more companies know about their customers, the more they can customize and personalize their products and services.

The CIOs are also interested in Web analytics because there's pressure to increase eBusiness to expand the digital channel.

Infrastructure

Everyone's trying to get out of the infrastructure business. It seems that the "commoditization" of IT is most evident in the infrastructure area. No one wants to manage desktops, networks, or—especially—help desks. Our CIOs expect to increase the outsourcing of these activities and explore other parts of their computing and communications infrastructures that can be outsourced.

There are also concerns about supporting an increasingly varied technology environment, not in terms of different manufacturers but in terms of additional devices, such as PDAs, pagers, smart cell phones, thin clients, and other devices used to access data, e-mail, and applications 24/7.

Security

The more commerce that occurs in cyberspace, the more numerous and severe security (and privacy) requirements become. All the CIOs we interviewed will spend more on security this year than they spent last year. The growing identify theft problem has stimulated additional investments in data security and network security; there remains considerable concern about wireless security, a concern that is hampering the desire for more and more broadband wireless communications.

Organization

The segmentation of technology into "strategic" and "operational" technology is driving some significant organizational changes. Many of our CIOs are interested in reorganizing their teams into layers of responsibility that fine-tune technology management roles. For example, many of the CIOs indicated that they were appointing deputies with specific responsibilities for applications, data management, security, infrastructure, and strategy, among other duties. Many were experimenting with offices of the CIO and technology directorates as mechanisms to distribute responsibility across their teams. The more savvy CIOs see this as a way to disconnect themselves from many of the more infrastructure-related management tasks: it's clear that CIOs do not want to be called when a network crashes or a server dies.

As more functions are outsourced, there's also increased interest in professional vendor management. Many of our CIOs expressed interest in the need to better manage their vendors, to write better requests for proposals (RFPs), and to monitor performance with diagnostic service level agreements (SLAs).

Management

Standardization is occurring at a rapid rate primarily because the technology industry itself is consolidating, not necessarily because companies have all discovered the wisdom of fewer rather than more vendors, applications, databases, and networks. Industry consolidation is driving a new standardization that our CIOs are well aware of—and quite happy about. Several noted how wonderful it must be to manage a fleet of but one kind of aircraft—the way Southwest airlines has managed its "infrastructure" for years. But standardization is also occurring because of complexity and the realization on the part of CIOs that increasing complexity simply cannot be managed over the long term—and there's no way it can ever be optimized over time. All the CIOs are pushing for less variation in their technology environments.

Governance remains a hot issue for all the CIOs. With more and more technology entering their domains, the need for clear acquisition, deployment, and support rules is at an all-time high. The CIOs stated they intend to restart the governance discussion with an eye toward consistency, simplification, and clarity.

Our CIOs have grown uncomfortable with traditional performance metrics and are feeling pressure to hit metrics that speak directly to business value (rather than technological operational efficiency). At the grassroots, simple asset and performance management tools are definitely back in style, while at the strategic enterprise level it's all about more customers, happier customers, and customers willing to spend more money. Technology investments need to speak directly to profitable growth.

Marching Orders

There were 20 CIOs in this roundtable-based survey. Although hardly scientific, it's important to note that there was amazing consistency among the technology leaders, suggesting to us that their plans may well represent a set of larger trends. The key themes were optimization, cost-effectiveness, creative sourcing, and the acquisition and management of standard technology layers—as well as that persistent theme about customer data, analytics, and personalization/customization. After all these years, it seems that data is still king.

Business Technology Trends to Worry about

What is going on in our industry, anyway? Here are five things to think about. Should we be happy or worried?

1. **The technology industry is consolidating**. CISCO continues to gobble up companies and even service companies are attracting mergers and acquisitions—and everyone's already heard too much about Oracle's acquisition of PeopleSoft and Seibel (and lots of others). Will this trend continue? Yes, with a vengeance. Why? Because commoditization, especially of infrastructure products and services, will continue with a vengeance. Differentiation in this space is tough—it's even tougher to generate profits from commodities, which require scale to make money. What does consolidation mean to us? Fewer choices (like what the cable TV industry gives us); and even fewer bells and whistles. The change is in the distribution of power among the vendors. First, fewer vendors now have more power; second, fewer powerful vendors means less competition and eventually higher prices (or at least less negotiat-

ing room). Is this good for the industry? Well, it's good for the deep-pocket survivors but ultimately bad for the consumers of technology products and services. If we fast-forward 20 years, technology consumers will be screaming for more government regulation of technology utilities.

2. **There are also major changes in the value and location of skill sets.** Undergraduates actually understood this earlier than industry pundits. Voting with their feet, thousands of them have abandoned the technology majors, including computer science, software engineering, and management information systems. They saw the handwriting on the wall almost three years ago, when technology and business process outsourcing began to increase so dramatically. Programming expertise is far less valuable in the United States today than it was in the 1980s or 1990s. Much of it is leaving the United States for cheaper pastures. It will never return. The only refuge is in skill sets like advanced architecture and complex data integration and data mining, areas less likely to be commoditized because they grow from digital technology innovation, which is still largely led by the United States (but perhaps not for long; see below). The problem is that the education and training industries are not responding quickly enough to reorient students to different careers. If educational and training programs remain in the twentieth century, there will be no valuable skills to market.

3. **Innovation is at risk.** Technology companies are hoarding huge stockpiles of cash. Why? Probably because they have less confidence in future revenue than they are revealing. Why not use the cash for more R&D? The Bush administration has influenced spending reductions in basic research—through the National Science Foundation (NSF) and the Defense Advanced Research Projects Agency (DARPA)—in computer science and information technology. Years ago, DARPA funded the lion's share of PhDs in the field, but no more. The private equity venture capital crowd is investing less and less in seed and early stage companies and thereby depriving them of innovation capital. This has already had a profound effect on computing and communications technology innovation. Instead of risking capital on seed and early stage companies—which, incidentally, have higher historical returns than later stage companies—they are behaving more and more like conservative bankers (who prefer to loan money to people who don't really need it). These trends plus the undergraduate boycott of technology majors will create an innovation drought.

4. **Governance is shaky.** Although there are no better ways to spend one's organizational hours than on honing a solid governance strategy, most companies still struggle with who-owns-what kinds of questions. It continues to amaze me how many companies just cannot get this right, cannot define and then consistently apply governance policies and procedures. In a strange sort of way, all the recent emphases on regulatory compliance have breathed new life into at least the governance of financial reporting. Why did it take an act

of Congress? Governance is good business, but far too many companies do it poorly. The critical aspect of this failure to get it right means that we continue to suboptimize the acquisition, deployment, and support of technology because we can't figure out who should be doing what, how, and when.

5. **Business processes remain mysterious**. If you ask your company exactly how it makes money and exactly what its costs are, you might be surprised by the answer. The problem is the word "exactly." Most companies have a general idea about how they make—and lose—money but they really don't know precisely how they do it. The same is true about their customers. Very few companies profile their customers accurately or objectively; and the same is true of business process visibility. Few companies can map their processes in ways that permit simulations, what-if analyses, or even basic descriptive analysis of how the company works.

Is there any good news?

Yes, technology is now cheaper and more reliable than it's ever been. We have sets of management best practices that actually make a lot sense, things like standardization, project and portfolio management, vendor management, and the like. Integration and interoperability technology is evolving. Whole new hardware and software architectures—which will stimulate whole new forms of transaction processing—are emerging. The major technology vendors continue to spend heavily in research and development, especially Microsoft and IBM. This spending will keep innovation alive as we determine what the overall national innovation investment strategy should be. All pretty good stuff. But control of the industry, measured by consolidation, skills, and innovation, is shifting. Fewer vendors, commoditization, devalued skill sets, and modest innovation will combine to change the industry in ways hard to imagine today. And without good governance and deep understanding of business processes and models, we'll continue to waste technology dollars.

It's always hard to tell just how much to worry. Some of my colleagues tell me that all of this is inevitable, that all industries go through a variety of stages until they settle down. I am often reminded that the IT industry is not all that old and that any number of perturbations is likely. So is the semipermanent handwriting on the way? Or is all this just part of the push and pull of evolution. Maybe fewer-rather-than-more technology vendors will be a good thing. Maybe targeted outsourcing is okay. Maybe innovation can be supported almost entirely by industry.

Depending on the news of the day or the latest survey detailing the state of the field, we interpret the trends differently. Some days I see chaos, but other days I see a relatively orderly progression toward a much more mature industry. Nick Carr's "IT Doesn't Matter" got everyone talking about the industry (to put it mildly), but long term I suspect his central thesis was correct (of course, IT "matters"). The real question is where the field will be in a decade or so. Carr simply described some trends that have some correlates in history with other industries. What might the reaction to the article have been if it had been innocently titled, "IT in Transition"?

Finally, there's the timing issue. As one of Murphy's best laws states—"everything takes longer than it takes"—we may well be at the beginning of a long maturation process or in the middle of a rapidly developing one. It's impossible to tell. My guess is that the field's transition is more evolutionary than revolutionary, but that opinion, of course, depends on the news of the day or the latest survey data detailing the state of the field!

Collaborate/Integrate: What to Do about Business Technology

We all need help sometimes. Not long ago I needed help developing a high-level strategy for a company that wanted to rethink its business technology investment strategy. I was asked: "So if we're going to invest in technology, what should be the big drivers, and what should be the filters through which we send these potentially huge investments?" I thought about the question for a while and came up with two words: "collaboration" and "integration." "What does that mean?" It means that investments in business technology should be made only if they're consistent with collaborative business models and enable technology integration and interoperability. The client then asked me to draw a picture (on the back of a napkin) of what I meant. Figure 1.6 was the result (when I got back to the office and launched PowerPoint).

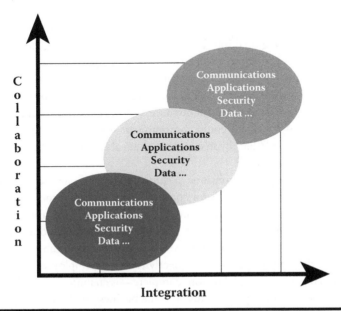

Figure 1.6   Investment filters.

The advice was pretty simple: stay out of the red zone. Make investments in business models and technologies that facilitate collaboration and integration: nothing more, nothing less.

But what does that mean?

Collaborate—Or Else

Collaboration comes in many flavors. You have to prepare generally for collaboration that will occur inside and outside of your firewall. You have to think about continuous versus discrete business models and transactions. You have to think about supply chain planning and management, customization, personalization, and eventually even automation, where significant numbers of your transactions will be automated. You need to think about customers and suppliers and even employees as "life cycles" to be managed and monetized. The notions of "whole customer management," "whole supplier management," and "whole employee management" should anchor your collaborative discussions. Connectivity is the watchword now, not just because the Internet makes it possible, but because connectivity enhances reach, service, expense management, and—therefore—profitability.

A key distinction? Continuous versus discrete transaction processing. Discrete transactions—like selling insurance policies, buying disk drives to be included in PC manufacturing, or buying or selling stock—used to be transactions that one could begin in the morning and complete by afternoon—or the next morning after a good night's sleep. Even today these transactions are continuous. One insurance policy is blended with another. Cross- and up-selling are continuous goals. Disk drive acquisition is integrated into PC manufacturing and buying and selling stock is simultaneously linked to tax calculations and estate planning. Tomorrow all of these transactions will be extended, continuous, and automated.

Another way to think about all this is to imagine what would be possible if your company had immediate and continuous access to its employees, customers, suppliers, and partners. What if you could communicate with all of these constituencies whenever you wanted? What if you could tell them about new deals, discounts, and opportunities any time at all?

One thing's for sure. If we continue to think about business processes as discrete, we'll miss profitable opportunities for continuous transaction processing. Worse, if you keep making investments in plant, equipment, communications, databases, and applications that are inconsistent with the collaborative, continuous world, you'll waste a ton of money positioning yourself to succeed in the past.

We're at a different place now. Connectivity among employees, suppliers, customers, and partners—though far from complete—is enabling interactive customer relationships, integrated supply chains, and the business analytics that permit real-time tinkering with inventory, distribution, and pricing. The strategies and business models were always there: for years we've imagined seamless connectivity and ubiquitous business. But the convergence of business and technology has made it more than just possible.

Integrate/Interoperate

This one's a little simpler: applications, data, infrastructures, and all of the rest of the gear that we buy have to integrate and interoperate. This means that you need to focus on enterprise application integration (EAI) and even Internet applications integration (IAI), because we're now replatforming first-generation Internet applications. Applications, databases, content, and knowledge must be integrated to support cross-selling, up-selling, supply chain planning and management, customization, personalization, and automation. It's great if there's a business imperative to collaborate, but if the technology doesn't integrate and interoperate, then it won't happen.

It also means that you need to reduce variation in your environment because variation exacerbates integration problems. You therefore need to standardize your environment around some significant discipline, which now becomes not just good management but necessary and sufficient to ongoing integration (and therefore collaboration).

Architectures must also be assessed for their willingness to work together and with the enterprise applications and databases you've selected. How about this: would your computing and communications architectures look different if you were wearing glasses when you deployed them—glasses that had one collaboration and one integration lens? Of course they would.

So that's the advice I gave to the client. Yes, it was high level. Yes, it was abstract. But it was also good advice: investors in business models and enabling technologies must drink the collaboration/integration Kool-Aid. Now you can take it to the next level.

Strategy, Anyone?

Let's say it clearly: if a company doesn't understand its competitive advantages and its current and future business models, it's doomed. Not only will it fail in the marketplace but it will waste tons of cash on technology along the way.

So what business are you in?

If the strategists in your company have difficulty answering this question, then you're in deep trouble—especially if you're a technology manager expected to make decisions about what to buy, build, in-source, or outsource.

Scenario-based planning can help reduce uncertainty about the future. The objective is not an elegant document suitable for publication in the *Harvard Business Review*, but a vehicle for provoking thought that involves several specific steps.

You need to **monitor trends** that pertain to your industry on a regular basis, including social, political, workplace, work habit, regulation/deregulation, national and global economic, and macro technology trends.

You need to **monitor and report on *known* and *anticipated* competitors**. The good news here is that people love to read stuff about the competition. This is because we benchmark and validate our behavior against our competitors. The huge danger is that if the competition you're tracking extrapolates only from its current business models—and that's all you track—you're likely to miss the out-of-the-box, unconventional competitors who can do serious damage to your market share. You should profile competitor business models and processes at least annually, including details about the products and services they offer, their channel strategies, and their market niches.

Based on all of the above—the environmental scan, competitor analyses, and existing business models—*future* **models and processes should be defined**. This is the essence of the scenario generation process. The key here is to simultaneously extrapolate from current trends *and* leapfrog current models into whole new business arenas. What, for example, will be the new model for customer service? What will your sales and marketing strategies have to look like? How will you cross-sell online and offline?

Key question: do you have the expertise in-house to think creatively *and objectively* about future business? If you do, beg, borrow, or steal their time; if not, hire some industry gurus (with deep industry knowledge—and empower them to speak candidly).

After you've modeled the future, **prioritize** the processes, products, and services that will keep you competitive. Keep the list short: a 20-item to-do list will always yield 15 orphans.

Then **convert the prioritized processes, products, and services into high-level technology requirements** with specific reference to communications, applications, data, security, standards, and people investments you'll need to make. You should also make a list of services that might be in-sourced, co-sourced, or out-sourced. And, yes, you should begin to price out the big-ticket items, like a communications infrastructure upgrade or an enterprise applications migration.

Create a "devil's advocate" process where new business models and processes are reality-checked.

Enough about the substance of the process. Let's turn to the politics. To build influential scenarios, you'll need:

- Buy-in and resources from *senior* management. Without both commitments you will fail.
- The right mix of people: you should populate your relatively small group (seven to ten) with mostly business professionals. The breakdown—ideally –should be: 60 percent with wide and deep business sense, 20 percent with

wide and deep business sense and wide technology sense, and 20 percent with wide business sense and wide and deep technology sense.

■ A time commitment from the participants of no less than one and no more than two days for the major events (like defining future business models and processes), and a continuous commitment of small time chunks to review the process along the way. This assumes that the owner of the process preps the group in the form of briefings and materials that provide explicit guidance about how the process works, scenario elements, and precisely what they will be expected to do (and not do).

■ Support: you'll need administrative support to organize and run the process. There will be at least one major event a year—a one- or two-day soirée for generating future business models and processes—and several short on-site events for reviewing materials (like competitor analyses). All of this must be professionally scheduled, organized, and facilitated.

■ For special events, you'll need a facilitator who understands the domain (insurance, manufacturing, pharmaceuticals, etc.) and the process. This is critical: if the facilitator is bad, the process will fail (and if you fail the first time you organize the event, you've failed forever). Facilitators must have engaging personalities and know as much or more about the domain as the participants. If the facilitator is a dud and doesn't understand the business models and processes that dominate the vertical industry, the process will break down and the political repercussions of your efforts could be "significant."

■ A budget: you will need cash to support the process. You have two options here. You can charge the participants or you can lure them in to your all-expenses-paid scenario development vacation. Try number 1 first; if it fails, go to plan B. Plan B is politically smart: if the sessions are productive you get double credit, and if they're not, at least you can't be accused of foolishly spending their money.

■ Finally, straw men: you will need to jumpstart the process. Because people are often better critics than creators, you need to have some straw men models and scenarios at your disposal.

These are the minimum prerequisites to success. If one or more is missing, you're toast.

Chapter 2

Organization

Five Flavors of Alignment

There are lots of ways to think about "alignment." Over the years I've basically abandoned the term but because it continues to persist in the literature (and I assume in the minds and hearts of technology professionals and business executives), perhaps we should continue to give it some due.

One of the problems I've had with the term is that it seems to be too vague and too inclusive. What *is* alignment? Rather than debate the definitions out there, let's look at alternative alignment flavors. I've identified five:

1. Strategic Alignment
2. Infrastructure Alignment
3. Operational Alignment
4. Innovation Alignment
5. People Alignment

Each of these is very different and each creates different expectations. They are discussed here because we all need to recognize the differences among the flavors and to ask ourselves how to service each one.

Let's look at the flavors in order.

Strategic Alignment

Strategic alignment is what most of us think about when we hear the term "alignment." The key here for practitioners is to make sure that technology investments are consistent with strategic objectives. For example, if a company decides that eBusiness will become a much more important part of the business, then it needs to make sure that its eBusiness infrastructure is secure, can scale, and is cost-effective. Chances are that such a company needs to invest in its eBusiness transaction-processing capability if its strategy is calling for more eBusiness. That in turn suggests that the decision to invest additional dollars in eBusiness has been made at the strategic level and that what remains is to make sure that the technology platform that supports eBusiness can grow with the business. This is a classic alignment test: if the company balks at the technology investments necessary to support its strategic objectives, then it will fail one of the most basic alignment tests. Other examples include the desire to do more cross- and up-selling and the need to integrate customer databases, the desire to acquire companies and the need for a standardized applications architecture and integration methodology, and the strategic need to reduce cost and the technology requirement to reduce variation, optimize sourcing, and measure performance. Strategic alignment is a great concept, but I suspect that there's often a disconnect between what corporate strategists want and what the technology professionals in the company are actually doing. The recommendation to improve strategic alignment is for strategic planning to require input from technology professionals or, put more bluntly, strategic planning cannot proceed without technology approval. Without such a tight coupling there will be gaps, and just when a company wants to execute its strategy, it may find that its technology infrastructure and applications portfolio will not support the strategy.

Infrastructure Alignment

Infrastructure alignment is about efficiency. Every company wants the best performance for as little cost as possible. But there's obviously more to infrastructure alignment. Reliability and security are hugely important to all users: look what happens when e-mail crashes! Like strategic alignment, infrastructure alignment assumes information about what the company plans to do, but it also assumes that companies will be relieved of fears about their ability to compute and communicate. Perfect alignment here is that everything "works" behind the curtain, that performance is consistently cost-effective.

Infrastructure alignment also assumes sourcing best practices. Because many infrastructure services have become commoditized, there's increased pressure to organize the acquisition, deployment, and support of infrastructure technology with the right mix of internal and external service providers. Alignment assumes the importance of vendor management, performance metrics, and delivery-based SLAs.

Companies that want additional infrastructure alignment invest in infrastructure control systems like Control Objectives for Information and Related Technology (COBIT) and IT Infrastructure Library (ITIL). The COBIT framework—according to the Information Systems Audit and Control Association (ISACA)—is:

> An IT governance framework and supporting toolset that allows managers to bridge the gap between control requirements, technical issues and business risks. COBIT enables clear policy development and good practice for IT control throughout organizations. COBIT emphasizes regulatory compliance, helps organizations to increase the value attained from IT, enables alignment and simplifies implementation of the COBIT framework.

According to ITIL and ITSM World, ITIL:

> Consists of 6 sets: Service Support; Service Delivery; Planning to Implement Service Management; ICT Infrastructure Management; Applications Management; The Business Perspective. Within these a variable number of very specific disciplines are described.

These control systems can help improve infrastructure alignment—but they also require significant investment and the governance to make them work.

Operational Alignment

Operational alignment is about flexibility, adaptation, and agility. While the applications, communications, and data architectures are reasonably well defined in well-governed organizations, there needs to be enough flexibility in the deployment of these capabilities to enable businesses to make the changes to their products and services that they need to stay competitive. Operational alignment is less about strategy and the anticipated need for consistency between next-generation products and services and the technology necessary to develop, deliver, and service them, than it is about servicing existing products and services. Words like tweaking should come to mind when thinking about operational alignment: when lines of business need to adjust their products or services, change their reporting requirements, or alter their marketing materials, they need their applications, databases, and communications to change with them. While this of course does not mean that they will frequently require whole new applications and databases, it does mean that applications and databases can yield the right things at the right time.

Like all of the alignment flavors, operational alignment also assumes a partnership between technology and the business, a partnership that encourages open communications, cooperation, and teamwork to deliver the best solutions as quickly as possible; where infrastructure alignment focuses more on reliability and cost-effectiveness, operational alignment focuses more on flexibility and agility.

Innovation Alignment

Innovation alignment is tough to achieve. It exists in companies that have an innovation culture—and not all companies do (in spite of lip service to the contrary). Perhaps the easiest opportunity for innovation alignment occurs within the relatively well defined area of R&D, an area that most companies have defined as important to their futures. Technology support for corporate R&D might focus on R&D processes, tools to enhance the R&D process, tools that contribute to innovation, and metrics to measure success/failure. There are also opportunities to exploit some new information technologies in the R&D process, such as online contests to "solve" complicated R&D.

Innovation alignment also requires the integration of strategic and operational alignment where new ideas are strategically viable and operationally feasible. This kind of integrative thinking is hard to achieve, but when successful can literally change the face of a company. Good example? Apple Computer struggled mightily until it developed the iPod. How did it innovate? The iPod had to be strategic and operational. There are other examples. Procter & Gamble innovates continuously. Rohm and Haas does the same thing. But U.S. automobile manufacturers seem to have problems innovating. The alignment challenge here is to identify the innovation capacity of the company and then focus resources accordingly. Tools for concept development, prototyping, and testing are among the resources that can accelerate innovation.

People Alignment

People alignment is a critical ingredient to all of the alignment flavors. We need people to execute the alignment agenda. But which people? With what kinds of skills?

Each of the alignment flavors requires a different set of skills and competencies. In fact, the flavors are so different that the necessary skills and competencies generally cannot be found in the same people. This has huge implications for companies seeking alignment. If you look at the five flavors, it's easy to see how the skills and competencies required for each differ so dramatically. Strategic alignment requires a top-down, holistic view of the business coupled by a purposeful view of technology, that is, how technology enables broad business agendas, not just specific transactions. Infrastructure alignment is about the details of architectures, cost-effectiveness, reliability, and security. Operational alignment requires skills in the delivery and support areas, as well as in the areas of flexibility and agility. Innovation alignment requires a great many creative skills. as well as the ability to detach from day-to-day infrastructure and operational activities. People alignment requires us to examine the skills of all the professionals responsible for alignment, assess the gaps, and fill them with the right people at the right time doing the right things.

Many alignment agendas fail simply because companies don't have the right people doing the right things. One of the toughest challenges is to assess the skills in your company with reference to the four flavors of alignment and then make the tough decisions about the mix of professionals in the company. Companies serious about alignment must make the tough decisions. How many can actually do this?

Alignment Nirvana

Obviously, achieving total alignment is difficult. When we think about alignment—and read testimonials to alignment success—we're usually reading about one or two alignment flavors—not the whole process. Alignment Nirvana is elusive because of the diverse skills necessary to achieve it; perhaps the best way to achieve it is to recognize the differences among alignment goals and processes and to pursue alignment as though it were five interconnected projects. The key—as always—however, is people. Without the right people pursuing these alignment objectives not much progress will be made—as suggested in Figure 2.1.

Alignment can obviously help companies achieve results, but to take full advantage of aligned opportunities we should recognize the different alignment flavors and organize accordingly.

Figure 2.1   Alignment flavors.

Cost versus Profit Centers

The Proof Is in the Attitude

I'm sick to death of companies that claim they're strategic technology investors when they're actually technology cheap skates. We know from industry analyses that "strategic" technology investors spend around 7 to 10 percent of their gross revenue on technology, while companies that are considered "tactical" investors spend 1 to 3 percent of revenue on technology. (Those in the middle I guess are "operational" investors.)

But let's be really candid here. Most companies—except for the really big 7 to 10 percent spenders—are technology cheap skates always looking to reduce technology costs. This means that spenders in the 1 to 6 percent range see their technology investments as cost centers—not profit centers. They really don't have all that much confidence in technology's ability to contribute to profitable growth through up-selling, cross-selling, or improved customer service; instead, they see technology as something that they must have to exist—like telephones, furniture, and company cars. This means that technology costs—like health care benefits and pensions—need to be reduced—regardless of the impact the reduction might have on productivity or morale.

Part of the problem—and this is the attitude part—is how many companies acquire, deploy, and support technology. Many of them—dare I really say this?—don't know what they're doing. You know the ones. They think that CRM applications will reduce or eliminate customer disdain or that wireless PDAs will cost-effectively keep us all connected so we can help the business grow. It's no wonder that these companies see technology as a cost center. There are also a bunch of companies that violate well-established best practices like standardization and performance-based contracting. These companies inevitably overspend on technology, which, in turn, will require them to tighten their technology belts (which is near impossible because they've already violated all of the acquisition best practices). Put another way, these are the companies that think that technology costs too much because they don't know how to acquire, deploy, or support it. Rather than point a finger at themselves, they declare technology an unmanaged expense and proceed to kill as much of the technology budget as they can (while everyone keeps complaining about the lack of service). Ultimately, technology becomes one of the company's major scapegoats, and the company embarks on a more or less constant search for a CIO.

It really is about attitude and money. Companies that see technology as a profit center see business models and processes differently from those that regard it as an unmanaged expense. They proactively look for ways to improve business models and processes with technology, not in spite of technology. They track technology trends and creatively apply technology to customer service, product personalization, and supply chain planning and management, among other activities that touch customers and markets. These companies invest in their technology profit centers in much the same way smart companies invest in excellent sales and marketing organizations.

So if the truth really be told, is your technology organization a cost center or a profit center? Maybe it's just confused, or, put more politely, a hybrid. When sales are off and customers are angry, does anyone call technology to the rescue? (We know what happens when the networks crash.) Does your CIO report to the CFO—or the CEO? Do the technology professionals at the company sit at the big table with the big dogs, or are they too busy retrieving data and chasing viruses to get any serious attention? Is technology a cost center or profit center at your company? Check out the spending trends, and then check out the attitude your company has about the role technology should play. Then you'll know if technology is about the reduction of cost or the generation of profit. If it's all about cost reduction, then try to get the infrastructure as efficient as possible—for as little money as possible—and learn how to manage chronic budget pain. But if technology is a profit center, then recognize that you're in a good place and try to have some real fun when you go to work.

Should Boards of Directors Govern Technology?

We recently completed some research on the role that boards of directors play in technology governance. We conducted a literature review and posted an online survey to determine what the state of the practice actually was. The results were pretty amazing—to say the least. More than a hundred technology executives responded to the survey. The findings reported here benchmark the state of the practice—and suggest how companies can improve business technology governance—assuming, of course, that they want to.

The work necessary to develop strategies, field applications, develop architectures, design infrastructures, and support the entire computing and communications environment—as Figure 2.2 suggests—all has components of governance. Note also the risk and planning context in which the layers exist. This context is especially important to the role that boards should play in business technology governance.

Many companies use review boards to evaluate their technology projects. These review boards are sometimes described as Executive Technology Committees, the Executive Technology Group, the Technology Steering Committee, or the Technology Advisory Board.

Boards of directors are typically organized around committees with specific responsibilities, but technology committees are relatively rare.

Many of the companies that do have technology committees on their boards of directors are technology companies. For example, HP, Cisco, Sun, and Microsoft have technology committees just like they have audit, compensation, and M&A committees. The difference is that technology company technology committees focus on corporate technology strategy—which new products to develop and market—and not on the internal use of computing and communications technology. Put another way, these committees would not look at the desirability or risk of installing an ERP application—but they would look at investing in a new search engine to compete with Google.

We undertook a survey of technology perceptions, governance, and, specifically, what companies are doing regarding board of director–level technology governance. The analysis of the survey data revealed all sorts of patterns and insights.

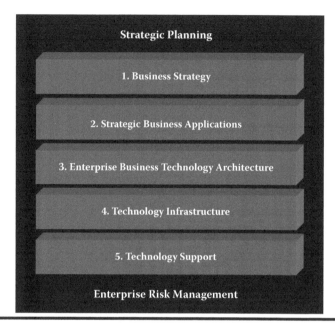

Figure 2.2 Layers and context of governance.

Responses to the question—**"What governance structures does your firm utilize for technology?"**—indicates that the vast majority of respondents use executive review boards (72.5 percent) or project management offices (62.7 percent) to govern technology. A very small percentage use outside advisory boards (5.9 percent).

The next question—**"How would you characterize technology governance at your firm?"**—revealed an amazing response: over 70 percent of respondents believe that their technology governance is "tight," while 27 percent think their governance is "loose."

The next question—**"What role does your firm's board of directors play in the governance of technology?"**—yielded some responses that in many respects define the state of the practice of board governance. Only 19.6 percent of the respondents stated that their boards of directors were routinely informed about the state of technology at their companies; 37.3 percent of their companies boards are informed about major projects, and 29.4 percent are informed only about "special" projects.

The next question—**"Has recruitment of directors for your firm's board been influenced in any way by a desire for technology experience?"**—suggests that an overwhelming number of companies (62.7 percent) in our survey do not regard technology experience as a prerequisite in any way to board membership. Only 7.8 percent of the respondents indicated that their companies prefer board members with technology experience.

The next question—**"Is there a technology committee or subcommittee of the board?"**—says it all: 74.5 percent of the respondents answered "no"; 19.9 percent of the respondents answered "yes." But the correlation of the 19 percent with the vertical industries represented in the survey indicated that companies that create, sell, and support technology are the ones that have technology subcommittees of their boards.

The next question—**"How often does the CIO, or another technology executive, present to the board of directors?"**—suggests that 19.6 percent of the companies invite their CIOs into the boardroom routinely but that 25.5 percent rarely do; 25.5 percent sometimes do; and 17.6 percent do so often. These results dovetail with the findings regarding the board's oversight of major and special technology projects, but suggest that 80 percent of board meetings are not interrupted by technology discussions.

"Does the CIO, or another technology executive, communicate to the board about technology matters between board meetings?" is a question that exposes the depth of technology involvement the board has with technology executives and technology initiatives. The data suggests that between-meeting communication about technology matters is very infrequent. Only 13.7 percent communicate between meetings and 51 percent rarely or never communicate between meetings; 9.8 percent often communicate; and 25.5 percent sometimes do.

The next question asks **"Do technology vendors present to the board?"** The data here is almost violent: over 90 percent answered "rarely" or "no."

In addition to the online survey we also conducted interviews with the CIOs, CTOs, and senior technology executives willing to spend some time clarifying their responses. The interviews were organized around a series of questions deigned to probe the responses from the survey. The open-ended questions (with selected responses) used to gather additional insight included:

- ■ "Our survey data indicated that relatively few companies have technology committees. Why do you think that so few companies have technology committees of their boards of directors? What do you think the real reasons are?"
    - The politics of board activity is complicated and brutal—there would have to be major political pressure on the board for a technology committee to be created ...
    - There's relatively little interest in technology at the board level ...
    - The board is already too busy—especially with compliance problems—to take on another task ...
- ■ "Our data indicated that there's confidence in how companies are acquiring, deploying, and supporting technology. Do you feel that way? Do you think that some of the issues should receive board-level attention?"

- We've gotten pretty good at running infrastructures and infrastructure management is the last thing we want to talk to boards about …
- Hardware, software, and communications are becoming more and more like commodities—which makes it easier to run technology organizations …

■ "What do you think the board's perfect role might be regarding technology?"
- Boards should be told about major technology projects …
- Boards should be told about major technology problems …
- A board committee might be formed if the company's strategy depended on technology and there were lots of big technology projects …

■ "What do you think the biggest obstacles are to board involvement in technology strategy?"
- Lack of understanding of technology problems …
- Lack of time …
- Politics, politics, and politics …

■ "Do you think that a board committee on technology would significantly improve technology decision making, or do you think that given all of the obstacles and constraints it might actually hurt the process?"
- A board committee would have limited impact …
- If the board really understood technology it could contribute …
- Only if it stuck to technology strategy—not operations …

These responses suggest a clear pattern (which is consistent with the data collected from the online survey).

The issues, challenges, and opportunities that boards *should* discuss include the five levels and context of business technology.

Level 1: Business Strategy

Boards should look for relationships between business strategies and technology requirements. For example, boards should understand the relationship between the desire for more eBusiness and the need for additional bandwidth, security, and Web analytics. Boards should guard against strategic business initiatives and technology disconnections; they should also be aware of the cost implications of fulfilling the requirements of new business models and processes. Boards should also inspect the organization of technology in their companies.

Level 2: Strategic Business Applications

Boards should be aware of major applications that the company plans to acquire or rent, especially applications that will change the way the company does business or that have large capital expenditure implications, such as CRM, ERP, and network and systems management frameworks.

Level 3: Enterprise Business Technology Architecture

Boards should discuss the general alignment of the overall "as is" and "to be" business strategy (and the strategic applications that support the strategy), and the overall technology acquisition, deployment, and support strategy for the company. Especially important is current versus future technology capabilities and technology gaps that could develop if the business model outstrips the company's technology infrastructure.

Level 4: Technology Infrastructure

Boards should discuss the technology infrastructure, especially its security, its ability to comply with regulations and audit requirements, its communications capabilities, and its general operational efficiency. Boards should receive scorecards on how well the infrastructure is performing over time and with reference to its competitors in the industry. Major infrastructure investments should be vetted with the board—especially given the importance of infrastructure to security, compliance, and online transaction processing.

Level 5: Technology Support

Boards should discuss the whole question of sourcing—often and in-depth. Why? Because sourcing speaks directly to core competencies: should the company in-source, co-source, or outsource its technology support? Should it in-source, co-source, or outsource business processes? What levels of support are required? High on the list for board review is disaster recovery and business resumption planning. What level of support in these (and related) areas is necessary, acceptable, cost-effective? These are all board issues.

Context 1: Strategic Planning

Business strategy and computing and communications technology are inseparable in 2008—and certainly for the foreseeable future. It is impossible to discuss the acquisition of more customers, up-selling or cross-selling existing customers, mergers, acquisitions, marketing, or sales without simultaneously talking about technology. Boards of directors should assume that discussions about business strategy will always require technology discussions. Put another way, it is impossible to talk about strategy without talking about technology. This perspective is clearly appropriate for the board: all strategic planning efforts should include technology initiatives and projects.

Context 2: Enterprise Risk Management

Huge security, compliance, and business risks are intertwined with technology. There are also risks connected with huge capital expenditures. Boards should inspect all security, compliance, and business risks and all large capital technology expenditures.

The data indicates that the preferred mechanisms for governing technology are executive review boards and project management offices. Relatively few companies have technology committees of their boards of directors. We also know that there are several Fortune 1,000 companies that have established technology committees of their boards and that technology companies have technology committees of the board though most of these committees that do not focus on internal technology issues, challenges, or opportunities.

There are several assumptions you need to make to determine the best way to govern technology:

- If you spend 4 percent or more (of gross revenue) on technology, then you should consider a technology committee of the board of directors because technology is consuming significant resources and is obviously intertwined with corporate strategy.
- If there are significant technology investments planned in the near term—and the likelihood of continued significant investment is high—then a technology committee should be established to track these initiatives.
- If technology will become an integral part of your overall business strategy, then a technology committee should be formed.
- If there are growing digital security, compliance, disaster recovery, and capital budgeting risks, then a technology committee should be formed.
- If your company's view of technology is strictly operational and tactical—and not at all strategic—and technology costs are below 4 percent of gross revenue—then there's no need for board-level oversight of business technology.

The *prescriptive* literature suggests that it's time for boards to assume meaningful oversight of technology investments and strategies. The *descriptive* literature suggests that there's relatively little board involvement in technology planning or oversight. The survey data that we collected (and the interviews that we conducted) supports the descriptive literature: there is relatively little board involvement in technology planning or oversight.

There are exceptions to the survey and interview data. Companies that are generally perceived as leaders in the strategic use of technology—companies like FedEx, Wal-Mart, and Home Depot—have institutionalized board oversight of internal strategic and operational technology. Companies that sell technology products and services—companies like EDS, Cisco, and Novell—also have board-level technology oversight, but these companies tend to focus on new technology product and service planning and review, not on internal operational or strategic technology.

This is a pivotal time in the evolution of technology governance. Technology is simultaneously becoming commoditized *and* strategic. The cost keeps rising as well, with many companies now spending 4 percent or more of their annual gross revenue on technology. While the majority of companies still use technology review boards and project management offices to govern technology (that govern well below boards of directors), companies whose technology budgets are growing and whose perception of technology is more strategic than operational will move technology up the governance hierarchy to the board level.

Just Enough Organization

Lots of companies wrestle with organizational structure. Consultants and gurus have all sorts of ideas about how to organize technology in just about every company in the world. But what should the basics look like? What are the pieces that should work for just about all companies—regardless of their vertical industry?

There are five primary pieces—all under the authority of a CIO:

- A governance organization
- An executive committee
- A business technology strategy organization
- A data and applications organization
- An infrastructure organization

Figure 2.3 suggests what all this looks like organizationally and hierarchically.

So what do these groups actually do? Figure 2.4 maps out at least the high-level activities they should pursue. Is this enough structure? Let's examine the parts a little closer.

The **office of the CIO** is obviously responsible for the whole business technology relationship. This is where the buck stops. No problem here—so long as the CIO has access to the most senior executives in the company. Ideally, this means that the CIO reports directly to the CEO and is a member of the company's executive team, though it's obviously possible to run a good technology shop while reporting to a CFO or a COO.

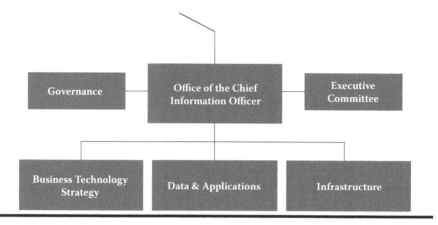

Figure 2.3   Simple organizational structure.

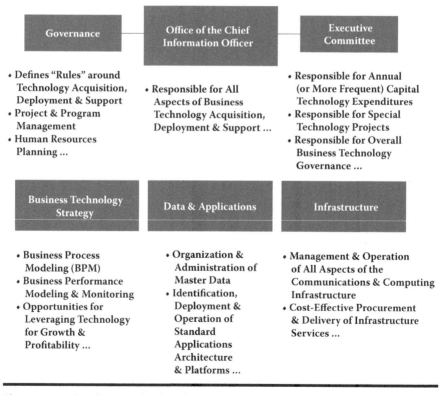

Figure 2.4   Simple organizational structure with primary activities.

The **governance** organization makes the rules about the acquisition, deployment, and support of technology. This is an incredibly important group and charter: governance has to be right or the company will quickly spin out of control. Specificity is key here—especially if there are multiple lines of business in the company. The rules about who does what and how disagreements are adjudicated are essential to a healthy business technology relationship. If there is ambiguity or inconsistency here, then the relationship will definitely be suboptimal—and expensive.

The CIO needs to staff this organization with some full-time and several part-time professionals (drawn from the business) who understand alternative governance models and organizational structures. The rules need to be compatible with the corporate culture and the management styles of the senior management team.

The governance organization should also be a dispenser of project management discipline, but not a disciplinarian for its own sake.

There should also be guidance about people coming out of the governance organization. The rules about hiring, firing, and rewarding technology professionals should be part of what the governance organization defines.

The **executive committee** should review business cases and (large) project plans. It should allocate capital technology expenditures on at least an annual basis. If there's not a lot of new technology projects, then the executive committee could perhaps meet only once a year, but if there are more than a few major projects or there are problems with major initiatives, then it should meet more frequently, probably quarterly.

The executive committee should comprise business and technology professionals. If there are multiple lines of business (LOB), then there should be a representative from each LOB. The committee should be composed of senior business and technology executives. A common mistake is to populate executive committees with more junior people or for the senior people to pass their committee responsibilities off to junior people. This practice makes it impossible for executive committees to function properly. If senior executives fail to participate in the technology program and project review process, then the wrong investments will be made. It's just that simple.

The **office of the CIO** should regard the governance organization and the executive committee as resources to technology strategy, planning, and decision making. In most companies there's no need for much more. Some companies will establish external advisory boards, but there's really no need to do this unless there's a branding or image-building requirement (when companies need to demonstrate to customers or investors that they're technology savvy) or there's a major initiative that could benefit from the perspective of professionals who have "been there and done that."

The **business technology strategy** organization should bond with the business to understand how the business operates, how it makes money, and how it needs to profitably grow. Business process modeling and business performance monitoring should reside in this organization. This team should look for ways to leverage technology to improve existing business models and processes as well as identify whole new business models and processes that could be enabled by new and existing technology. This organization tilts in two simultaneous directions: first toward the business (multiple lines of business, if that's the corporate structure) and second toward the data and applications organization, which will be responsible for actually implementing business technology investment recommendations.

The **data and applications** organization should exploit the existing data and application architectures and platforms—and push standardization. It should focus on the company's master data and the reduction of applications that do not provide clear operational or strategic value to the company. It should also define the current and future data and application architectures. It should aspire to agility. It should form close partnerships with the **business technology strategy** and **infrastructure** organizations.

The **infrastructure** organization should own all of the enabling computing and communications technology including of course all basic hardware and software. This organization should direct the acquisition of all infrastructure technology and decide on optimal sourcing strategies. It should drive cost out of operational technology/infrastructure delivery. It should focus on standardization, performance metrics, and vendor management. The "engine" should be constantly tweaked for efficiency. The infrastructure organization should coordinate exquisitely with the data and applications organization as well as the business technology strategy organization—but much more with the data and applications team than the business technology strategy team.

What about coordination?

Figure 2.5 suggests that all of the organizations in this simple structure are linked in continuous cooperation. But the major relationships are the ones between the business technology strategy organization and the data and applications organization, and between the data and applications organization and the infrastructure organization. These are the interrelationships that will make or break even the simplest technology organization. If there's less than solid communication and coordination among these groups, gaps, and shortfalls will appear.

All this is intended to get us to think about what's core and what's not about our technology organizations. Do you have too much organization? Too little? Might it be possible to streamline your current organization? How many divisions or departments do you really need?

The proposed simple organization structure addresses all of the right areas—governance, capital expenditures, strategy, data, applications, and infrastructure. One feature of the simple organization structure is its ability to absorb additional requirements, such as the need for a vendor management office—which could fit within the governance organization. In other words, the organizational principle should be to work within existing organizational structures rather than constantly changing them to accommodate what might appear to be major organizational requirements. The rule of thumb should perhaps be to always retreat to the

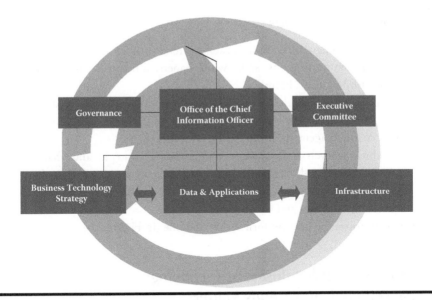

Figure 2.5   Simple organizational structure with primary interrelationships.

existing structure before adding additional organizations—that have to be staffed and managed.

Tuning Up the Business Technology Organization

Take a hard look at your business technology organization. What do you think you do well—and poorly? Here's an agenda for the team. See what makes sense for your organization; assess how well you understand trends—and optimal responses to the trends—as well as some best practices you may or may not be practicing.

Industry Trends: Do You Know What's Happening—And How to Respond?

Trends to Bet On ...

- Business is becoming more collaborative, with more and more integration of the supply chain, customization, and increased eBusiness ...
- Technology is getting better—and integrating ...
- Management "best practices" are emerging, adding new discipline—and pressure—to the technology acquisition, deployment, and support process ...
- Expectations about the value of technology are morphing in two directions: "technology is a commodity" and "technology is a strategic driver of competitive advantage" ...

Responses to the Trends ...

- Embrace the changes: Communicate the trends inside your company through internal communications, short white papers, links to Web-based thought pieces. Build a new "brand" ...
- Proactively interpret the changes for the lines of business: Why should they care about the trends? How will they affect business processes, competitiveness, cost management, profitability, growth? ...
- Redefine the levels of technology around what is "strategic" and what is "operational"; tilt toward the identification and implementation of technology that has clear strategic value, while improving the discipline around operational technology delivery and support ...
- Create above the line; perform below the line (in Figure 2.6) ...

Do You Know What Business, Technology, Organizational, and Trends Matter?

Trends to Bet On ...

- Business—like technology—is integrating and interoperating ...
- Competitors are "conventional" and "unconventional"—especially in the global marketplace ...
- The pace of technology change is still rapid, but there are new metrics for assessing just how ready it is and how it might be exploited ...
- Organizations are rethinking the way they organize technology; the roles of CIOs, CTOs, and other senior technology professionals are changing ... some of the new, highly valued skill sets include negotiations, vendor management, and portfolio management—all linked to business value metrics ...

Responses to the Trends ...

- Use the scenario planning process to stimulate discussions—with the businesses—around emerging business models ...
- Lead the scenario planning effort with technology dollars; build credibility with the business units by leading strategy—not just technology—discussions ...
- Derive technology investments from the scenarios with specific business value ROI ...
- Invest in competitive intelligence to track what the competition is—and is not—doing ... Benchmark some of your investments against what the competition is doing ...

Figure 2.6 Strategic versus operational technology.

- Develop a technology hit list comprising the technologies likely to affect the business models and processes identified in the scenarios you develop; communicate the possibilities ...
- Reengineer the business technology organizational structure around target business models and processes (derived from the scenarios and enabled by the technology clusters) ...

Have You Optimized Business Technology?

Trends to Bet On ...

- As more and more technology gets commoditized—and as the cost of technology continues to rise as a percentage of gross revenues—there's increased pressure to link technology investments to business goals and outcomes: the "language of business" is now the language of technology ...
- Business value metrics are what sell today—and for the foreseeable future ...
- The "strategic" and "operational" segmentation is creating expectations about value, sourcing, and leadership—expectations that require technology professionals to develop new personal brands and technology organizations to segment activities "above the line" and "below the line" ...
- Near- and offshore outsourcing is now on the top of everyone's list as a way to manage costs ... While it's far from perfect, there are opportunities for all sourcing flavors, including down-the-street outsourcing ...
- The now famous "IT Doesn't Matter" article that appeared in the *Harvard Business Review* was half-right: business technology optimization is about dis-

cipline and cost management below the line and profitable growth above the line …

■ Identify the pain in the lines of business, then identify the sources of pleasure …

Responses to the Trends …

■ Use pain/pleasure matrices to build credibility and then bona fide influence; commiserate with the business—not the technology organization … ask the tough question: who do you work for? …

■ Push for strategic influence built initially on operational credibility …

■ Align your behavioral strengths, weaknesses, and predispositions to the relief of business pain and the delivery of business pleasure …

■ Create "partnerships" with the business; use your behavioral skills to build credibility on your way to influence … the "end state" is business partners that see you first as business professionals and second as technologists …

What about Business Technology Management?

Trends to Bet On …

■ Business cases are becoming more rigorous—and necessary to secure funding for even small-scale projects …

■ Business cases come in at least two forms: the short form and the long form … the short form is a one to three page document that describes a project's costs, risks, and (expected) impact … the long form is a seven to ten page document that contains the requisite TCO and ROI data …

■ Business cases should link directly to business pain and/or pleasure …

■ Business cases have several critical success factors (CSFs) that when satisfied increase the probability of support:
  - Well-defined governance
  - Resource availability and management
  - Senior management support
  - Relative importance/cost/risk positioning
  - Measurement and tracking
  - Good ongoing communications to all stakeholders …

■ Governance—especially in decentralized organizations—should be clear, unambiguous, and actionable—and should speak to:
  - Business and technology trends
  - Organizational structure/processes
  - Change management
  - Funding

- Compliance
- Collaboration
- Customization
- Supply chain planning and management
- Partner management

■ Acquisition options are growing: companies are outsourcing more and more technology to down-the-street, near-shore, and offshore vendors ...

■ Shared risk is increasingly becoming part of sourcing arrangements ...

■ More and more companies are formalizing their project management methods and tools and aggregating projects into programs and whole portfolios ...

■ Digital "dashboards" are being used to track project/program/portfolio progress ...

■ A special project management discipline is the process by which projects are objectively assessed, expanded, or killed ...

Responses to the Trends ...

■ Develop—and follow—business case templates ...

■ Develop and track critical success factors ...

■ Link business cases to explicit measures of business pain and business pleasure ...

■ Develop "operational" definitions of ROI and TCO models—endorsed by your company's financial professionals ...

■ Define governance clearly, unambiguously, and actionably ... according to explicit governance parameters ...

■ Conduct an "optimization audit" to determine the extent to which existing technology investments are paying operational and strategic dividends ... This is especially important given the investments that have been made in large applications platforms (like ERP applications) ... What are the strategic opportunities enabled by the standardized platform? How are they being pursued?

■ Explore the potential of business process/performance management–based approaches to measurement and operational efficiencies ...

■ Invest in project management discipline and project/portfolio/program dashboards ...

Are You Communicating?

Trend to Bet On ...

■ There's more pressure on technology to communicate effectively with the business than the other way around ...

Responses to the Trend ...

- Build a communications program (as an adjunct to your larger marketing program) ...
- Identify the best communicators in your organization and focus them on oral or written communications ...
- Develop "technology translation guides" for the business ...
- Establish alternative communications mechanisms, such as liaisons, task forces, and steering committees ...

Summary

Do you believe the trends? Are your responses consistent with industry best practices? Do you believe that your business technology engine is running smoothly or does it need a tune-up?

Would You Survive an Alignment Audit?

What if an auditor walked into your office and presented you with a set of business/IT "alignment" questions. The audit objective (in this nightmare) is to determine if you're spending too much, too little, wisely or stupidly, on IT.

How would you answer the following questions?

- To what extent are your communications, applications platforms, and corporate standards aligned with business objectives?
- Have outsourcing/in-sourcing/co-sourcing acquisition options been evaluated against a set of measurable core competencies?
- Have preparations been made for "information warfare"?
- Do your communications and computing infrastructures seamlessly support your eBusiness plans?

What if the auditors asked how you track the most promising—and reject the least interesting—technologies. How would you answer these questions?

- What should you do about data warehousing, data mining, and business intelligence?
- What individual or hybrid broadband technologies have you selected?
- Can you run your business on Java applications?
- What are your plans for (inside and outside your firewall) systems management?

What if the auditor then wanted to know how well or how badly certain things are done? Could you provide *quantitative* insight into your basic processes? Could you describe how you:

- Manage small and large-scale software development projects?
- Manage subcontractors?
- Train and retain key employees?
- Model business processes?

What about the competition? How would you do here?

- Do you know who your conventional and unconventional competitors are?
- Do you know what they're up to? How they're strategically and tactically using IT?
- What's your plan to respond to them?
- Do you have a process for monitoring the competition's plans?

These are the kinds of questions a good alignment auditor would ask. Your grade would be based on how well you answered these and lots more questions about your computing and communications infrastructure, your applications portfolio, your organizational structure, how you recruit, manage, reward, and retain employees, how you make in-sourcing and outsourcing decisions, how you pay for IT, and—most importantly—how you define and prioritize the business requirements that should drive all of your IT investments.

How would you do?

You're not unique. Every company faces alignment challenges from within, from outside competition, and even from the IT industry itself. You're challenged from within by your culture—which may have been a little slow to respond to Internet marketing, customer relationship management, and cross-selling. You're challenged from the outside by old and new competitors, especially by those leveraging technology to penetrate new markets and integrate supply chains. You're also challenged by IT itself, especially its rate of change and its underappreciated complexity.

If the truth be told, the technology you rely so heavily upon is less and less understood by its creators and implementers. Complexity is the result of overload: as more and more technology is created and applied, and as we depart from the traditional requirements → design → development → deployment model to one that recognizes all variations of what used to be linear life cycles, we find ourselves buried in eBusiness requirements, new technologies, legacy opportunities and challenges, and cost/benefit/ROI models that should scare the heck out of us. Distributed Internet computing is the conceptual, physical, and operational opposite of centralized computing. While we've made enormous strides in Internet computing, we've also created computing environments that are more complex, more expensive, and less reliable. This is the unavoidable result of the increasingly heterogeneous communications and computing infrastructures and architectures that we've created.

Politically and bureaucratically you're probably a company of business units with—and for good reason—high levels of technology autonomy. This means that there are "enterprise" and "divisional" business and IT missions. The enterprise mission likely pertains only to the computing and communications *infrastructure,* while the divisions worry about infrastructure *and* business applications. Your alignment strategy must recognize these distinctions. You're also expected to share data, keep everything secure, and deliver five 9s of reliability.

Chances are good that you're spending too much on IT. Chances are also pretty good that you're technology—not business requirements—driven. And chances are you're struggling to understand the traditional and "e" business models and processes that define the essence of what you are so you can make the right IT investment decisions.

Figure 2.7 presents an alignment scorecard. How did you do?

You Report to Who?

Beyond the endless discussions about death march CIOs who report to CFOs, and Cheshire CIOs who've landed seats at the big table courtesy of their CEO-reporting relationship are huge issues around how to make IT "work" in your company. Here are a few of them:

- The reengineering of IT organizations will surface as one of the major corporate imperatives of the new millennium: companies will look to IT to (really) integrate with the business and provide competitive advantage; organizations that fail to assume this new role will be ousted in favor of new regimes that "get it."
- Speed and flexibility will become as important as consistency; "good ol' boy" relationships will be (partially, not completely!) replaced by strategic partnerships that will be judged by performance—not historical inertia.
- As skill sets become obsolete faster and faster, there will be pressure to change IT organizations at a moment's notice. This will dictate against large permanent in-house staffs organized to protect their existence. New applications pressures will kill entrenched bureaucracies and give rise to a new class of results-oriented hired guns.
- The emphasis on business/IT alignment will increasingly focus on business requirements that in turn will lead to business applications and computing and communications infrastructure specifications. Given the pace of technology change, it's essential that your organization infers requirements and produces specifications quickly and efficiently. This will require companies to tilt

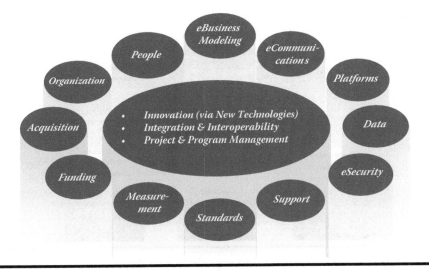

Figure 2.7   A business/IT alignment scorecard.

toward staff with these kinds of capabilities as they proportionately tilt away from implementation skills. IT organizations will be driven by "architects" and "specifiers"—not programmers.

■ Companies will find it increasingly difficult—if not impossible—to keep their staff current in the newest business technologies …This means that IT organizations by default will have to outsource certain skills … The approach that may make the most sense is one that recognizes that future core competencies will not consist of in-house implementation expertise but expertise that can abstract, synthesize, integrate, design, plan, and manage IT.

How many of the above drivers hit home?

The components of your organization strategy appear in Figure 2.8.

Business Strategy Linkages

If you live in a decentralized organization—where the central IT organization owns the enterprise computing and communications infrastructure and the lines of business own their applications—pay very special attention to IT organization. Unless you're prepared to fight lots of religious wars between central IT and the lines of business, organize your internal IT professionals in ways that support the lines of business. If your current organizational structure in any way, shape, or form encourages an adversarial relationship between central IT and the lines of business, then your organizational structure is flawed.

Figure 2.8   The components of your organization strategy.

Assessment of Core Competencies

Let's make some assumptions about where you are today and where you're likely to be tomorrow. These assumptions will help you think about IT products and services acquisition as well as organizational structures.

■ Business processes necessary to sustain profitability and growth must be flexible and adaptive; "entrenched" or "traditional" processes will not sustain profitability or market share … Organizations pay "lip service" to the value of thinking "outside the box," but seldom actively encourage or reward it.

■ Initiatives like "business process engineering," "total quality management," "process improvement," and similar attempts to change organizational processes for higher profits and greater market share, play out as expense reduction efforts—not as strategic initiatives that provide long-term vision … There is very little evidence that these efforts have long-term payoff, except as "political" processes that create the impression—both inside and outside of the organization—that there is a logical process at work.

■ Because of the evolution of the technology field itself, many organizations are now staffed with professionals who have a "bottom-up" view of the nature and purpose of information and software systems.

■ Efforts to retool and retrain IT professionals have not proven cost-effective: in fact, the amount of time, effort, and money spent on retooling and retraining has seldom—if ever—resulted in measurable returns on the investments … The effort necessary to reach these professionals is disproportionate to the return.

■ The basic discipline necessary to convert business requirements into applications can only be practiced in organizations with repetitive missions, with professionals trained in the discipline, and in organizations deeply committed to rewarding disciplinarians and punishing violators.

■ Process improvement that lasts and has a measurable impact is fundamental and can be found in generic disciplines like design and engineering ... not in fads like "BPR," "TQM," or other evangelical movements that ultimately trace their discipline to design and engineering.

■ Those who create and market information technology exploit this chaos to their own competitive advantage by selling "silver bullets" to IT managers vulnerable to promises that are seldom—if ever—kept. IT costs will continue to grow disproportionately to profitability ... The market forces that will drive this ratio include increased employee acquisition, support, and retention costs, increased costs of doing business due to increasing regulation, and the costs connected with maintaining huge corporate technology infrastructures.

In light of these realities, you have a number of organizational options available to you. You can continue to support (read: care and feed) a large in-house IT staff—and organize accordingly—or you can begin the transition to a more creative IT products and services acquisition strategy that will require you to make some significant organizational changes.

As your business evolves, it's essential that you undertake a brutally candid assessment of your core competencies today and—especially—what they should be tomorrow, and then begin to define the organizational structures that will exploit the "right" competencies.

Acquisition and Support Requirements

So what do you need?

The bottom line is simple: if you haven't conducted any alignment assessments, then you cannot organize effectively. If you've organized before you've made these assessments, then you're already nonaligned because it's impossible to cost-effectively map your IT requirements around a predefined organizational structure before you know the requirements!

The core competency process discussed above will help a lot here. Asking tough questions about what you need to do—and should do—will help you determine your IT requirements and help you, in turn, map your acquisition and organizational options. This is no time for the faint of heart. You must candidly assess what you should do and then define your organizational structure.

Optimal Organizational Structures

One of the steps you can take that will help you transition from perhaps where you are today to where you might very well need to go tomorrow is described below. It describes an approach to organizational alignment that builds from the above assumptions about your situation and current and future core competencies.

The best way to interpret the approach is to read it as an open letter to your company. The organizational structure described below can work within a centralized or decentralized organization, though the clear bias is toward a decentralized structure.

What follows also works within alternative sourcing scenarios. If, for example, you're decentralized but insist on in-house requirements, specification, implementation, and support, then you can use the model to help you make it all work.

The "open letter" format is intended to personalize new organizational requirements. It was constructed in response to the problems plaguing most IT organizations and companies struggling with what to do about IT. Please read it with these assumptions in mind and—much more importantly—as something that you might perhaps resend in your company.

An Open Letter to the Business Technology Community

It's time for us to rethink how we acquire, deploy, and support IT and how we should organize ourselves to effectively apply IT to our business models and processes. This letter is intended to explore the parameters of that organization and offer a set of specific suggestions for making IT the strategic weapon it's destined to become. Let's begin with a description of the new business/IT agenda—which really describes a new business/IT partnership.

The New Business/IT Agenda

There are clear objectives which together prescribe a new agenda for information technology at our company.

IT must align with current and anticipated business processes, products, and services; if alignment cannot be determined, then investments in existing or new infrastructures or applications should not be made.

The ultimate purpose of IT is to ensure efficiency, profitability, and growth, not to champion "technologies."

IT is as major a contributor to business strategy and planning as any other "conventional" business activity or function; without (well conceived, implemented, and supported) IT, there are no business processes, products, or services; IT is therefore as "legitimate" a corporate stakeholder and provider as marketing, financial controls, and other "core" business activities.

Our IT organizational structures must adapt to changing business priorities; the ability of IT to adapt to new competitor challenges and business opportunities is essential to its ability to contribute to profitability and growth.

From Here to There

Decentralization is appropriate: our businesses are moving too quickly to be organized or managed centrally. The decentralization of IT is a natural and appropriate extension of the decentralized business environment. While one might argue that centralization/decentralization swings with the political winds, it's difficult to imagine it ever swinging back to where applications development becomes separate from their business units or users. What is possible—and desirable—is the "centralization" of the "infrastructure"—defined in very specific ways—because there is a lines of business and enterprise benefit to the central management of infrastructure services.

Our internal IT organization must evolve from "control" to "collaboration" and "facilitation." IT is too often seen as an obstacle to progress and growth, not as a facilitator of business.

IT needs to identify a short list of enterprise (corporatewide) infrastructure areas in which to invest—and then invest in them consistently and predictably. These areas include:

- The design and development of a world class communications network.
- Methods for organizing, accessing, and securing data.
- World class mobile computing, virtual office, and electronic commerce infrastructure technology.

IT also needs to identify a set of activities that will add business value to the lines of business—activities that are appropriately conducted at the enterprise level. They include:

■ The setting of standards boundaries that simultaneously provide room for the businesses to operate in and offer the cost and performance advantages of less-rather-than-more-variation in our communications and computing environment.
■ Process improvement initiatives.
■ The comanagement of any enterprise outsourcing activities.
■ Procedures for aligning systems and technology investments with business strategies.
■ The facilitation of reuse (of applications, databases, development architectures) and the reduction of redundant technical activity in the lines of business.
■ Leadership in enterprisewide initiatives (like major upgrades).
■ Enterprise hardware and software (license) acquisition.
■ Contracting and subcontracting.
■ Hardware and software asset acquisition and disposition.
■ Selected security administration and business resumption planning.
■ Overall security policy.

IT should organize accordingly:

■ IT should evolve to a proactive decision-making and problem-solving body: the technology decision-making organization should comprise not only technology professionals but business representatives as well.
■ The central IT organization should establish a program office (PO) that will manage all outsourced activities, all account executive activities, and those "negotiations" activities that characterize so many of the interactions with the businesses. This PO should be staffed by central/enterprise IT and representatives from the lines of business.

- The office of the CIO of the enterprise should create deputy CIO positions to be filled by technology representatives from the lines of business.
- Enterprise IT should organize according to the targeted enterprise activities, according to the percentage of support that is outsourced, and according to what the businesses need and will find useful. The organization should be defined via a partnership with the lines of business (who—as "clients"—have a clear vested interest in the way enterprise IT is organized). The central IT organization has a clear vested interest in defining an organization the businesses will find useful. This is not a call for reengineering, which when done in-house nearly always fails; rather, the suggestion is to identify—with the help of the divisions—a slate of activities and capabilities the businesses would find valuable and then backfill the organization into these requirements.
- The central IT organization should establish centers of excellence on a temporary basis; for example, when there is a cross-divisional need like in the areas of Year 2000 compliance or eBusiness, centers of excellence, staffed by enterprise and lines of business professionals.
- IT should take the lead in massing the talent and technology to develop solutions to problems that all the businesses face. Once the problems have been solved, the technology should be exported to the businesses, making room for the next center (or "tiger team"). These centers collectively represent the "special services" that the central IT organization provides to the lines of business.
- Central IT should organize a small set of (excellent) "consultants" who will support the businesses in the enterprise areas. These consultants should not be charged on a fee-for-service basis. Instead, they should be (a) charged to tax or (b) embedded in the rates. However, over time—and once value has been demonstrated—then a "declining subsidy" funding model can be implemented. Such a model provides non-fee-for-service support initially but converts the support to fee-for-service over time.

The central IT organization should adopt a new attitude about its relationship with the businesses.

- It should partner with the businesses, actively seeking their involvement in key decisions about infrastructure and other enterprise activities. Failure to get buy-in results in unnecessary and unproductive conflict.
- The central IT organization should adopt the "consulting mind-set," which would see the divisions as clients, not as adversaries.
- The central IT organization should work with the businesses to develop charge-back and investment procedures for paying for IT services. This source of enormous conflict can be reduced or eliminated.

The central IT organization should rethink charging/funding mechanisms.

- It should identify (with the businesses) those services that should fall into the traditional charge back model, those services that should be fee-for-service, those services that should be non-fee-for-service, and those services that should be funded centrally (via some model that puts skin in the game from all sources); ambiguity here must be eliminated.

There are special occasions when the enterprise will subsidize business costs, such as for major technology refreshes and events like the Year 2000 conversion effort. But this funding will come with "strings": the enterprise will require the divisions to comply with certain conditions of acceptance, such as hardware/software asset acquisition practices, adherence to standards, and enterprise systems management.

Services

The central IT organization should organize itself to provide sets of ongoing and special (temporary) services organized in some specific ways. Business strategies should drive the whole process. Business strategies (which must be clarified and validated) developed by the lines of business lead to lines of business IT strategies that, in turn, provide input to the enterprise IT strategy (defined as services). These services represent the specific services that the lines of business (as clients) would accept, reject, or modify, as appropriate, and include such activities as desktop, laptop, and PDA management, data center management, communications management, applications management, and security management.

Mechanisms

In order to deliver the above services and build the kind of relationships with the divisions that will benefit the company, the central IT organization needs to organize itself adaptively.

Alternative funding mechanisms should be explored, separating day-to-day operational expenses from infrastructure investments. While traditional charge-back mechanisms can be used to pay for day-to-day operational expenses and—via a built-in cushion—some infrastructure reinvestment, there should also be a central fund for major investments. This fund can be generated via a corporate tax or via new allocations from the enterprise. Incentives should be created for the lines of business to invest directly or indirectly in infrastructure investments and reinvestments.

In addition, those activities that the enterprise considers to be of great importance should be centrally funded if the businesses are unlikely to fund the activity. A prime example is business resumption planning and disaster recovery. Other activities—like process improvement, end to end planning, and related "disciplines"—often go unfunded by the businesses. If the enterprise considers such activities to be of great importance, and the incentives to invest at the lines of business level are inadequate, then the enterprise should (a) change the incentives or (b) fund the activity centrally.

A core competency analysis should be conducted for the purpose of determining which support services should be provided by in-house personnel and which should be provided by outside consultants and vendors. Economies of scale, efficiencies of operations, expertise considerations, and an overall core competency assessment should drive decisions about what to do in-house and what to outsource.

Industry trends are clear, however. Many companies are stripping out those activities that dilute their missions and are enhancing those activities that represent the core or essence of their business. Moreover, the pace of technology change, the obsolescence of skills, and the volatility of the industry all suggest that alternatives that permit us to move quickly should be explored.

We should adopt a life cycle–based approach to in-sourcing/outsourcing options, with the predisposition to control the business strategy → requirements → specification → design process and manage the implementation and support process.

We should monitor industry trends to determine when to move to hybrid or outsourced IT products and services. For example, in 1990 very few organizations outsourced their help desks, whereas by 2000 nearly 70 percent of all Fortune 1,000 companies outsourced some help desk activities (with the trend expected to grow dramatically). Industry trends are important to monitor because they reflect the maturity and cost-effectiveness of products and services.

We should select the right in-sourcing/outsourcing model depending on the circumstances.

■ In-source when the tasks involve requirements → specification → and design—and when in-house expertise is deep and available.
■ Outsource implementation via complete and "transitional" outsourcing models where there is a high potential for "knowledge and process transfer" and where the transfer area is a targeted core competency.
■ Outsource when the target is at the back end of the life cycle, when the prospects for knowledge transfer are low, and when the area is not—and should not become—a core competency.

There are also options surrounding the ownership of hardware and other computing assets. Emerging trends indicate that an increasing number of organizations are leasing computing equipment of all kinds. Leasing versus buying options should be analyzed thoroughly and often.

The PO should address the opportunities and risks associated with outsourcing (among other issues). Once decisions have been made, the PO should coordinate vendor support.

Investments in the right personnel are critical to success. As we move toward a pure service model, organizational decisions, and decisions about in-sourcing and outsourcing, and our need for the "right" talent will rise dramatically.

Our needs will migrate from mainframe-based programming to client/server and network-centric systems integration and then—inevitably—to the Internet as our primary communications and computing platform. Skill sets will have to be enhanced in systems integration, architecture design, and project/program management to make this journey successful.

Organizational Structure

As we reorganize, there needs to be:

- An emphasis on services.
- Consulting support for each of the service areas.
- A PO to manage the percentage of work that is outsourced, the account executive structure, and the central IT organization/lines of business prioritization of work; the PO comprises representatives from central IT organization and the divisions.
- A technology council that links the services and management of the central IT organization to the lines of business and divisions.

People

It's naive to believe that behavior will change by redrawing organizational boundaries or by codifying new responsibilities. In order to make the proposed technology organization effective several things must be true:

- Skill sets must be reexamined; skill sets that supported mainframe-based applications, data center operations, and related activities are less valuable today—and will certainly be less so in the future—than architecture design, systems integration, distributed applications (so-called network centric applications), project management, and program management skill sets.

■ Incentives must be reexamined; we must revisit the reward structure to make certain that the skills, talent, and activities that mean the most to the company are generously rewarded, while those of less importance are rewarded accordingly. It is essential that the "right" message be sent here: employees must believe that (a) there is a clear vision for the business/technology relationship and (b) they will be rewarded for their dedication to this relationship.

A new breed of business/IT professionals must be fielded, professionals with an understanding of broad and specific technology trends, business trends, and how to convert the intersection into system requirements and system specifications. Such professionals will work directly with the businesses to understand how technology can be cost-effectively aligned with business strategies.

And Away We Go

There's obviously lots to do. And it won't all happen overnight. The reality of our profession is that there will still be brushfires to extinguish, vendor crises to manage, and financial disasters to avoid. But while all this chaos continues to swirl around us, we nevertheless need to think about how to make our business ↔ technology organization less contentious and more efficient. A series of discussions will begin immediately to decide how to implement the kinds of changes described here. Thanks.

This generic organizational structure can be implemented—complete with embedded biases—in your organization.

Organization Effectiveness Metrics

It's critical that you measure the effectiveness of the organizations you create. Annual surveys, interviews, and other instruments should be used to determine if things are working—or not. It's best to have the assessments made by consultants with no vested interest in the results.

Depending on what you choose to outsource, you should also develop a set of metrics that will permit you (a) to first compare what you've got now to what was the case before outsourcing and (b) to determine if the outsourcer's performance is up to snuff. Of course, there should also be metrics to determine if in-house professionals are performing adequately, should you decide not to outsource.

Who's Minding the Technology Store?

Time to Promote the Gurus

Who's in charge of tracking business technology trends in your company? I mean really "in charge"? Lots of places have in-house gurus, but very few have created formal positions to track the major technology trends that can affect their companies. I must confess that I've always found this amazing given the pace of technology and business change. Maybe it's time for all of us to rethink our technology watch strategies.

Tracking the Right Technology Trends

So how do you identify the technologies most likely to keep your company growing and profitable? The explosion in technology has changed the way you buy and apply technology and has forever changed expectations about how technology can and should influence your connectivity to customers, suppliers, and employees.

What you need is a technology investment agenda that helps you identify the technologies in which you should invest more and those that get little or none of your financial attention.

The agenda ultimately must be practical: while blue sky research projects can be lots of fun (especially for those who conduct them), management must find the technologies likely to yield the most growth and profitability, not the coolest write-up in a technical trade publication. But this can be tough especially when there's so much technology to track—and relatively little certainty about what your business models and processes will look like in two or three years.

The trick is to identify the right technologies at the right time and make the most cost-effective investments possible. Or, stated a little differently, it's hard to innovate if you don't track trends in computing and communications technology.

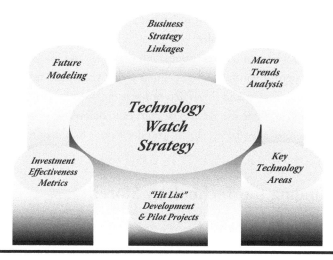

Figure 2.9 **The components of your technology watch/investment strategy.**

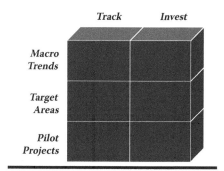

Figure 2.10 **Technology watch requirements and planning.**

Components of a Technology Watch Strategy

The components of a technology watch strategy appear in Figure 2.9. Figure 2.10 converts it into a matrix that can be used to determine where you are today and where you need to go.

Figure 2.10 can help with the prioritization of technology requirements as well as steps you might take to plan for the exploitation of new technologies.

Business Strategy Linkages

As always, it's essential that you define the business models and processes that you'll pursue over the next two to three years. Some might argue for a longer lens, but it's tough enough to extrapolate out two to three years. These models and trends will provide the anchor for assessing emerging technology trends.

Macro Technology Trends

Let's identify some technologies that should appear on everyone's list, technologies that will have an impact on a wide range of horizontal and vertical industries:

- Objects
- Wireless
- Peer-to-peer
- Optimization
- Web services
- Artificial intelligence
- Customization and personalization
- Data warehousing and data mining for business intelligence
- Enterprise applications integration through service oriented architecture
- Security authentication and authorization

No doubt there are others. This is an almost generic list; the key is to distill it down to those likely to have the most impact on your business.

Key Technology Areas

Simplicity is important here. A long list of cool technologies doesn't help many companies with their business/technology alignment. The key is to reduce the number to those that can be monitored and piloted. This is the proverbial technology hit list, as famous for what's on it as for what's not.

"Hit List" Development and Pilot Projects

The purpose of technology monitoring and assessment is to develop lists of technologies likely to affect your business. Hit lists are excellent devices for rank-ordering and screening technologies. They also focus attention on specific technology opportunities.

The most promising technologies should be piloted. Pilots should be sponsored by all those who might benefit from the application of the technology. In other words, don't go off and do pilots all by yourself in some obscure part of the company. Quite the opposite approach is recommended here: involve as many technology and line of business professionals as possible, and publicize the progress the pilot application is making (or not making). The purpose of the pilot is to determine if the technology will cost-effectively solve problems that to date have proved difficult and expensive to solve.

Pilot projects should be real projects. They should have project managers, schedules, milestones, and budgets. They also need dedicated professionals to objectively determine where the promise really lies (see Metrics below).

Pilot projects should not last too long: a pilot project that requires six or more months to yield the classic go/no go result is much less likely to succeed than one that yields an answer in 60 days. In fact, if you institutionalize the piloting process, your ability to attract funds to conduct technology pilots will correlate with how quickly you've delivered results in the past.

Technology Investment Effectiveness Metrics

Investments you make in new technologies (and in the pilots that justify these investments) should be measured over time to determine if the technology is delivering on the promise you expected. Metrics should be developed that address the rationale for the technology's deployment, metrics such as cost, speed, effectiveness, and the like, as well as business value metrics, like customer satisfaction, market share, and profitability.

Continuous Improvement

All this needs to keep happening: an effective technology watch strategy continues forever. You need to model your business models and processes continuously as well as the technologies likely to enable them. Some companies institutionalize the process in the form of in-house R&D labs, "skunkworks," or "incubators."

Five Hours to Influence

I was recently asked the following question: "If you had five hours to communicate a message to the business side of the aisle, what would it be?" Reasonable question. Here are the topics I'd cover if I had five hours with the nontechnology senior management team—five hours to communicate what technology is all about—five hours to deliver a "program" of issues and opportunities—five hours to get them thinking the *right way* about business technology.

First, it occurs to me that the communications program should be designed to be delivered as a whole or in parts, or in abbreviated form, with all of the parts compressed into a single presentation. Why all this fidgeting with the pieces? Because senior executives have attention-deficit disorder and there's no way to predict how long they'll sit still or how much time they'll actually commit to learning more about technology. Don't believe this? Test it by announcing a three-day program on "Business Technology for Nontechnology Executives" and see how quickly the screaming begins.

Three modules make sense to me:

■ Technology architecture and infrastructure
■ Technology challenges and opportunities
■ Trends and best practices

The first module—**technology architecture and infrastructure**—should be designed to explain the basics: hardware, software, databases, communications, and services. I suspect that many nontechnology executives don't understand "architecture" or "infrastructure." We need to make them feel comfortable about what they don't know, making sure that we don't embarrass anyone or make anyone feel uncomfortable about their knowledge of the basics. It should be treated as an "overview" of current technology, so the executives feel as though they are being updated rather than educated. (I'm sensitive to this aspect of bonding with executives: several times a year I present to the Wharton Advanced Development and CFO-as-Strategic Partner Programs—all very senior executives. The presentation to them is around "what they need to know" to optimize business technology management, not on lecturing them about what they don't know.)

The second module—**technology challenges and opportunities**—should be designed to communicate the complexity of running technology architectures and infrastructures, and to communicate opportunities for business technology integration, especially the use of technology for cost management and competitive advantage. Examples here include network reliability, security, data synchronization, 24/7 eBusiness transaction processing, organization, and governance. The purpose of this module is to communicate the challenges that technology managers face as they deliver cost-effective technology services to a growing number of professionals. The module should also communicate opportunities for cost management and competitive advantage.

The third module—**trends and best practices**—should present some emerging technologies that could help the company save money and make money. This could be a fun module because it would demonstrate that there are technologies that can really help the company do some interesting and useful things. Some of the technologies to be covered would include business intelligence, Web analytics, and selected Web 2.0 tools and techniques.

The overall objective of the program would be to bring executives and managers up to speed on technology environments, on technology challenges and opportunities, and on technology trends and best practices.

The intended "effect" of the program should be to:

■ Deepen executive understanding of business technology and the important role it plays
■ Increase executive appreciation for the complexity of managing technology globally
■ Excite executives about technology as a significant lever for cost management and strategic advantage

Form? Lots of short videos, examples, case studies, and stories about the competition—that will really get them interested and keep them engaged. Can you spell "edutainment"?

Grading Industry Cultures

When I was at CIGNA (the giant health care company you may love or hate, depending on whether or not you've seen Michael Moore's *Sicko*), I experienced a mutant corporate culture: it had a senior management team with its own biases and predispositions and a set of policies and procedures that were the result of a massive merger between the Insurance Company of America (INA) and Connecticut General (CG). But the corporate culture was also the product of the insurance industry; insurance executives saw the world pretty much the same way—and that way was to think about technology as a cost center, definitely not a strategic weapon with which to clobber the competition.

Industry cultures define a lot about how companies in different industries acquire, deploy, and support technology.

The insurance industry is a late adopter of technology. If the truth be told, most insurance executives really don't like technology very much. They see technology as a giant pain in the ass, something they cannot get along without (though wish they could), and something that costs way, way too much money. The major insurance players were all late to the Internet and are still late, leaving lots of insurance sales to Internet companies like eHealth (www.ehealth.com) and Health Benefits Direct (www.hbdc.com), not to mention all of the "quote companies" like Insweb, Netquote, and Iquote, which take money from the insurance companies every time they channel a policy on their behalf. They cling to legacy claims processing systems that have long since crossed the cost/benefit line and are reluctant to make investments in business intelligence and service-oriented architecture. They even still wrestle with build-versus-buy decisions, as though operational technology never commoditized and outsourcing was still just an experiment. Overall industry grade? C.

The casino industry sees technology as a way to mine data to riches—on the backs of gamblers who lose on Monday, but not Tuesday, and who really like to check into casinos from the back door, among other quirks that together "profile" the high rollers (those who lose lots of money). Their investments in CRM are paying off; they are extracting more money from the high losers than ever before. Overall industry grade: B+ for effectiveness (but a D for social responsibility).

The financial services industry is committed to technology on all levels. It's safe to say that they are operational and strategically committed to technology as a lever in their efforts to snare customers (or, as they say, "clients") from cradle to grave. Some banks spend lavishly on technology and some only aggressively. Executives like Jamie Dimon (JP Morgan Chase; Bank One) and Jack Brennan (Vanguard) strongly believe in technology and spend huge amounts of money on new financial products, new service offerings, and especially on the retail end of the business. Vanguard's use of the Web is nothing short of game-changing. Overall industry grade: B+.

The retail industry loves technology—especially the big guys. Wal-Mart, FedEx, and UPS, among others, all spend a ton on operational and strategic technology. They have pioneered data warehousing, supply chain management, mobile tracking, and a whole host of cost saving and revenue generating projects. Thank these companies every time you track your online packages via the Web. Grade: A– (they would have gotten an A, but they've had a lot of hiccups in the RFID space).

Industry cultures tell us a lot about technology adoption, the way technology is acquired and sourced, and the expectations that managers and executives have about the contribution technology can make to cost management and revenue generation. What grade would your industry get? Do you know? (I am always amazed at how little we know about our direct and indirect competition.) Take a look around outside your building. See what your vertical is doing with technology. Profile it and your company's approach to technology. Give it a grade within the vertical and also generally. The answer key should have something to do with using technology to manage costs, technology for strategic advantage, flexible sourcing strategies, and the creative use of performance, customer, and supplier data. Final question: Are you happy with your vertical? Are you well matched with your industry? (I absolutely hated the insurance industry's view of technology and ultimately got tired of trying to convince senior management that the Internet was for real and, yeah, we really do need to move to a standardized release of Windows.) I realize that these are tough questions, so maybe it's just better to improve your company's standing in the vertical where it lives.

Whatever Happened to Mentoring, Meritocracies, and Sabbaticals?

Whatever Happened to Mentoring?

I don't mean the casual bonding that sometimes occurs between newer and older employees, but formal mentoring programs designed to accelerate the company knowledge acquisition and communication process.

When new people come into an organization, they should be given a month to find a mentor, not only to show them the proverbial ropes but to help them plan their careers in the company. Mentors should be assigned to work with new hires for what equates to one day a week, for at least several months. After that, the mentoring should continue for as long as the employee and mentor are with the company, or until the relationship needs to be changed because of the trajectories of either career. One day a month for life sounds about right.

Mentoring is like continuous orientation. It increases the probability of a successful employee/company match and therefore helps with retention—and succession. The worst thing that can happen is to spend lots of time and money recruiting people who leave before they make any useful contributions to your company because they were lost somewhere in the shuffle. Formal mentoring is good business, and to make it work, positive and negative incentives should be used to make the programs viable.

Whatever Happened to Meritocracies?

Speaking of incentives, which ones do you use to keep good people? And how do you use them to send the right messages to the people you don't want to keep? There are lots of arguments here. Some think that the quintessential incentive is money, that no matter what else you offer there better be enough cash (in various forms) to please your star performers. There's a lot of wisdom here. People need to buy food, educate their kids, and pay off their homes. One thing's for sure: if you underpay your top performers, you will lose them. We can argue forever about how much is enough, but if you don't pay it you'll lose people (to the competitor that has a database of your good people). So you have to find the right number and stay just above it for as long as you want to keep them on the job.

But money's not the only incentive. Evidence suggests that environments that respect their employees and offer them the right learning opportunities keep their employees. Trust results from a mutually respectful and beneficial relationship between employer and employee. Profound, huh? Actually, while we all pay lip service to platitudes like this, they do keep us balanced—*especially when meritocracies lose to golf handicaps.** What does this mean?

If there's one aspect of a corporate culture that demoralizes employees at all levels, it's the perception (which is too frequently reality) that factors other than merit determine rewards. You've seen it and I've seen it. Frat boys, sorority sisters, and golfing buddies who are anything but brilliant get promoted and rich because of who they know, not what they know or how they perform. When this kind of reward structure exists, it infects organizations at all levels. People become cynical, angry, and disenfranchised when they believe that no matter how hard they work, how right they are, or how well they perform, they won't be appropriately rewarded. So what happens when golf handicaps drive wealth creation? Several things. First, given the message that's sent loud and clear to the troops, the get-along/go-along culture will reduce your overall competency to mediocrity. Many of your employees, in other words, will adapt to the rules of the game that the buddy system plays by. They won't rock the boat, think outside the box, or—God forbid—challenge authority, because they understand that if they piss off the ruling boys—or gals—they'll never get rich. So they begin to spend more time working on their relationships with the ruling elite than with customers, suppliers, or partners. The obvious result here is that business suffers. Next, the star performers who really want to

---

* See "Meritocracy vs. the Golf Culture," *Business Finance,* August 2002, for a great discussion about how the rules for advancement change the higher you go in the organization.

improve the business—and who are uncomfortable with good ol' boy/gal rules—leave your company to work for one of your competitors (who may or may not play by the same rules). Third, the company will eventually collapse under the weight of these rules if they continue to grow in number and complexity or if they spin out of control into what we've recently seen in the form of corporate anarchy, arrogance, and irresponsibility.

Whatever Happened to Sabbaticals?

Sabbaticals? You bet. When key people work really hard for a long time with consistently impressive results, you need to occasionally give them a rest. Is this that complicated? Look at the companies that offer sabbaticals and see what kind of loyalty they generate.

Performance reviews have been around for a long, long time. They are some of the most political processes in your company. Some of your employees are so good at gaming reviews that actual performance has little to do with an employee's assessment. In highly political organizations, people spend a lot of time figuring out how to game performance reviews. In meritocracies, people spend time organizing and presenting performance evidence.

How should you do this? First, publish the process and the outcomes, which range from promotions, raises, bonuses, new responsibility, demotions, and dismissals. Each year employees should participate in the development of performance objectives, which should be used at the end of the year to assess how well the objectives were met. The employee's immediate supervisor along with a two-person "independent" board should be involved in the review. Am I crazy? Am I suggesting that we get people to agree on what they should accomplish during the year and then review their progress? That three people can do this "objectively"? If the culture supports all this, the answer is yes. But if it doesn't, forget about it.

Overall, we spend too much time worrying about people trivia and not nearly enough on how to grow loyal productive people. Think about mentoring, (positive *and* negative) incentives, meritocracy, sabbaticals, and objective performance reviews. When used right, they're all great tools.

Has Anyone Been to Nordstrom's?

One snowy Sunday morning in December I spent some time—a lot of time, in fact—on hold with, and occasionally actually speaking to, "technical support" representatives from Dell.* Six months prior I purchased a pretty spiffy Dell desktop to complement my trusty Compaq Armada laptop (that just keeps going and

---

* In fact, I wrote this entire section while on hold with Dell.

going). I listened to the on-hold voice tell me over and over again that I could just go to Dell.com for technical support, because the scripts that the organic technical support team used to troubleshoot problems were the same scripts that the digital technical support team used. This advice struck me as peculiar; if I could really get the answers I needed from the Web, then why was Dell spending so much money frustrating me with 800-number support? Was the voice implying that I was an idiot to actually want to speak with someone? I bounced from service rep to service rep, ending with a (live) Dell support professional telling me that she did not know how to solve my problem. (My DVD player quits every time I try to play a DVD—not exactly a world class problem.*) She walked me through the troubleshooting scripts, we reinstalled drivers, etc., but nothing worked.

What I experienced was the worst of all worlds. After several hours of Christmas music, and after being rerouted five times, it occurred to me that maybe we haven't come all that far—at least in the computer industry—with customer service. This assessment was punctuated by my being told that if the problem was a software problem, I would be charged a fee for the help—even though I paid for three years of support (learning during the service experience that my warranty only covered hardware)—or I could call the software manufacturer myself to discuss my problem.

The experience with Dell was redefined after an experience with the Nordstrom retail chain. I find it hard to imagine a Nordstrom service representative telling me that I had to contact the manufacturer of the shirt whose sleeves were falling off because Nordstrom supports only the boxes in which the shirts are sold—or if I wanted the shirt repaired or replaced, I'd have to pay an additional fee or take a trip abroad to solve my problem. If you've shopped at Nordstrom's you know that there's essentially nothing they cannot do for you; the customer is—literally—always right.

Do you pay more for this service? Of course. Truly excellent service is embedded in the purchase price, and for those who want to make the price/service trade-off, the rewards are clear. Dell of course is not the only vendor whose "support" is far from perfect. In fact, given that Dell (and other hardware and software vendors) worries more about being cheap than supported, when one buys a Dell one should expect to receive the same service as one would receive at K-Mart or Wal-Mart, because these chains are often the low-cost retail provider; it would cost Dell—and therefore us—way too much to provide Nordstrom-like support at K-Mart—or any retail chain that guarantees low prices every day.

So how should the industry deal with complexity, support ambiguities, ineffective customer service, and service loopholes? As a customer, I think it's simple:

---

* I subsequently posted a message to a community board only to discover that lots of people have the same problem; I got some good tips on how to solve the problem from perfect strangers who were happy to receive a "thank you" as payment for their services. Maybe they worked for Nordstrom's during the day.

so long as desktop and laptop operating systems and applications software is so complex, the product of so many different vendors, and subject to so many failures and conflicts, whoever sells the (hardware + software) *system* should be responsible for supporting what they sell. They should not be able to point a finger somewhere else, charge for fixing problems that are bundled in their own branded boxes, or cut customers loose to solve problems on their own. Is there another retail industry that treats its customers this way? Only the low-cost ones. So what do we want? Cheap prices or great support? Yes.

All of this explains why desktop/laptop support is one of the fastest growing outsourcing targets and why technology consultants for personal residences are popping up all over the place. We all need more help with fewer headaches. If I manufactured the hardware and software, I'd try to interrupt these trends; I'd try to own my customers. How about a little CRM? Maybe Nordstrom's has the bar too high. How about JCPenney?

Do You Have a CTMO?

Does your company have a chief technology marketing officer (CTMO)? If not, then maybe it's time to find one. If you're a small company, then maybe a CTC (a chief technology champion) will do, but if you're a large company—or (especially) a large public company—then you need to think about who creates, distributes, and maintains the information technology "message."

What are the pieces of a good technology marketing strategy?

First, consider what you're "selling." You're selling hardware, software, services, image, and perception. When everything goes well, everyone thinks that the technology people are really pretty good, that things work reasonably well—and for a fair price. If the hardware and software works well, but the image is poor, technology is perceived to be a failure, just as bad hardware and software—but good perceptions—will buy you some time. Like everything else, you're selling hard and soft stuff, tangible and intangible assets and processes.

Next consider who you're selling to—noting from the outset that you're selling different things to very different people. Yes, you're selling hardware, software, and services (along with image and perception) to everyone, but the relative importance of the pieces of your repertoire shifts as you move from office to office. Senior management really doesn't care about how cool the network is or how you've finally achieved the nirvana five-9s for the reliability of your infrastructure. They care about the 20 percent you lopped off the acquisition project you just launched, or how company data is finally talking to each other and that you're now able to cross-sell your products. Yes, the content *and form* of the message is important.

Public companies have a unique challenge. Increasingly, technology is included as a variable in company valuation models. This means that the analysts that cover public company stocks look at technology infrastructures, applications, and best practices to determine how mature a company's technology acquisition, deployment, and support strategies are. CIOs, CTOs—*and CTMOs*—talk to these analysts, fielding their questions and otherwise molding their understanding of the role that technology plays in the current and anticipated business.

What's the brand of your technology organization? If you were a professional sports team, what would be a good name for your organization? Would you be the Innovators? The Terminators? Put another way, if you asked the analysts who cover your stock to word-associate technology and your company, what would they say? Disciplined? Strategic? Weak?

What about collateral materials? Does the technology organization have its own Web site? Its own brochures? Case studies? White papers? Reference-able "accounts" (internal customers who are happy with technology's services)? Are there newsletters and technology primers? Is there information about the competition?

Is there a scorecard (accessible from a dashboard) that keeps track of how well—or poorly—the major projects are doing?

Is there a technology "road show"? A consistent message about the role that technology plays in the company, how technology is organized, what matters most, the major projects, and technology's contribution to profitable growth—among other key messages—is essential to running technology like a business.

Most importantly, are their dedicated resources for technology marketing? I cannot emphasize enough the value of internal and external technology marketing. The technology story at your company—assuming that it's mostly good—needs to be packaged and sold on a continuous basis. Invest a little here and the payback will be substantial.

Do you have a CTMO? Do you need one?

Another Audit

One of the steps that more and more companies are taking is the conduct of "optimization audits." Great … just what we need: another audit, another acronym (OA), and another question to answer when someone higher in the organization than you asks about how optimization audits work—and if they're required by some government agency.

They're not required; they're not part of anyone's formal compliance agenda. But they do make a whole lot of sense. Several companies I work with have requested them because they've made some major technology investments, and they'd like to know if they're getting the bang for the buck they expected (and were told to expect by the vendors who provided the hardware and software and the consultants who assisted in the implementation of the monster applications or rejuvenated infrastructure).

Optimization audits look at existing computing and communications infrastructures and applications and assess their potential value to sales, marketing, growth, and profitability. These audits are different from the more conventional TCO or ROI assessments that companies often make before they approve business cases for new technology projects. *Optimization audits focus on unexploited business value from investments already made.* Put another way, they're designed to answer the question: "What the heck did we get for the $100M we just spent?—and you better not tell me that all we got for all that cash was a zero latency network."

The greatest need for OAs is in companies that have made major investments in ERP, CRM, and network and systems management (NSM) applications. The price tag for these investments can easily exceed $100M. But there's a life cycle problem with these mega applications: implementations tend to consume so much time, money, and effort, that payback tends to be tactical and operational for way too long—and to the relative neglect of strategic payback. For example, let's assume that a company implements an ERP system to integrate disparate financial reporting systems. Most of the effort is devoted to the consolidation of financial data and the standardization of financial reporting. While operational efficiency is obviously valuable, the existence of a common transaction processing platform enables much more than standardized reporting of financial data. An ERP application, for example, can integrate back-office, front-office, and virtual office (Internet) applications. If the databases are also standardized across these applications, then cross-selling and up-selling may be possible, along with supply chain integration and even dynamic pricing. CRM applications can help define "whole customer" models with long-term life cycles that can be monetized year after year. These are the kinds of dividends that enterprise applications can yield if they're pushed to their full capacity—capacities that even the vendors themselves often fail to stress. In their desire to sell operational solutions they sometimes fail to sell the longer-term strategic impact of their technology.

OAs are designed to answer the following kinds of questions:

■ Now that we have a standardized (ERP, CRM, NSM) platform, what are the quantitative tactical and operational returns on the investment we're seeing?
■ What are the potential tactical and operational benefits we're *not* seeing?
■ What strategic benefits are we seeing?
■ What strategic benefits are we *not* seeing?
■ How can the business be transformed by the efficiency of the platform and its possible extensions?

OAs take a top-down approach to holistically model the company's information, product, and service processes and their relationship to the standardized platform they've implemented. The top-down profile is informed by the existence of the enterprise platform (which, more often than not, is implemented from a set of bottom-up priorities). The last step is the connection to business value metrics, like sales, growth, and profitability.

OAs should be conducted by companies that have implemented large enterprise applications or massive infrastructure platforms for primarily tactical or operational reasons. Although these reasons are solid, they're incomplete. Additional strategic payoff should be defined—and pursued—as vigorously as the companies pursued tactical and operational payoffs. But remember that strategic payoff is only meaningful when it's defined around business—not technology—metrics. The days are long gone when a CIO can authorize a $100M project to make some applications talk to one another or manage technology assets more cost-effectively. It's no longer about just cost management: it's now—and forever—about growth and profitability. Optimization audits are all about finding the optimal path from technology to profitable growth.

The Whole Context and Nothing but the (Whole) Context

I like to talk about the effect that "politics" has on business technology decision making. Seems that everyone relates to "politics" and the impact it has on corporate behavior. This time I'd like to expand the "context" discussion to include the rest of the variables that influence the technology acquisition, deployment, and support processes and, for that matter, all corporate behavior.

Politics is one aspect of the overall context that influences decisions. The others include the culture of the company, the quality and character of the leadership, the

Figure 2.11   The whole context.

financial condition of the company, and the overall financial state of the industry and the national and global economies. Figure 2.11 says it all.

The three most obvious pieces of the puzzle include the pursuit of collaborative business models, technology integration and interoperability, and of course the management best practices around business technology acquisition, deployment, and support. Three of the other five—politics, leadership, and culture—are "softer"; two of them are "hard" and round out the context in which all decisions are made.

Let's run through the variables. As suggested earlier, it's important to assess the political quotient of your company. Some companies are almost completely "political": a few people make decisions based only on what they think, who they like (and dislike), and based on what's good for them personally (which may or may not be good for the company). Other companies are obsessive–compulsive about data, evidence, and analysis. In the middle are most of the companies out there, with some balance between analysis and politics.

Corporate culture is another key decision-making driver. Is your culture adventurous? Conservative? Does your company take calculated risks? Crazy risks? Are you early—or late—technology adopters? Does your culture reward or punish risk takers? When they tell you to "think outside the box," is that code for "I dare you to challenge the status quo"? It's important to assess your corporate culture accurately. Technology investments must sync with the culture (as well as the rest of the variables that comprise the total decision-making context).

What about the leadership? Is it smart? Is it old—nearing retirement? Is everyone already rich? Is everyone still struggling to get back to where they were in 1999? Is it embattled, struggling to retain control? Is the senior management team mature or adolescent? Is it committed to everyone's success or just its own? Is it compassionate or unforgiving? The key here is the overall leadership ability of the senior management team. There are some really smart, skilled, and honorable management teams out there, and there are some really awful ones as well. Trying to sell a long-term technology-based solution to a self-centered team with only its personal wealth in mind simply won't work; trying to sell the same solution to a team that embraces long-term approaches to the creation of broad shareholder value usually works very well.

How well is the company really doing? Is it making money? More money than last year? Is it tightening its belt? Has the CIO received yet another memorandum about reducing technology costs? Is the company growing profitably? Is there optimism or pessimism about the future?

Is your industry sector doing well? Are you the only defense contractor losing money? The only pharmaceutical company without a new drug pipeline? Or is everyone in the same boat? Is the general economy looking good, or are there regional, national, or global red flags? What's the confidence level for the sector and the economy? Where's the smart money going? It's essential to position your company within the larger economic forces that define national and global bear and bull markets.

Be sure to touch all of these bases as you prepare to launch a new technology effort. While the business case may be strong, there are other factors that can dramatically influence the outcome of the process. Pay very close attention to politics, culture, leadership, the company's financials and the overall national and global economies. If the lights are all red, maybe it's a bad time to propose any changes or any large technology investments. But if there are some red—but mostly yellow and green lights—then perhaps it's time to work the context to your advantage. One thing is for sure: ignoring any of the pieces will jeopardize your chances of success.

What Kind of Technology Center Are You, Really?

We know from industry analyses that "strategic" technology investors spend around 7 to 10 percent of their gross revenue on technology, while companies that are considered "tactical" investors spend 1 to 3 percent of revenue on technology. (Those in the middle I guess are "operational" technology investors, whatever that means.)

But let's be candid: most companies—except for the really big 7 to 10 percent spenders—are technology cheapskates always looking for ways to reduce their technology expenses. This means that spenders in the 1 to 6 percent range see their technology investments as cost centers—not profit centers. They really don't have all that much confidence in technology's ability to contribute to profitable growth through up-selling, cross-selling, or improved customer service; instead, they see technology as something that they must have to exist—like telephones, furniture, company cars, and, yes, expense accounts (though I think expense accounts are generally treated more gingerly). This means that technology costs—like health care benefits and pensions—need to be reduced—regardless of the impact it might have on productivity or morale.

Part of the problem is how many companies acquire, deploy, and support technology. Many of them—should I actually say this?—really don't know what they're doing. You know the ones. They think that CRM applications will reduce or eliminate customer disdain, or that wireless PDAs will cost-effectively keep us all connected so we can help the business grow, or that multiple instances of multiple ERP applications will promote business agility. It's no wonder that these companies see technology as a cost center: all they do is overspend on the wrong stuff at the wrong time with the wrong expectations. There is also a bunch of companies that violate well-established deployment and support best practices like standardization and performance-based contracting. These companies inevitably overspend on technology which, in turn, requires them to tighten their technology belts (which is near impossible because they've already violated too many acquisition best practices). Put another way, these are the companies that think that technology costs too much because they spend too much. Rather than point a finger at themselves, they declare technology an unmanaged expense and proceed to kill as much of the technology budget as they can (while everyone keeps complaining about the lack of service). Ultimately, technology becomes one of the company's major scapegoats as it embarks on a more or less constant search for a CIO.

It really is about perspective and money. Companies that see technology as a profit center see business models and processes differently from those that regard it as a cost center. They proactively look for ways to improve business models and processes *with* technology not *in spite of* technology. They track technology trends and creatively apply technology to customer service, product personalization, and supply chain planning and management, among other activities that touch customers and markets. These companies invest in their technology profit centers in much the same way that smart companies invest in excellent sales and marketing organizations.

So if the truth really be told, is your technology organization a cost center or a profit center? Maybe it's just confused, or, put more politely, a hybrid. When sales are off and customers are angry, does anyone call technology to the rescue? (We know what happens when the networks crash.) Does your CIO report to the CFO—or the CEO? Do the technology professionals at the company sit at the big table with the big dogs, or are they too busy retrieving data and chasing worms to get any serious attention?

Check out the spending trends, and then check out the attitude your company has about the role technology should play. Then you'll know if technology is about the reduction of cost or the generation of profit. If it's all about cost reduction, then try to get the infrastructure as efficient as possible—for as little money as possible—and learn how to manage chronic budget pain. But if technology's a profit center, then recognize that you're in a good place and try to have some real fun when you go to work.

But what if you're not sure? What if your company sometimes treats technology like a profit center and sometimes like a cost center? It turns out that you are not alone: lots of companies have schizophrenic technology organizations, and like golf shots we fail to commit to, you are probably not terrific at technology cost management or technology-driven profitable growth. So what to do? Tee up a real discussion about the role that technology should play and design a playbook that favors one or the other perspective. Things go better when we know who we really are.

Who's in Control?

Everyone's been complaining about Sarbanes–Oxley and other government-induced compliance formulae for several years now (everybody, of course, except the auditors and consultants who make a ton of money on compliance and related activities). Technology has become part of the compliance process in some very important ways. Let's talk about the role that IT governance plays in compliance and the frameworks out there to help us all stay legal. The COBIT framework—according to the ISACA, as noted earlier in the chapter—is:

An IT governance framework and supporting toolset that allows managers to bridge the gap between control requirements, technical issues and business risks. COBIT enables clear policy development and good practice for IT control throughout organizations. COBIT emphasizes regulatory compliance, helps organizations to increase the value attained from IT, enables alignment and simplifies implementation of the COBIT framework.

According to ITIL and ITSM World, ITIL:

Consists of 6 sets—Service Support; Service Delivery; Planning to Implement Service Management; ICT Infrastructure Management; Applications Management; The Business Perspective. Within these, a variable number of very specific disciplines are described.

Although the UK Government actually created ITIL via the CCTA, it is rapidly being adopted across the world as the standard for best practice in the provision of IT Service. Although ITIL covers a number of areas, its main focus is certainly on IT Service Management (ITSM).

IT Service Management (ITSM) itself is generally divided into two main areas—Service Support and Service Delivery. Together, these two areas consist of 10 disciplines that are responsible for the provision and management of effective IT services.

I must admit that several years ago I wasn't a huge fan of these frameworks, but I have come around primarily because I've seen large and medium-sized organizations use them effectively. I'm especially happy about the readiness of our industry to implement the frameworks. Trends like hardware standardization, common software architectures, and well-defined support processes have made it possible to use frameworks to monitor and leverage technology.

So what's going on with these frameworks?

First and foremost, the adoption of ITIL and COBIT is part of the maturation of the technology profession. Both frameworks embed best business technology management practices. Do they relate to each other? Yes, COBIT is a higher level business value framework while ITIL is a lower level infrastructure service performance framework. The ideal configuration is therefore a combination of both frameworks where ITIL measures internal technology efficiencies and COBIT interprets them in the context of business value. In fact, the latest versions of these frameworks talk to each other, enabling integration.

Like so many governance frameworks, tools, concepts, and ideas, COBIT and ITIL have gained notoriety recently because of their contribution to regulatory compliance. IT auditors are encouraging their clients to think about these frameworks to improve compliance—and make everyone's life easier. While compliance is a nice by-product of their use, the primary reason for framework adoption is business technology discipline.

So where are you on this governance → compliance path? Have you examined COBIT and ITIL? They're worth a look. Not only will they keep the IT auditors at bay, but they'll help you manage your technology and better connect its performance to business metrics. Just make sure you track where the consultants are going.

Discipline

Over the past year I've seen a lot in business technology discipline (or not). I spent a day at a large enterprise where its representative explained how the company had implemented 11 ERP systems and multiple instances of them. When I got up off the floor and promised them huge savings by reducing the variation in their back office environment, they told me that they really weren't interested in the savings because that would require too many meetings, too many arguments, and—well— just too much discipline. They really didn't like discipline (or arguments), so they planned to stay pretty much the way they were, thank you very much.

I then traveled to a company that had lots of old applications, lots of new applications, lots of redundant applications, and no real standards for application deployment or support. Their solution to the problem was to build the world's largest data warehouse to which everything could connect and from which every question known to humanity could be answered. While they supported all of their disparate applications, they planned to invest $250M in the data warehouse project over five years. This time I needed a defibrillator to remain conscious as I explained that if they reduced the variation in their applications environment, they wouldn't need the data warehouse. But someone—in authority—then said that they always wanted a data warehouse because they heard data warehouses—and data marts— were really cool.

Yet another company I work with thought that the project managers in the project management office were way too mean and that they had to be disciplined. "Isn't the PMO the dispenser of PM discipline?" I asked, only to be told that the project managers had taken their disciplinary mission way too seriously, so seriously in fact that no one liked any of the project managers any more. So the company decided to de-discipline them through a 12-step program.

What's up with discipline, anyway? Is it just something that guys like Jack Welch and Larry Bossidy write about? Does anyone actually practice what they preach? I have concluded that very few of us are disciplined. Of course there are exceptions. Engineering teams tend to more disciplined than marketing teams. Product R&D teams are more disciplined, by and large, than finance teams. But what about information technology teams? Are they disciplined? Only when the culture supports the use of logic and evidence (instead of emotion and rhetoric). In other words, it's impossible to be disciplined when everyone around you is crazy—or, worse, just doesn't care about the benefits that accrue from more rather than less discipline.

Best practices are all about discipline, repeatability, and predictability. But who practices best practices? Do you? I do only when I expect to be rewarded for doing so, but if I expect to be harassed for being disciplined I usually pass. What's the lesson here? Discipline starts at the top, has a proud history, and is embedded in the furniture. If it's not, then it just won't stick.

So the first step is to assess the discipline quotient (DQ) at your company. If it's low, then lower your expectations. If it's high, then you're already disciplined. If you don't really know—or the company is disciplined on Monday but never on Tuesday—then the DQ assessment is more complicated. The question then becomes: can this dog hunt? (aka: can this company discipline itself?) If you fall into the last category, try a few things to test the water. You might be pleasantly surprised—or deeply disappointed.

Making Money with IT: Three Ideas for Revenue Generation

Most IT organizations are cost—not profit—centers. Senior executives (except for the CIO and CTO, of course) are always trying to reduce technology expenses. A friend of mine—a CIO at a major insurance company—gets a memorandum every quarter from the CEO asking him to reduce technology expenses by 10 percent. He keeps telling him that if he were able to reduce technology spending by 10 percent—quarter after quarter—eventually technology would be free. This silly dance has been going on for years.

But there may be another way to skin the cat. Instead of trying to cut costs quarter after quarter, year after year, how about if we think about generating revenue from technology? By revenue I don't mean that usual challenge thrown at CIOs and CTOs ("use IT to generate more sales and profit") but revenue generated by selling technology expertise and capacity.

How might this work?

Do you have any really good architects at your company? In a previous life, I entertained offers from companies in my industry for the services of my team of architects. My boss at the time thought the idea was crazy, that our people should not behave like consultants (even though that is what they were doing in-house). He really didn't understand the potential, not just to make money in the short-term, but the possibility of defining the industry's enterprise architecture in much the same way that Wal-Mart defines industry technology standards. The offers were in the $250 to $400 per hour range and several companies wanted significant amounts of time to help them with all sorts of application, communication, and security architecture problems. We estimated that we could sell several person-years of effort without compromising our internal workload. We could have easily generated over $1M in consulting fees a year. Consulting? Why not? If you have the talent and the capacity, why not monetize the team?

Do you have excess capacity anywhere else? Do you have storage, bandwidth, or content management available to the right bidder? At Villanova University, for example, we have excess capacity on our WebCT (distance learning) platform. Why not lease excess capacity to companies (or universities) that have distance learning requirements they need to satisfy, but don't want to go through the trouble of implementing and hosting their own course management system? What other capacity might we—or you—have?

Finally, what about providing extreme outsourcing services to sister or brother companies that have decided that technology is no longer core to their mission? It's possible to provide applications, communications, data, and security support services for companies in the same business as you (that aren't direct competitors, of course). Could you do it? Yes, if you've taken your own business technology relationship to the right place—if you're already well versed in business technology acquisition, deployment, and support best practices. You might be surprised at how experienced you really are and how many companies might want your services. This is a whole new business and you'd have to feel comfortable about getting into the technology service business, but there are significant upside possibilities here.

So the next time someone asks you to cut your budget once again, or the next time someone makes an impossible technology = increased sales and profit argument, suggest some old fashioned ways to make money: earning it as a technology provider. Crazy? Not as crazy as you think. More and more companies are opting out of the technology business by increasing their outsourcing activities. Might the best and brightest in specific vertical industries compete with offshore providers? Maybe it's something to think about.

A Little Exercise Goes a Long Way: Internal Focus Group Problem Solving

The Idea

We all know that internal "politics" can stifle creativity and innovation. But what if you could neutralize the politics by preserving anonymity? Years ago when I was CTO at CIGNA Corporation we engaged a consultant to set up an anonymous question-and-answer (Q&A) system that would permit technology professionals to post questions to the leadership team about projects, plans, strategies, and the like, without attribution. Professionals could input their questions, which were displayed on a large screen for everyone to see.

The technique worked pretty well until everyone realized that there really wasn't a way to trace questions (or other comment) to the source. Once that realization sank in, some interesting questions and comments began to appear on the large screen—questions and comments that were, to put it mildly, inappropriate. So we scrapped the idea and returned to closed doors and good old-fashioned gossip to get some new ideas and candid comments into the mix.

But much more recently, I've discovered another way to get technology professionals to participate in honest-to-God problem solving—without attribution. The idea is simple enough: create an internal focus group protected by anonymity and present it with real problems to solve. The group should be large enough to encourage creative diversity and should be "protected" from recriminations by a senior executive committed to preserving the not-for-individual-attribution status of the group. Participants also need to believe that their work will be brokered directly with the decision makers who can actually affect change. It turns out that while technology professionals love to vent, they prefer to try to fix problems. They also want some air cover if they're going to share their candid recommendations.

Templates

The following templates were recently used in a Fortune 500 company to address four specific areas:

- The organization of IT
- eBusiness
- Technology communications and marketing
- The optimization of the SAP R3

In each case, the group was provided with a current state and future state template to guide the problem-solving session. I facilitated the sessions as the neutral third party. The recommendations were sent directly to the CIO of the company—who provided the air cover for the group. In every significant sense, the sessions were "closed." The only output was the recommendations themselves.

The first problem was simple: how should IT be organized at the company. The following two templates guided the discussion (Figure 2.12 and Figure 2.13).

Note that in each case there's an assessment of the current state and future state. The first discussion is necessary to benchmark the analysis; the second to realistically identify future options. Both states are assessed with reference to strengths, weaknesses, opportunities, and threats (SWOT).

The next three problems included eBusiness, the communications around and marketing of IT, and the optimization of the company's primary applications

Current State	Strengths	Weaknesses	Opportunities	Threats
Governance Strategy				
Reporting Relationships				
Accountability & Incentives				

Figure 2.12 The organization of IT—Current state.

Future State	Strengths	Weaknesses	Opportunities	Threats
Governance Strategy				
Reporting Relationships				
Accountability & Incentives				

Business Case

Figure 2.13 The organization of IT—Future state.

	Current State	Strengths	Weaknesses	Opportunities	Threats
Company Strategy					
Optimization					
"Friendly Data"					

Figure 2.14   eBusiness—Current state.

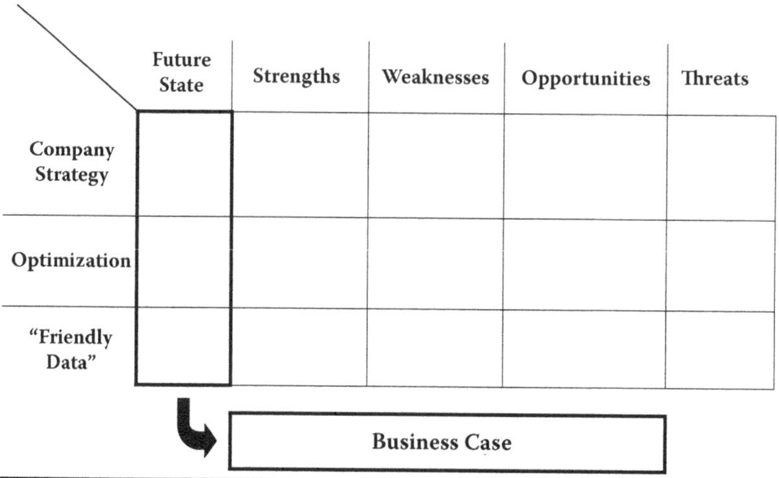

	Future State	Strengths	Weaknesses	Opportunities	Threats
Company Strategy					
Optimization					
"Friendly Data"					

Business Case

Figure 2.15   eBusiness—Future state.

	Current State	Strengths	Weaknesses	Opportunities	Threats
Company Strategy					
Internal C/M					
External C/M					

Figure 2.16   The communications and marketing of IT—Current state.

	Future State	Strengths	Weaknesses	Opportunities	Threats
Company Strategy					
Internal C/M					
External C/M					
	Business Case				

Figure 2.17   The communications and marketing of IT—Future state.

	Current State	Strengths	Weaknesses	Opportunities	Threats
Company Strategy					
Optimization					
"Friendly Data"					

Figure 2.18 The optimization of SAP R3—Current state.

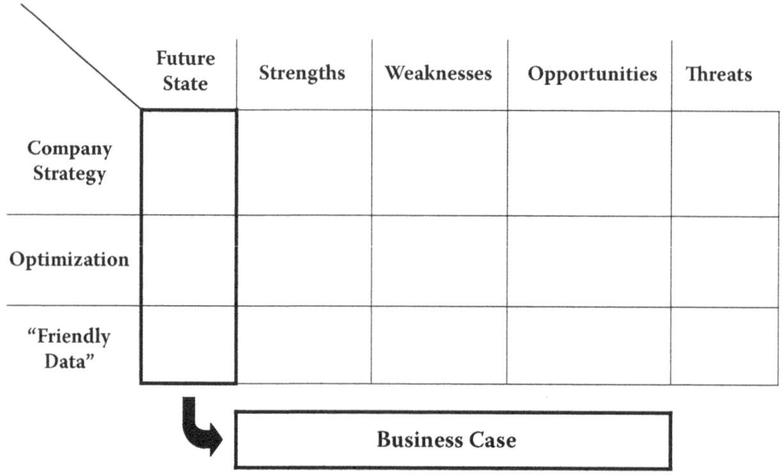

	Future State	Strengths	Weaknesses	Opportunities	Threats
Company Strategy					
Optimization					
"Friendly Data"					

Business Case

Figure 2.19 The optimization of SAP R3—Future state.

platform, SAP R3. In each case there was a current state assessment following by a future state one, as well as a SWOT analysis. The outcome here was a set of recommendations.

Figures 2.14 through 2.19 present the templates used to organize the discussions.

Examples

The actual exercises yielded some very interesting recommendations. Let's look at a few of them.

Recommendations from the Organization of IT Exercise

After assessing the current state—describing the existing organization of IT at the company—the focus group turned to the future state. Here are a few of those recommendations:

- There should be dedicated business IT directors for each business unit (BU) regardless of its relative size. Why? Because "sharing" IT directors sends the wrong message about the importance of IT or the commitment that corporate IT has to the business; IT directors who work with more than one BU also need to sometimes struggle to find resources to build credibility and create influence across the BUs ...
- The organizational structure should be simplified:
  - There are too many direct reports to the CIO ...
  - Similar functions—e.g., infrastructure-related functions—should be grouped together ...
  - A "strategy" function should be created that focuses on the short- and longer-term opportunities, competitor intelligence, and (very applied) R&D ("skunkworks") ...
  - The project management office (PMO) should be focused on projects *and* portfolios within and across the BUs ...
- Create a team of internal consultants that would service business IT directors in the delivery of services and solutions; the internal consultants could carry the standardization and governance messages and provide the BUs with arms and legs to jumpstart technology projects ...
- Governance "rules and regulations" should be explicit, published, and developed simultaneously from the top and the bottom; they should speak directly to "operational" (infrastructure) and "strategic" (benefits realization) opportunities and constraints ...
- Individual performance incentives should be defined and followed:

- Guidance about the distribution of performance should be provided early in the performance evaluation process and driven by personal development plans prepared on an annual basis …
- Expectations about performance should be explicit and provide "air cover" for dealing with especially poor performers …
- A renewed effort should occur to address especially poor performers, especially since resources are scarce and poor performance should not be even passively rewarded …
- Performance rewards for excellent performers should also be clear, consistent, and meaningful …

Recommendations from the eBusiness Exercise

- eBusiness is generally underexploited in the company; specific opportunities should be piloted to demonstrate the value of increased eBusiness …
- The eBusiness infrastructure's capabilities should be communicated and "marketed" as a cost-effective way to pilot eBusiness applications (because the infrastructure has already received significant investment) …
- The company should seek to, where appropriate, copy the successes of its competitors that have had eBusiness success …
- Explicit metrics should be used to evaluate the impact of eBusiness pilots and initiatives, metrics such as end-customer satisfaction, end-customer profitability, internal efficiency, partner satisfaction, etc.…
- Strong executive leadership would help advance eBusiness efforts tremendously …

Recommendations from the Communication and Marketing of IT Exercise

- IT at the company should be "communicated" and "marketed" like a product or service that retailers market to their customers …
- IT should develop a communications campaign designed to educate, describe, and illustrate the value of technology through mechanisms such as:
  - "CIO Grams"
  - Newsletters
  - "Road Shows" (for multiple audiences)
  - "The Value of ERP," "eBusiness," etc. half-day sessions
  - A Consumer-Oriented Web Site …
- The communications and marketing initiatives should be focused internally *and* externally:

- Internally the messages should focus on the business value of technology ...
- Externally the messages should focus on the use of technology for competitive advantage, cost management, and competitive positioning, especially as technology contributes to the company's ability to integrate new business processes and whole new companies into its technology platforms ...

■ The company should leverage its influence with its major vendors, especially SAP—and especially through a consortium of vertical companies—to help solve current and expected problems ...

■ Formalization of half-day "Business–Technology Exchanges" where the business describes its objectives and challenges and IT describes where it thinks it might help ... the open exchange of problems/opportunities might facilitate an ongoing communication between the business and IT ...

Recommendations from the Optimization of SAP/R3 Exercise

■ There are opportunities to demonstrate the value of R3 in several ways that range from the basic to the strategic including:
- Deal directly with the training issues—there are still many that find R3 hard to use, hard to change, etc.
- Develop pilot "dashboards" to demonstrate the value of data extraction from R3; more specifically, because there have already been requests for dashboards from the businesses, we should find champions, assign teams, and pursue some specific pilots ...
- Focus on high-value, high-visibility projects like "customer analytics," especially with reference to visibility into profitability and the profiling of "good" and "bad" customers ...

■ Leverage the company's influence with SAP and its supporting vendors ...

■ Emphasize—and demonstrate—the strategic value of Business Warehouse (BW) ...

Conclusions

What did we learn from the closed sessions? First, and most importantly, we learned that technology processionals can be creative and resourceful when given the right opportunity. We also learned that the quality of recommendations directly correlates with the environment in which they are developed. Closed sessions with executive air cover generate solid recommendations; open sessions—"Town Meetings," for example—generate lesser quality recommendations.

Focusing on specific issues and challenges also helps. The group understood that there were four areas on the agenda—not five or ten—and that no more would be added to the planned session. They performed like internal consultants asked to step out of their day-to-day roles to help rethink approaches to these areas. They responded extremely well to the new consulting role.

Finally, we learned that the approach should be formalized and distributed across the organization. Participation should rotate over time. The results of all of the closed session recommendations should be assessed by the executive sponsor and then communicated to the whole organization as input to ongoing quality improvement initiatives. In a very real sense, these sessions contribute to the ongoing management agenda; a little exercise does go a long way.

Of PMOs, VMOs, and XMOs: Why So Many Management Offices?

Everyone wants new management offices. It seems that a preferred response to management problems of many kinds is to create a new office responsible for something fairly specific. The ones that come immediately to mind are project management offices (PMOs), vendor management offices (VMOs), and process management offices (PMOs—again—causing, of course, some confusion among the acronym crowd). What are these offices and who are these people? Why are there so many of them?

Project Management Offices (PMOs)

PMOs gained popularity more than a decade ago when everyone started to realize that technology projects were "different" from other projects (or so they thought), and when the failure rate for technology projects began to skyrocket. But perhaps the most important driver of the creation of PMOs was the percentage of gross revenue that was being spent on technology. In the 1980s, the percentage was below 1 percent, but by 2000, it had grown to a range of 3 to 8 percent—higher in some companies where technology was truly seen as "strategic." The rise of the project management discipline also correlates with the creation of PMOs, and some of the discipline's progress can be seen in the professionalization and certification of project management. The ascension of the Project Management Institute (PMI, www.pmi.org) is probably the best example of how a discipline grows through courses, workshops, and formal certifications.

PMOs usually subscribe to a specific project management philosophy—and there are many philosophies championed by all sorts of gurus. (I Googled "Project Management" and got 454,000,000 hits.) It's a not-so-small cottage industry: individuals and companies buy an enormous amount of PM stuff every year, and there are countless consultants who will provide all the PM expertise you need.

Process Management Offices (PMOs)

Process management offices gained popularity when the business technology field itself matured past requirements to keep networks up and running and applications from crashing all the time. Once infrastructures and architectures stabilized, we started worrying more about business technology optimization than about keeping the ship afloat. Processes—like supply chain planning and management, CRM, sales force automation, and inventory control—had to be improved and then optimized. Many companies nominated chief process officers who often congregated in process management offices. Perhaps the most visible example of the use of process officers to improve business technology effectiveness is at General Motors, which has created process officers in supply chain, product development, customer experience, production, and business services. These process officers work with the line of business CIOs—and the enterprise CIO—to tighten the relationship among technology, business goals, and key processes.

Vendor Management Offices (VMOs)

VMOs became popular at about the same rate as outsourcing increased. More and more companies realized that they needed special expertise to manage their vendors, that the development of RFPs and the development of comprehensive SLAs were just as important as removing latency from their communications networks. The challenge here, however, was newer—and therefore less understood—than either project or process management. Companies are still struggling with vendor management, especially as the nature and depth of outsourcing activities increase. VMOs will become even more important as the field continues to bifurcate into "operational" and "strategic" layers where the former is likely to eventually be completely outsourced. The expertise necessary to optimize the client–vendor relationship is still very much in development; best practices here are changing as the nature of outsourced offerings change.

Why So Many Management Offices?

All these offices—with the possible exception of VMOs—are defensive. If projects were approved, run, and assessed well there would be no need to create a new layer of management (bureaucracy) to get things right—they're already okay. Project management offices (PMO[I]s) are created to address a problem—to improve the way companies launch and run major projects. Similarly, process management offices (PMO[II]s) are usually created because the process police either don't exist or are organizationally weak. Process management officers are often created to define and defend business processes that software (like CRM, SFA [sales force automation], SCM [supply class management]) clearly cannot sustain by itself. The processes themselves must be well understood, defined, and accepted (by all levels of management) in order for them to generate business value.

VMOs are part defensive and part exploratory. The pace of outsourcing requires many companies to jumpstart their vendor relationships to new levels of management, cooperation, and partnership.

Ultimately, all of this is about governance. Key management processes must be defined and the responsibility for their implementation assigned. But shining a very bright light on processes so key to success is in itself a defensive strategy. Put another way, if key management processes and disciplines were already deeply embedded in a company's culture and modus operandi, it wouldn't be necessary to introduce and reinforce the practice of what should already be best practices.

Governance itself is cultural. What kind of culture allows projects, portfolios, and programs to spin out of control? What kind of culture permits supply chains to run unattended? What kind of culture deals with vendors inconsistently? Clearly, corporate cultures that have a tough time with discipline generally are likely to have a tough time with governance specifically.

Best Practices

- PMOs (I and II) and VMOs (and other offices designed to do specific things) should not be conceived as defensive organizations staffed with people whose second career choice might have been law enforcement. Discipline is not about search-and-destroy, punishment, or retribution. Discipline is about efficiency and productivity and is ideally fueled by positive—not negative—incentives.
- Those who staff management offices cannot default to inflexible discipline: management offices really need to help, not hinder, business processes. They should "commiserate" with business managers who are not gurus from the disciplines to which their management offices pay allegiance. In fact, for example, while the concept of a "project management office" may be a really good idea, companies should not try to re-create the focus or commitment that the Project Management Institute maintains day after day. Best practices here should extract those project management procedures, rules, and tools that will work for their organizations and cultures, not the one-size-fits-all approach sometimes advocated by process gurus. The concept of "fit" with organizations, cultures, and leadership styles is critical to the success of management offices.
- Feedback is critical to success. How does the company really feel about the contributions that the PMO or VMO is making to the business? Do managers creatively work around the management offices? Is the cost of maintaining the offices outstripping the value that they add? Obviously, if the troops refuse to follow the leaders, the war is unlikely to be won.

Finally, if you look hard enough, you'll see any number of new management offices popping up. Here are a few to ponder:

- People management office
- Customer management office
- Security management office
- Supplier management office
- ERP management office

Good luck with your office of choice.

Chapter 3

People

Time for New Skills: People Readiness for the Second Digital Revolution

We expect a lot from leadership, from our vendors, from ourselves, from our customers, and even from our investors. We need skills in specific new areas (as well as some of the same old skills).

So what are the skills we'll all need in the early twenty-first century? What skills are necessary to optimize the business technology relationship? Let's return to the distinction between strategic and operational technology that we discussed previously and the layers of each—as suggested by Figure 3.1. Let's use this picture to identify the skill sets necessary for business technology convergence.

Business Strategy Skills

Here's a list of business strategy skills we'll need:

- **Collaboration**—Knowledge about the interconnected marketplace and internetworked companies; knowledge about what happens inside and outside of companies—the collaborative mind-set; knowledge about how customers, employees, partners, and suppliers interconnect.
- **Customization and Personalization**—Knowledge about mass personalization, behavioral models to correlate online and offline behaviors, wireless

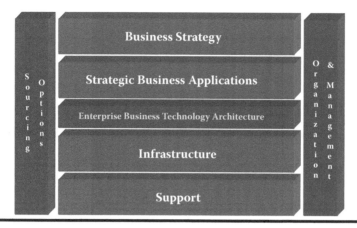

Figure 3.1 Technology layers.

personalization, and personal and professional CRM, among other related areas.

■ **Supply Chain Management (SCM)**—Knowledge that includes supply chain concepts, models, and tools. Integrated SCM (by vertical industry) would be a central focus here along with the technologies that enable SCM as well as SCM standards, technologies (such as exchanges), and some of the leading SCM platforms.

■ **Business ↔ Technology Convergence Strategy**—Knowledge that examines methods for developing and assessing collaborative/integrated business technology strategies; knowledge about the current scenario that's driving your collaborative business strategy and the plan for integrating computing and communications technology in your company.

■ **Competitor Intelligence**—Knowledge about specific competitors including information about their sales, marketing, profitability, key employees, strategy, tactics, and so forth.

Business Applications Skills

Here's a list of business applications skills we'll need:

■ **Business Application Optimization**—Knowledge that looks at major technology and business processes and how they can be optimized with a variety of business applications, like CRM, ERP, and other applications.

■ **Core Business Applications Management**—Knowledge that identifies the applications that make money for the company, as well as the applications that define the company's competitive advantages; knowledge about how to make them perform optimally together.

■ **Business Analytics**—Knowledge about the processes and technologies that yield insight from sales, marketing, customer service, finance, accounting, technology infrastructure, and competitor data; knowledge about the forms that analyses can take.

Enterprise Business Technology Architecture Skills

Here's a list of enterprise business technology architecture skills we'll need:

■ **Applications Architectures**—Knowledge that looks at how mainframe (single tier), client–server (two tier), and Internet/Intranet (three tier → *n* tier) applications have changed and what the trade-offs among the architectures (defined around flexibility, scalability, reliability, etc.).

■ **Business Scenario Development**—Knowledge about current and emerging business models and processes and the ability to map them in current and future competitive contexts.

■ **Communications Architectures**—Knowledge that focuses on existing and emerging communications networks especially including the role that wireless access and transaction processing will play in emerging collaborative, business models and processes.

■ **Data Architectures**—Knowledge about the role that data, information, and knowledge will play in collaborative transaction processing; knowledge about existing database management platforms, data warehousing, data mining and knowledge management, especially as they contribute to business intelligence.

■ **Enterprise Architectures**—Knowledge about the overall business–technology architecture, especially how it's defined and how it adapts to changes in business and technology; the overall blueprint for business technology optimization.

■ **Enterprise Technology Architecture Modeling**—Knowledge about the overall organization of technology that supports overall business goals, especially as all of this integrates and works as seamlessly as possible.

■ **Security Architectures**—Knowledge about security and privacy inside and outside of corporate firewalls; knowledge about authentication, authorization, and administration technologies and tools; knowledge about security integration and interoperability.

Infrastructure Skills

Here's a list of infrastructure skills we'll need:

■ **Messaging and Workflow**—Knowledge that examines the platforms that support all varieties of communication and how communications technology enables communication and transactions among employees, customers, and suppliers inside and outside of the corporate firewall.

■ **Automation**—Knowledge about intelligent systems technology and the application of that technology to personal and professional automated transaction processing, monitoring, E-billing, and the like, including methods (neural nets, fuzzy logic, expert systems) and how these methodologies can be embedded in tools and applications.

■ **Database Management and Analysis**—Knowledge that positions data, information, knowledge, and content—of all varieties (static, dynamic, text, video)—and how it can be managed for alternative purposes, as well as data, knowledge, and content management platforms, next-generation database management applications (especially object-oriented DBMSs).

■ **Integration and Interoperability**—Knowledge that describes the technical requirements for making disparate, incompatible applications, standards, data, platforms, and architectures communicate with one another, focusing on enterprise applications integration (EAI) and Internet applications integration (IAI), wrapper/glue technologies like XML, as well as more conventional middleware. The knowledge should focus on the need for—and objectives of—integration and interoperability including cross-selling, up-selling, customer service, alliance building, and so forth.

Support Skills

Here's a list of support skills we'll need:

■ **Business Technology Metrics**—Knowledge designed to introduce professionals to ROI, expected value analysis (EVA), TCO (and other) models for assessing business technology effectiveness. Business case development and due diligence should also be included here.

■ **Security and Privacy**—Knowledge that examines the concepts, models, tools, and technologies that enable security architectures, authentication, authorization, administration, and business resumption planning. The technologies would include encryption, biometrics, PKI (public key infrastructure), and smart cards, among others.

■ **Project and Program Management**—Knowledge about project management processes, methods, and tools as well as program management processes, methods, and tools. The range of areas would include several varieties of business technology project management and several varieties of program management, including business technology acquisition strategies, managing outsourcing, service level agreements, and so forth.

■ **Procurement and Asset Management**—Knowledge about how to optimally procure and manage computing and communications assets.

- **Partner Management**—Knowledge that includes approaches, methods, and tools for managing relationships with distributors, resellers, service providers, and so forth.
- **Vendor Management**—Knowledge that includes approaches, methods, and tools for managing relationships with distributors, resellers, service providers, and so forth.
- **Regulatory Trends**—Knowledge about regulations and regulatory trends in specific industries and hit lists for tracking legislation that could have a significant impact on business policies, processes, and procedures.
- **Business Technology Acquisition Strategy**—Knowledge that examines all aspects of the technology procurement and support process, especially including in-sourcing, co-sourcing, and outsourcing.
- **Professional Communications**—Knowledge that helps people understand the form and content of professional written and verbal communication. especially as it involves the communication of business technology.

How much do we know about all this? When we talk about education and training, this is the range of knowledge you want your people to have. When we talk about skill sets for the second digital revolution, these skills are front and center. What kind of progress are we making?

Feel My Pain

Let's continue with what technology leadership will require in the early twenty-first century (and perhaps a lot longer).

There's a communications trend growing out there—and I'm not talking about digital communications. More and more, business executives expect their technology partners to communicate with them in ways that are business—rather than technology—focused. More to the point, they expect technology professionals to see the world the way they do.

Here are three emerging communications → "bonding" trends:

- Understand where the business feels pain—and how it would define pleasure. Remember that the business expects technology to reduce its pain—defined, of course, around cost reduction. But it's more than that. Business managers worry about their supply chains, their competitors, their manufacturing, distribution, and—always—their margins. The technology agenda needs to speak directly to their pain points—which, when relieved, can become the sources of wide and deep pleasure. If you become a dispenser of pleasure as you reduce pain, your credibility will rise—which will reveal the second path to a business technology partnership.

- We hope that when technologists walk into a room, the business managers don't run for cover or—worse—attack them mercilessly for their sins (network crashes, Web site debacles, ... you know the drill). Nirvana here is influence—defined in terms of how the business thinks about how and where technology can help. Does the business respect you enough to confide in you, to commiserate with you, to invite you to brainstorm about its strategy? Who do you drink beer with?
- If you're influential, you can shape both operations *and* strategy. If you get operations straightened out, you can spend most of your time—with your new partners—thinking about competitive advantages, revenues, and profitability. There's no better place to work, no better way to spend your time.

Here are three steps you can take to widen the communications channel between you and the business:

- Make a list of the things that cause your business partners pain, and then rank-order them—from their perspective, not yours. Think like them. The more you do, the better the list will be. Work with your partners to validate and improve the list. Then spend some time brainstorming about what your business partners think are the really good things that can happen for them—once their pain gets relieved.
- Honestly assess your credibility with the business. If it's high, then think about how to become influential. Some tips here include working through your partner's prism and then supporting the execution of your partner's plans. Once a baseline credibility is established, then transition to influencing important operational and strategic processes. But if your credibility is low, then you have to build it up slowly but surely, principally by delivering effective pain relievers—that is, reducing costs while increasing reliability.
- Use your new-found influence to contribute to strategic planning. The best way to do this is to initiate ideas, models, and pilots. Your partner will appreciate your skin in the game. The perfect outcome here is for your partner to rely upon your insight so much that it would be inconceivable for a new strategic initiative to launch without your fingerprints all over it.

IT Begins in the Classroom

What trends do we see in the education of next generation technology professionals?

What Should We See?

Students who were ecstatic about computer science, computer engineering, and management information systems (MIS) from 1995 to 2000 were not very excited about careers in these fields after 2000, mostly because of the collapse of the technology job market: in fact, from 1999 to 2004 the whole world altered its view of technology from strategic to operational. During this time, a number of new courses came online in academia that focused directly on eBusiness, supply chain planning, and even digital security. Some of these courses were timely, but some were not—especially the eBusiness ones that argued on behalf of the "new economy"—which had lost a lot of its luster by 2001.

It seems to me that educators need to focus on where the field is today—and is likely to be in three to five years—if not ten. Infrastructure technology *is* a commodity, but there's still a ton of strategic leverage to be gained through the efficient application of (especially) front office/customer-facing technology. I think that the way we acquire, deploy, and support (especially) infrastructure technology and our applications portfolios are changing so fast and so profoundly that the data centers of the 1990s will be unrecognizable by 2010. I think that the whole business technology relationship is morphing into a symbiotic partnership that will require CIOs and CTOs to understand business models and processes as well, or better, than computing and communications technology. Much of the data we collect at Cutter substantiates these trends.

So What Should We Teach?

Computer science programs need to focus less on programming languages and much, much more on architectures, integration, and interoperability; much less on algorithms and discrete structures and much more on software engineering best practices. I'm suggesting that computer science jettison its strict mathematical foundations in favor of courses (and internships) that link operating systems, data architectures, and algorithmic problem-solving techniques to specific classes of problems that graduates will face when they hit the trenches. Although the next version of Microsoft Office has to be written by someone, I'd prefer it if our software architects and engineers treated problem solving holistically, anticipating the new Web services-based service-oriented architectures (and event-driven architectures) likely to redefine the way we all think about software applications and transaction processing. These are the trends that are driving a few—but not nearly enough—academic curricula.

I think academic MIS programs have a tougher challenge. Because most MIS programs are in business schools, there's more pressure on the graduates to link what they've been taught to real problems—a great pressure to demonstrate relevance. I think MIS programs need to acknowledge Nick Carr's ("IT Doesn't Matter") commodity challenge and distinguish between "strategic" and "operational" technology, the latter of course being the commodity. Since MIS majors tend to be technologically broad rather than deep, the strategic/operational distinction is actually a very useful one: why not focus more on strategic technology than commoditized operational technology? And what about technology management? With more and more outsourcing, it seems to me that project, portfolio, and vendor management might be good skills to develop. Academic MIS programs really need to respond to the operational/strategic distinction and—given the trends in these areas—rethink their course and degree offerings.

So what might an MIS curriculum look like? In addition to "the basics" like data communications, database management, and enterprise applications, twenty-first-century MIS programs could focus on business analytics, supply chain optimization, digital security, and lots of technology management skills. Over and over again I hear companies express interest in hiring people who know how to write business cases for technology projects, how to manage projects (and portfolios), how to manage vendors, and how to effectively communicate all this orally and in written documentation. A third option would be to "verticalize" MIS curricula, redefining courses around the requirements of specific industries, like pharmaceutical, financial services, manufacturing, and insurance industries. All this would result in three or four curriculum layers: one for the basics, one for strategic technology, one for technology management, and one optional layer that's vertical.

Business technology alignment should begin in the classroom. There are clear trends in the practice of our field. These trends should be reflected in the academic programs that prepare students for successful business technology careers. There's a growing gap between trends in the industry and trends in academic curricula. For the health of our industry, this gap needs to narrow.

Decision-Making Discipline: An Executive Course on Multicriteria Selection Methods

Very often I am asked for recommendations about how to proceed with an operational or strategic technology initiative. The typical questions include: "What should we buy?" "What are the best options for us to consider?" "How should we organize the decision problem?" These are process questions more than anything else—and there are some methods, tools, and techniques that can be applied to simple and complex business technology acquisition, deployment, and support problems.

Very recently I was asked to help a company think about how it might design an executive course in methods, tools, and techniques for multicriteria decision making. Here's a description of the course and an example of how the primary multicriteria selection method can be used to solve a real problem.

The executive course and the methods embedded in it should be positioned in the larger context of business technology acquisition, deployment, and support *discipline.* One of the pillars of a mature business technology strategy is the discipline practiced by business technology decision makers. The course we developed should help increase acquisition, deployment, and support discipline.

Course Content

The new executive course was inspired by a desire to exploit the power of behavioral science and quantitative approaches to business technology decision making, descriptive and prescriptive models in individual, group, and organizational settings, expected value, utility theory, the multicriteria analytic hierarchy process (AHP), and risk analysis, all applied to business technology management problems.

The objective of the course is to examine how decision support modeling (and off-the-shelf software) can be applied to the solution of problems that business technology managers face all the time. Upon completion of the course, business technology decision makers understand a broad range of decision analytic tools that can be applied to a variety of business technology management problems.

The new course consists of an overview and three modules. The overview discusses the role of decision technology in supporting value-based decision making for organizations and provides an overview of the modeling approaches used in the course. It also introduces some demonstration problems used to demonstrate the applicability of the models, tools, and techniques to business technology decision making. The modules drill down onto two classes of methods, tools, and techniques—decision analytic methods, tools and techniques; and tools and techniques that use decision analytic-based methods to develop business outcomes and project management plans.

The overview of the methods, tools, and techniques that together represent the broad decision analytic family includes:

- Requirements models
- EVA models
- Multicriteria decision/evaluation models
- Business process modeling
- Asset management methods and tools
- Life cycle models
- TCO models
- ROI models
- Project management models
- Due diligence methods, tools, and techniques
- Business case modeling

The business technology problems to which the tools can be applied include:

- Supply chain planning and management
- Transaction processing modeling
- Hardware selection
- Software selection
- Outsourcing decisions

■ Business technology strategy development
■ Business scenario development
■ Manufacturing modeling
■ Business technology forecasting
■ Training planning
■ Business technology investing (R&D)
■ Network modeling
■ Architecture modeling
■ Technology business case development

The next part of the course is the "flagship" module where participants solve specific problems designed to demonstrate how the methods and tools work. The kinds of problems likely to find their way onto the list include:

■ Selection among competing ERP applications (e.g., SAP, Oracle, and PeopleSoft)
■ Selection among alternative laptop computers to buy for faculty and students
■ Determination of bandwidth necessary to support back office, front office, and Internet applications transaction processing
■ Web site redesign project planning
■ Evaluation of alternative approaches to CRM
■ Development of TCO and ROI models that inform the go/no-go hardware and software acquisition decisions
■ Development of forecast of business demand for your products and/or services over the next three years; the development of forecasting models that provides qualitative and quantitative forecasts
■ Development of business cases to build data warehouses to permit cross-selling and up-selling
■ Development of a project plan for a multiyear effort to migrate 5,000 laptops to a new hardware and software standard; the identification of key dependencies, constraints, and costs
■ Development of a rank-ordered list of R&D projects
■ Evaluation of alternative wireless providers

The goal of the problem-solving exercise is to successfully implement one or more of the methodologies to solve a complex decision problem.

Participants are informed about the course's life cycle on the first day of the three-day class where we describe the three module approach and the course's conclusion as a solution to a real business technology problem. Modules one and two consume the first two days of the course; module three—the project—consumes the third. The class transitions from a relatively conventional lecture-and-learn format to a group problem-solving exercise.

In the pilot class of 20 participants, we worked on a single problem: e-mail. Faced with an e-mail system that was stressed by increased traffic and security challenges, we launched a project to explore alternative e-mail architectures.

AHP was selected as the tool to evaluate alternative architectures. AHP is a multicriteria decision-making tool that structures decision problems into a hierarchy that permits alternatives to be evaluated according to criteria weights and alternative scores.

Expert Choice is the software application we use to support the evaluation and selection process.

The participants organized themselves into groups that developed the hierarchy of criteria and subcriteria, identified the alternatives, and then evaluated the alternatives with reference to the weighted criteria and subcriteria. The problem involved the selection of an optimal e-mail architecture.

Three e-mail architecture alternatives were identified by the team:

- Microsoft Exchange
- Sun One
- Outsourcing

The first two were conventional—products offered by major vendors. But the third alternative was to outsource all e-mail to a third-party provider. Figure 3.2 displays the large hierarchy of criteria and subcriteria that was developed (a snapshot taken from the *Expert Choice* software application that supports multicriteria decision making).

The results of the process were as follows:

- Microsoft Exchange: 38.5 percent
- Sun One: 37.9 percent
- Outsourcing: 23.7 percent

This means that according to the analysis of the three criteria with reference to the weighted criteria and subcriteria (see Figure 3.2), MS Exchange "won"—but not by a lot. The outsourcing alternative did not score all that well.

What Next?

We have had some success with the executive course. But there are several more steps we plan to take. Because the original course did not have a modeling or simulation module, and because business technology professionals are now highly focused on BPM (business performance/process management and the modeling of "as is" and "to be" business models and processes), we plan to add an interactive modeling module. Software tools exist—like Extend, among others—that support workflow and intra/extracorporate transaction modeling. We plan to integrate these methods, models, and tools into the next version of the executive course.

Goal: To find a strategically valuable messaging architecture that supports email and related act
- Total Cost of Ownership (L: .351)
  - Implementation Cost (L: .361)
  - Technical Support (L: .266)
    - Administration (L: .347)
    - Software Maintenance/Licensing (L: .275)
    - Help Desk/User Support (L: .210)
    - Hardware Maintenance (L: .169)
  - Training Cost (L: .213)
  - Acquisition Cost (L: .160)
- Risk (L: .323)
  - Long Term Vendor Viability (L: .446)
  - Compatibility of Emerging Architecture (L: .446)
  - Performance Risk (L: .065)
  - Functional Risk (L: .043)
- Operational Efficiency (L: .124)
  - Security (L: .414)
    - Vulnerability of server code (L: .432)
    - Virus Protection (L: .292)
    - SPAM filtering (L: .276)
  - Reliability (L: .282)
    - Percentage of Users impacted by down-time (L: .448)
    - Frequency of Down-Time (L: .327)
    - Survivability (L: .225)
  - Technical (L: .180)
    - PGP (L: .889)
    - Simultaneous connection to several mail servers (L: .111)
  - Scalability (L: .125)
    - Installed Base (L: .486)
    - User Capacity (L: .318)
    - Tune-ability (L: .197)
- Features (L: .088)
  - User Features (L: .600)
    - Address Book (L: .295)
    - Spell Checking (L: .295)
    - Search Mechanism (L: .222)
    - Multiple Mail Accounts per User (L: .188)
  - Operational Features (L: .400)
    - Variable User Storage Size (L: .400)
    - Transmission Size (L: .272)
    - Mail Filtering (L: .150)
    - Renders HTML Mail (L: .089)
    - Compose HTML Mail (L: .089)
- Compatibility (L: .062)
  - Compatibility with existing support systems (L: .750)
  - Compatibility with existing mail clients (L: .250)
- Future (L: .051)
  - Mobile Devices (L: .667)
  - Unified Messaging (L: .333)

Figure 3.2   E-mail architecture hierarchy, criteria, subcriteria, and weights.

Theory versus Practice: Who Owns IT Education and Training?

The interplay between "theory" and "practice" in IT education is well documented. Scholars and practitioners have been writing about it for decades. Much of these discussions have been about the roles that each community should play: educators should educate; practitioners should apply; educators should communicate principles; practitioners should train. But the relationship is far more complicated than the simple definition of roles. There are issues that surround the pace and trajectory of change in theory and practice. There are issues surrounding the evolving roles of "educators" and "trainers," and there are even issues surrounding the responsibilities that theory and practice have to their constituents.

The Practice of IT

During the period from 2001 to 2005, a quarterly online survey sponsored by the Cutter Consortium collected data from CIOs, CTOs, technology managers, CEOs, CFOs, technology consultants, and vendors about the content of the field, the skill sets necessary to succeed, and the technologies most likely to be applied, neglected, or decommissioned. More than 1,000 professionals responded to the surveys. The survey data was subsequently presented to—and validated by—the Villanova University CIO Advisory Council in 2005, which consists of 25 CIOs and CTOs from the Philadelphia region. The data suggested that the practice of the field is organizing itself around five layers and two flanks. Figure 3.3 presents the business technology layers and flanks that can be used to identify and describe the skills necessary to succeed in the early twenty-first century.

*The Joint Task Force for Computing Curricula**

During the same period of time, the Joint Task Force for Computing Curricula of the Association for Computer Machinery (ACM) for the early twenty-first century identified five areas of computing degree concentrations:

■ Computer Engineering
■ Computer Science
■ Information Systems

---

* Joint Task Force for Computing Curricula, Computer Curricula (2004). Overview Report (Including a Guide to Undergraduate Degree Programs in Computing). The Association for Computing Machinery (ACM), The Association for Information Systems (AIS), and The Computer Society (IEEE-CS). November 22.

Figure 3.3   The layers and flanks of the practice of IT.

- ■ Information Technology
- ■ Software Engineering

These areas represent the academic programs that the Joint Task Force believes represent the state of the field and the educational outcomes we should pursue. It identifies a suite of "computing" and "noncomputing" areas it believes comprehensively represent the knowledge and skills areas that students in each of the five degree areas should possess.

Theory versus Practice

The list of knowledge and skills areas identified by the Joint Task Force that define the components of the five degree programs were derived from academic programs and curricula that have evolved over a long period of time. The Cutter Consortium survey data, however, identified knowledge and skills areas from a practitioner's perspective. Table 3.1 presents the two sets of knowledge/skills areas side-by-side. The contrast is dramatic. The Joint Task Force's list only barely correlates with the list developed from the practitioner surveys. The lack of correlation between the two lists suggests that we revisit the distinction between "theory" and "practice," and the role that we'd like relevance to play in the design and delivery of early twenty-first century technology curricula. The Joint Task Force list speaks directly to enabling technology and very indirectly—almost not at all—to the industry problem-solving context in which technology lives—or dies. Twenty years ago this distinction made much more sense than it does today. But today it's hard to distinguish between business and technology at all, given that nearly all business transactions are enabled by technology.

Academic programs should acknowledge the widening gap between theory and practice, especially because it has enormous implications on their graduates' ability to find work—which leads to the second point about the lack of correlation between the Joint Task Force/ACM and Cutter practitioner skills lists. A not so close inspection of the Joint Task Force list indicates a failure to comprehend the trends in near-shore and offshore outsourcing. Increasingly, operational and tactical tasks like systems development, application maintenance, and help desk support are being outsourced to near- and offshore partners. Too many skills areas on the ACM list ignore these outsourcing trends. In fact, if we correlated the Joint Task Force list with outsourcing trends, we would find another widening gap. When we layer outsourcing trends on to the situation, we see industry turning to offshore providers to satisfy its operational requirements rather than U. S.-educated professionals who are not receiving enough of the knowledge or skills that industry values (or is willing to pay for, compared to offshore provider rates). Today those requirements are relatively low level operational requirements, but over time offshore providers will rise up the food chain to more strategic technology capabilities (from the lower to higher layers in Figure 3.4). It's these latter areas that should catch the attention of U.S. educators because the sourcing battle for Layers 4 and 5 is nearly over.

Other important areas to consider are architecture and optimization. One of the most important corporate knowledge areas today—in fact, the essence of business technology convergence and optimization—is enterprise architecture. Enterprise business technology architecture is the linchpin among business strategy, strategic applications, technology infrastructure, and technology support. As business is enabled by technology and technology defines new business models and processes, the importance of enterprise business technology architecture is growing by leaps and bounds. **This emerging core competency for the practice of the technology profession is completely unrepresented in the Joint Task Force's list of knowledge and skills areas—though it is an entire layer in our practitioner survey.** Similarly, business technology optimization is an opportunity area for educators. More and more companies are struggling to optimize the performance of their software applications, networks, database management platforms, and infrastructure.

Perhaps technology curriculum should not be so fine-tuned. It's not clear why we need five different overlapping flavors of academic technology degrees. Although distinctions between computer engineering (CE) and the other disciplines are relatively easy to appreciate—especially because of the role that hardware plays in CE programs—the differences between information systems (IS), IT, software engineering, and computer science (CS) are much harder to understand.

Perhaps there should be only three flavors: computer engineering, CS, and IS that address the relevance problem from several perspectives. (The focus here will be on the relationship between CS and IS; CE will likely remain primarily hardware focused and in engineering colleges within the nation's universities.)

CS programs may need to focus less on alternative programming languages and much, much more on architectures, integration, and interoperability; less on algorithms and discrete structures and much more on software engineering best practices. Another way of saying this is that CS programs should focus less on Layers 4 and 5 and more on Layers 1, 2, and (especially) 3.

Table 3.1   ACM Joint Task Force Knowledge and Skills Areas and Practitioner Areas

ACM Task Force Areas	Practioner Areas
Computing Knowledge and Skills	**Business Strategy Knowledge and Skills**
Programming Fundamentals	
Integrative Programming	Collaboration
Algorithms and Complexity	Customization and Personalization
Computer Architecture and Organization	Supply Chain Management
	Business ↔ Technology Convergence Strategy
Operating Systems Principles and Design	
	Competitor Intelligence
Net Centric Principles and Design	
Platform Technologies	**Business Applications Knowledge and Skills**
Theory of Programming Languages	
Human–Computer Interaction	Business Application Optimization
Graphics and Visualization	
Intelligent Systems (AI)	Core Business Application Management
Information Management (Data Base) Theory	Business Analytics
Information Management (Data Base) Practice	**Enterprise Architecture Knowledge and Skills**
Scientific Computing (Numerical Methods)	Applications Architectures
	Communications
Legal/Professional/Ethics/Society	Data Architectures
Information Systems Development	Security Architectures
Analysis of Technical Requirements	Business Scenario Development
Engineering Foundations for Software	Enterprise Technology Architecture Modeling
Engineering Economics for Software	
Software Modeling Analysis	Enterprise Architecture
E-business	
General Systems Theory	**Organzation and Management Knowledge and Skills**
Risk Management (Project, Safety Risk)	
Project Management	Reporting Relationships
Analysis of Business Requirements	Centralization and Decentralization
Embedded Systems	Governance
Circuits and Systems	Procurement and Asset Management
Electronics	Business Case Development/Business Technology Metrics
Digital Signal Processing	
Very Large Scale Integrated Circuit (VLSI) Design	Project/Program Management
	Procurement and Asset Management
Hardware Testing and Fault Tolerance	Partner Management
	Vendor Management
Mathematical Foundations	Regulatory Trends
Interpersonal Communication	Professional Communications

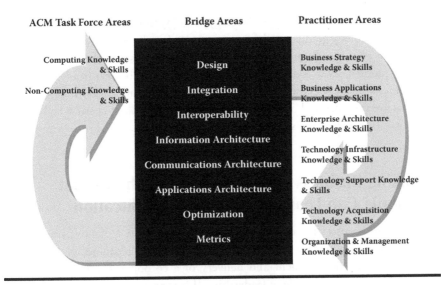

Figure 3.4 Knowledge and skills areas with bridges.

In addition to the basics like data communications, database management, and enterprise applications, twenty-first-century IS programs should focus on business analytics, supply chain optimization, digital security, and lots of technology management skills—in short, the list of practitioner knowledge and skills areas. Over and over again we also hear companies express interest in hiring people who know how to write business cases for technology projects, how to mange technology projects (and portfolios), how to manage vendors, and how to effectively communicate all this orally and in written documentation—all with constant reference to enterprise business technology architecture.

CS programs can enable IS programs while at the same time maintaining their own identity. The knowledge and skills areas proposed by the Joint Task Force should all be extended to link to the knowledge and skills on the IS side. Clearly, the programs need to be coordinated. Figure 3.4 suggests how this might work. The Joint Task Force knowledge and skills areas appear on the left and the practitioner knowledge and skills appear on the right side of the figure. In the middle are some "bridges" that might shrink the gap between the two areas. These bridges might become required for both CS and IS curricula and help CS programs become more relevant and IS programs more grounded in the enabling technology that supports business processes and transactions.

Conclusion

The gap between what we teach in colleges and universities and what we actually do in business is widening. But there are steps we can take to narrow the gap and respond to where business technology is going and what the world expects from our technology graduates without compromising the essence of computer and information systems education. We need to better understand the breadth of the relevance problem. Next we need to better understand the bridges from "theory" to "practice." Some are suggested in Figure 3.4. The underlying issues are philosophical: what are the roles and responsibilities of early twenty-first-century technology educators? This is the core issue.

Tweaking Business Technology Leadership: What Academia Can Learn from Executive Education

This chapter discusses the changes that were made to the Villanova undergraduate, MBA, and executive MBA (EMBA) programs in response to the lessons learned from the development and delivery of a corporate executive education program in business technology leadership. This is an unusual curriculum development model because executive education programs are usually derived from academic programs, not the other way around. In this instance, several academic courses were designed and modified directly in response to a corporate executive education program developed by Rohm and Haas, the global specialty chemicals company.

The Business Technology Leadership Executive Education Program

The program focuses on two closely related objectives: the wide and deep understanding of business and technology trends and the components of effective business technology leadership. The program increases awareness of the changes occurring in the industry as well as what effective leaders need to understand about emerging business and technology.

The program consists of modules that build on one another: the final module is a "capstone" exercise that solves a real problem. The program focuses on the new role that technology should play in the enterprise, a role that assumes a partnership between business and technology, between business metrics and technology performance. The program is interactive and hands on. When participants complete the program they have the knowledge and skills to change the business technology relationship. They also own a perspective on business technology that that will translate into improved business performance. Perhaps most importantly, participants also learn about themselves and their leadership abilities through leadership assessments conducted during the program.

A unique feature of this program is its approach to leadership development. The program optimizes the intersection of content, techniques, and hands-on exercises. It is not a conventional lecture/learn/test development program. Instead, the program applies business best practices in technology acquisition and related techniques to a variety of real problems. Participants build on their skills and enhance their core competencies while solving the kinds of complex problems they're likely to find in their professional worlds.

Among the program's modules are:

1. **Business and technology trends that matter** include the business models and processes likely to have a significant impact on companies—not the latest fads. Some of these include SCM, mass customization, cross-selling, and up-selling, among other "real" business model opportunities.

2. **Technology trends that matter** focus on emerging technologies likely to impact business models in the short-term such as RFID, Web services, SOA, Web 2.0, Voice-over-IP (VoIP), and business intelligence—and not on technologies that are more concepts than workhorses.

3. **Business technology optimization** stresses the importance of business metrics such as customer satisfaction, sales growth, cost management, and profitability. The core message here is that the value of technology investments should only be defined around important business metrics. The program stresses the importance of technology's requirement to understand and embrace the language of business, not the language of technology.

4. **Business technology management** looks at current acquisition and deployment and supports best practices: what makes sense—and what doesn't? Does it make sense to outsource the back office? The front office? Everything? Nothing? Are business cases driven by the right ROI metrics? Is enough attention paid to project management? Portfolio management? The program also looks at alternative business technology organizational structures. What should reporting relationships look like?

5. **A special feature of the program is its focus on the leadership abilities of the participants.** The program works with all participants to identify their leadership strengths and weaknesses with the objective of helping each participant realize his or her leadership potential. Behavioral assessments are administered to each participant; behavioral profiles are developed and used to help participants better understand leadership challenges. As part of the program, each participant develops a personal development plan designed to enhance his or her business technology leadership potential.

6. **The communication of the business technology "message" is also examined during the program.** Who describes what business technology projects are ongoing and what their impact will be? Should there be a "Chief Business Technology Marketing Officer"? Is someone responsible for the elimination of "techno-speak"?

The final component of the program is an exercise designed to solve a specific problem inside the company. With the participation of business leaders, program participants break into groups to develop an acquisition, deployment, support, organizational, or governance strategy designed to satisfy short- and long-term requirements.

There are some short lectures, but most of the time is spent discussing the issues and performing exercises organized around the program's major themes. Participants are challenged to think creatively about how to solve business problems with technology and how to optimize business technology investments.

The Program's Impact

The program has been delivered to nearly 100 Rohm and Haas professionals. It is safe to say that the "awareness" level around the need for business-metric-driven technology is high at the company. Tiger teams have been developed to address specific problems and the whole business technology relationship now operates at a higher level than it did a couple of years ago. The technology organization has been reorganized in an effort to provide better service to internal and external customers. The eBusiness strategy has been redesigned and business technology professionals have been placed in all of the company's lines of business to facilitate the communication and prioritization of business requirements. The company's intranet now describes key technology initiatives that are linked to business value. There is now a "road show" that contains the new business technology message.

Impact at Villanova University

Curriculum development at universities is notoriously slow and painful. Curriculum committees often strangle new ideas to death: it can literally take years for new courses to be deployed. In response to political pressures from one group or another, professors may take a year to develop a single new course.

Our experience at Villanova University, however, has been good. We have been able to develop some new courses in business technology at both the undergraduate and graduate levels. In fact, four new courses have been developed and revised over the past few years that track closely with the message embedded in the Business Technology Leadership Program. The evolution of the undergraduate and graduate program courses in response to the design and delivery of the executive education program represents a departure from the usual academia-knows-best approach about curriculum development. In fact, the approach to curriculum development was driven by the industrial executive program—not internal academic research.

Why did it work? **Because the undergraduate MIS, EMBA, and MBA programs all adopted a relevance mantra**. This commitment to curriculum relevance fueled the development of parallel courses to the executive education program. Of course, the five-day Business Technology Leadership Program became semester-long courses. All the courses focus on the business value of technology and on the leadership qualities necessary to fully integrate technology and business. Leadership is defined around business—not technology—metrics. Special emphasis is placed on the emerging business models that technology will enable, and the acquisition, deployment, and support of technology that simultaneously saves money and contributes to profitable growth. In short, the courses—like the executive program—see technology through business eyes, not through the eyes of technologists searching for elegant architectures or infrastructures for their own sake.

The four courses include:

- The MIS undergraduate **Capstone Course** on business technology convergence
- **Value Creation through Technology** in the EMBA program
- **Strategy-Driven Technology** in the EMBA program
- **Business Technology Management** in the MBA program

The **undergraduate MIS Capstone Course** begins with the following message:

> This course examines business, technology and management, treating them as an integrated whole. While you may have had Systems Analysis and Design, Database Management, Enterprise Applications, Data Communications, and a whole host of business courses, this course will provide a framework for understanding how all of these pieces fit together. The purpose of the course is to ground students in the relationship between business and the communications and computing technology that enables, extends, and supports existing and future business models and processes. Ultimately, all of this is about the expansion of business models and the exploration of the information technology that helps deliver and sustain them—and makes them flexible and profitable. We'll concentrate on the integration of business models and processes, computing and communications technology, and the management tools and techniques that enable business and technology to work seamlessly together.

The **Value Creation through Technology EMBA course** begins like this:

> The course examines the relationship between business models and processes and computing and communications technology. Through lectures, in-class discussions, group projects and presentations, and mini-cases, a variety of topics will be addressed, including emerging

collaborative business models, technology integration, business technology management best practices, technology organizations, and technology people management. The course is intended to provide students with the content and best practices necessary to optimize investments in business technology. The learning objectives include knowledge about predominant business models and processes, the range of available data, applications and communications technology, business technology management best practices including total-cost-of-ownership (TCO) and return-on-investment (ROI) modeling, business case development, and project/portfolio management. The main purpose of the course is to ground students in the relationship between business and the communications and computing technology that enables, extends, and supports existing and future business models and processes. The course is for managers, not technologists.

The **Strategy Driven Technology EMBA course** is hands on:

The course requires the development of a business technology strategy for your company. The goal here is to develop a strategic business technology management plan with all of the necessary components, such as business cases for specific technology projects (like ERP or CRM projects), the financials around TCO, ROI, and strategic EVA, organizational strategies, people strategies, and a plan to monitor mainstream and emerging technologies. A presentation designed to "sell" the program is also required. Students are required to develop a business technology strategy that enables profitable growth.

The **MBA Business Technology Management course** focuses on optimizing the acquisition, deployment, and support of business technology. It is a course that describes management best practices and requires students to demonstrate their understanding of the steps necessary to optimize technology investments. The course also looks at technology due diligence and a variety of case studies that demonstrate how companies succeed and fail at technology management. Like the other courses, the technology management course is relevant to what happens in the real world.

Lessons Learned

Without question, the role of technology is changing. Business managers and executives see technology as part operational and part strategic. The operational perspective is about the cost-effective acquisition of commodities and the strategic perspective expects technology to improve business results. **The way we train our** technology managers and executives needs to acknowledge these perspectives and the weight each one receives. "Curriculum" needs to align with the strategic perspective more closely than the operational one. Although this is not to say that operational technology is unimportant, it is clearly to say that technology needs to earn strategic points if it's to remain in any sense "core."

We've also learned that the best form of executive education is active learning, where executives and managers participate directly in problem solving as part of the executive education and training process. The program in Business Technology Leadership ends with a real problem-solving exercise. Put another way, there needs to be a point to executive education and training beyond the inherent goodness of knowing new things. We have learned that education and training needs to be purposeful if it is to have impact.

We have learned that there is synergism between executive education and training and undergraduate and graduate education—if extraordinary effort is made to link the two curricula. Our synergism began with the executive program; the undergraduate and graduate program changes followed the successful Business Technology Leadership Program's delivery. We used this success to prevalidate the addition of the four courses in the MIS, MBA and EMBA programs. Without the early success of the executive program we would have found it nearly impossible to develop and deliver the undergraduate and graduate courses. We also learned that changes to academic curricula are slow and painful unless there is a senior champion and sympathetic academic administration driving it.

Finally, we've learned that all curricula—executive and academic—are moving targets. What "works" today will fail tomorrow. Business technology best practices change. Expectations about technology's contribution to business change. We have revised the Business Technology Leadership Program and the four undergraduate and graduate courses several times in just two years. In fact, all of the curricula have changed each time they have been delivered. This is unheard of in "production" executive education and even more so in higher education. Managing the lack of alignment between the need to change and the costs associated with change management represents a substantial challenge to executive and academic education progress. We have learned that this challenge must be acknowledged and managed from the outset if the programs are to be effective, timely, and relevant.

How's the Team Doing? An Unbalanced Scorecard

Lots of people I know strongly believe that business technology alignment depends almost completely on the quality and availability of the right people at the right time. Do you agree? Take a look at Figure 3.5—an unbalanced scorecard. It's a tool to help you profile your people according to their capability, energy, ambition—and a few other characteristics.

Clearly, the goal is the assembly of a bunch of smart, sane, energetic, and appropriately ambitious professionals.

But what does **smart** mean?

Figure 3.5 presents at least three kinds of knowledge which, of course, need to be integrated. **Generic, structured knowledge** includes facts, concepts, principles, and formulae that describe what things are and how they work. Finance is a good generic, structured field. Computer science is another one. College students major in these fields. **Industry-specific knowledge** comes from different sources. A little comes from colleges and universities, but most of it comes from on-the-job experience, training, and industry certifications. **Company-specific knowledge** comes from time spent in the trenches of your particular corporate domain. We often place great value in institutional memory, but be careful about how easily distorted such memory becomes. People with political agendas are terrific at rewriting history to match their current vested interests.

When we talk about "smart," we're talking about depth in the three knowledge classes as well as the ability to integrate them into insights, inferences, and decision making. But whereas "intelligence" is fed by integrated knowledge combined with raw intellectual horsepower, energy and ambition are measured independently. Have you ever tried to measure them?

Some of your people are really smart, and some are not. Some work at understanding existing and emerging business technology trends, and some don't. Some even work at increasing their natural energy levels, but most don't.

Some want your job; some are clueless. Some are evil; some are sweet. Some got where they are mysteriously; some really earned it. Who are the "keepers"?

If you're in charge, you need a large bag of tricks—and the will to frequently reach into it for just the right one. There's not too much you can do about raw horsepower—we're born with the basics—but there's a lot you can do about the availability and insertion of knowledge, especially industry- and firm-specific knowledge.

What about the "jerk factor"?

If you're new to an organization—as I've been several times in my career—after a week or so of "observation" you begin to make lists. One of them is a list of the people who are so far over the top that you find yourself slipping into a state of buyer's remorse, wondering how you could have been so stupid to accept the new position. People of course fall into all sorts of categories. Some are hopelessly rude and arrogant. What do we do about these people (who have buddies just like them all over the place)? What do we do about people who disrupt, blame, and undermine? People who complain all of the time? People who have nothing to offer but bitterness, anger, and jealousy?

People can be smart, ambitious, and energetic, but arrogant and caustic. Who do you want on your staff? To whom do you entrust major business technology initiatives? How do you make the trade-offs?

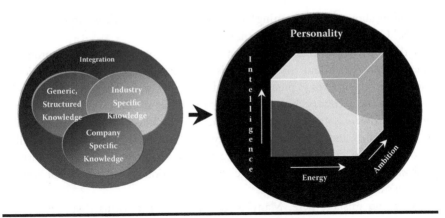

Figure 3.5   The people placer: An unbalanced scorecard.

If you have lots of smart people with no energy or ambition, you have a problem. But it's actually more dangerous if you have dumb people with tons of energy and ambition. The military has known for centuries that officers can be smart *and* arrogant, but never arrogant *and stupid.*

When companies are making lots of money, people (and companies) suffer fools amazingly well, but when times get tough, tempers and patience grow short. When times are good, you should find what the jerks do best and isolate them accordingly; when times get tough, you should prune them from your organization. Ask your high performers who they avoid and why they avoid these people. A consensus of opinion usually represents reality.

Use Figure 3.5 as a scorecard. Grab a handful of darts (with specific names on them) and start firing at the cube on the right. How does the team look?

Three Brands for the Millennium

It's time to plan your next move.

Although the technology industry still supports tons of people, spending and hiring trends don't look all that robust. In fact, there are lots of senior technology professionals still looking for work. What's going on? Is the demand for our services fading? Are we becoming obsolete? No, but there's a big change in the works. Put another way, in five years do you think you'll be doing what you do today? I recently asked 25 senior technology managers at a major public company this question—and not one of them raised a hand.

The distinction I've raised before between operational and strategic technology is a good place to start planning how to reinvent yourself. Operational technology is what all of the "IT-is-a-commodity" crowd keeps talking about; you know, the argument that IT is no longer strategic. Strategic technology is where the action is—and likely to stay. But what do these apparently divergent interpretations of the field tell us about career planning? Tom Peters suggests we think about "personal brands." Good advice, but what brands will sell?

I think there are three. And all of them focus on solutions—not problems. Operationally, the brand that will sell is optimization. Technology professionals who can sell themselves as practical-yet-adaptive infrastructure jockeys will always have work. The necessary skills here include the ability to cost-effectively design and support hardware, software, and communications architectures that directly enable business models and processes. Scalability, reliability, interoperability—and all of the other "ilities"—are assumed to be part of the skills repertoire that operational professionals will have. The language these professionals will use is not techno-speak: it's the language of business.

Make no mistake here. Many of the infrastructure skills that were highly regarded five years ago will not be held in the same esteem five years from now. Lots of infrastructure technology has already been commoditized and outsourced; more will follow. Infrastructure optimization will be about creative commodity management and bullet-proof performance.

If you're not happy with the infrastructure brand, how about branding your-self around strategic technology? If you have wide and deep business knowledge, understand how you—and your competition—make money, and if you under-stand the range of back office, front office, and Internet applications through which all the customers, transactions, and money pass, then you can become a business technology strategist. But earning one's stripes here requires creativity about how existing and emerging applications can increase market share and profitability. Like the operational brand, the strategic brand is primarily about business, not technol-ogy. Business technology strategists sound (and dress) more like consultants than technologists; brand success here requires a lot of finesse.

The third brand that I think will play well in the early twenty-first century is busi-ness technology management guru. Given what we spend on business technology, keeping the books will become more and more important. But the big brand will be about ROI, vendor management, program management, and performance metrics, among other skills that help companies acquire, deploy, manage, and measure business technology investments. Knowing when and how to outsource, how to craft a partner agreement, and how to track the impact of investments on profitability and growth will be the kinds of activities that will define your twenty-first century management brand.

These three brands suggest how you might think about your next move, how to reinvent yourself. How will colleagues describe your special value to the company in five years? What kinds of skills do you think will sell? Which ones are likely to be devalued? Here are some thoughts. Programmers should move from coding to integrating to architecting; database administrators should move from database management to warehousing to mining; back office/front office applications spe-cialists should move from ERP to extensible transaction processing to scenarios that define future business models and processes; and managers should move from asset management and TCO to portfolio management and strategic ROI.

Finally, all of the brands require some business success staples, like the ability to effectively communicate complicated ideas, to compromise, negotiate, and prioritize—and, we hope, your personality doesn't need a major overhaul (because all three brands require some degree of savoir faire).

So which brand do you like?

Can you get there from here?

Can We Handle the Truth?

There's a great scene in the movie *A Few Good Men* when Jack Nicholson tells Tom Cruise that he "can't handle the truth."

What about us? Can we handle the truth?

How honest are we about our ability to deal with the problems that have held business technology alignment back for decades?

I was having dinner with an industry colleague recently and after a couple of glasses of wine, we started to tell each other the truth (or at least versions of the truth that were much more accurate than the ones exchanged before the wine). I described the conversation to a friend who told me that I should have recorded it and published it anonymously for the field to read. Well, here it is—and try to pretend that my name is Joe Klein (he's the guy who anonymously wrote *Primary Colors*—a fictitious look at the Bill Clinton campaign that also became a movie).

My colleague described the senior management team at his company as really pretty clueless about computing and communications technology—not in the bits and bytes sense (which, we both agreed, they shouldn't have to understand)—but in terms of the strategic relationship between business and technology. Here are some of the observations: "They think technology's a commodity that can be bought at sales" … "They think that as machines get more powerful they should cost less and less—and replace more and more people" … "They think that consultants know more about the company than we do" … "They think that the people who do technology are really not all that good, that all that 'stuff' is way too complicated, way too quirky, unreliable and way too expensive."

Then he trashed his vendors who seemed to know a lot about processes that he couldn't find at his company, no matter how hard he looked. They also kept him on this upgrade treadmill that was deliberately designed to keep his company in a constant state of churn.

Because he lived in a decentralized world, he argued that the ("god damned") matrix at his company was worse than the one Keanu Reeves surfs around in, that there were just too many people with bold lines and dotted lines running through them, and that no one can have two or three bosses and survive the corporate jungle for very long. Sipping some wine, he matter-of-factly offered, "It's why people who live in matrix organizations eventually go crazy."

As he reached for his third glass of wine, he ranted about all of the "killer apps" he has to kill. Seems that there are all kinds of people at the company susceptible to *vendormarketitis*. In the past year alone, he had to kill grid computing, biometric authentication, and even a Segue, among a bunch of other things that the inmates barely understood—but had been told at a cocktail party these were killer apps capable of catapulting the company to the "next level."

He ranted about his inability to adequately reward excellent—or punish poor—performance, how he had to keep hiring more and more people to do fewer and fewer jobs because he couldn't remove anyone. He said that human resources (HR) wasn't very helpful here. He wondered aloud what HR actually did at the company.

Charged with developing the company's technology strategy, he asked the people who run strategic planning to define the "as is" and "to be" business models so he could determine which technology investments should—and should not—be made. But the planners complained that it's impossible to know how the company expects to make money in a few years, that no one can predict the future. When he asked the planners how he was expected to optimize technology investments with less-than-specific information, they persuaded him to just do the best he could—but to make sure that the overall cost of technology goes down over time.

While everyone wanted to "standardize" technologies and processes, no one wanted to play bad cop; in fact, no one even wanted to play good cop. Lip service was all he got. When push came to shove, they all wanted to call their own shots. Every time he tried to enlist the support of senior managers to redefine technology governance they ran for the hills. A few months later the same execs asked him to quantify the cost savings attributable to the standardization he had promised.

At this point, **I** drank a third glass of wine.

"People," I said, "it's all about the people."

"How long did it take you to figure that out," he said.

Sometimes the truth hurts.

The Real Truth

I have received a lot of e-mails about my article, "Can We Handle the Truth?" Seems that a lot of us think that the truth is, well, *the truth*—at least from the technology side of the house. But a healthy percentage of the communications were from the other side, the managers who use technology, approve huge technology budgets, and otherwise define corporate strategies. You know, from the senior management team—the "SMT"—that has to be persuaded that technology investments make business sense. I also heard from some vendors.

Here's a sampling of what I received:

The propeller heads need to understand that technology is only important if it helps business make money. The further removed from that goal they stay, the more irrelevant they are to operations and strategy. I really don't care if they think I don't understand what they do. Their job is to make me successful.

When I got that e-mail I cringed but—just for the heck of it—I forwarded it to the same guy who drank all the wine last time to reality check the comments. Here's his reply:

Fine, we're propeller heads. But what the hell is this guy talking about? What are we? Servants? **Everybody** works for the business. This guy's no rocket scientist.

Another one wrote:

Tell the guy who drinks the wine to get real. If he wants perfection he needs to move off the planet. Standards are not straight-jackets. And whoever said that business wasn't messy. It's hard to develop strategies. Hard to organize companies. Hard to manage people. Grow up.

Then a vendor chimed in:

I love how "vendors" are always the fall-guy. We do the dirty work for lots of companies. We train our people and when money is tight negotiate our fees. Where's the problem here? We know the business—it's our job to know the business. Here's a truth: without us, there would be no applications, databases, or networks. Give me break. And if he can't tell the difference between a fad and a solution, then he's in the wrong business. Killer apps? … what is this … 1999?

So what do we have here? Very different cultures, very different agendas—and multiple versions of the truth.

Alignment's like a religious war. But let's talk perspective.

1. The business technology relationship is morphing into a place where everything that isn't overtly strategic is a commodity. The business performance management trend is about business technology optimization or, put another way, alignment on steroids. If you're stuck in the trenches, then you think the "SMT" is stupid about technology; if you're part of the SMT then you think the people in the trenches just don't get it. These perceptions need to marry.

2. Killer apps are investments that simultaneously reduce costs and increase growth and profitability. If you even think about them without these two

goals in mind, then you're hopelessly stuck in the twentieth century—and if you don't think systematically about costs and benefits then you probably shouldn't be in business.

3. People will always be nearly impossible to organize and manage; it makes more sense to accept this rather than to try to change it. The exception to this advice is situational: if your company is tanking, then there'll be a bigger appetite to deal honestly and directly with people issues. Seize these moments to do the right thing for the company (and all of the employees expected to work hard to turn things around).

4. If we don't partner well with vendors, we'll ultimately fail. Expertise is specialized and even die-hard in-sourcers will eventually need help. The pace of technology change and the economic pressures over which we have little control will make at least co-sourcing inevitable. The key is to partner with vendors who know your sector and technology well. But don't delay. It's essential that you develop a short list of bona fide partners ASAP.

5. "Strategy" is owned by everyone. Gone are the days when technology pros can claim that business pros need to prime their agenda with detailed scenarios comprising business models and processes. Business and technology cannot exist without each other. Strategy is a team sport.

I don't think these five "perspectives" are very controversial. Maybe we argue so much because we're under so much stress, or because we've been trained to be suspicious about the other side's motives. The key idea was expressed in one of the e-mails I received. All this stuff is "messy." There's no perfect business model, architecture standardization, or killer app. While it's fun to talk about "disruptive" technologies, conversations about balance and compromise are more realistic, more adult. Alignment is much more about cooperation and negotiation than anything else, and maybe that's all the truth we need.

Do You Speak Business?

Everyone seems to agree that the form and content of "alignment" has forever changed. But all the conventional arguments about business and technology "silos," the commoditization of IT, and new technology leadership skill sets—while legitimate—miss some important points. Let's look at the evolution of the business technology relationship from "alignment" to "partnership" and three things that must be absolutely true to take the relationship to the next level. These things can be located along continua that you can use to determine how sophisticated your alignment-to-partnership strategy really is.

Figure 3.6 identifies three paths in the alignment-to-partnership journey. We have to appreciate business pain and pleasure, we have to become more than just credible, and we have to define business value around strategy. If you understand these paths, you can redefine the business technology relationship—I mean *really* redefine the relationship.

Pain → Pleasure

Let's assume that you understand where the business feels pain—and how it would define pleasure. Remember that the business expects technology to reduce its pain—defined of course around cost reduction. But it's more than that. Business managers worry about their supply chains, their competitors, their manufacturing, distribution, and, of course, their margins. The technology agenda need to speak directly to their pain points—which, when relieved—can become the sources of wide and deep pleasure. If you become a dispenser of pleasure as you reduce pain, you're credibility will rise—which will reveal the second path to business technology partnership.

Credibility → Influence

We hope we're credible. We hope when technologists walk into a room, the business managers don't run for cover or—worse—attack them mercilessly for their sins (network crashes, Web site debacles ... you know the drill). Nirvana here is influence—defined in terms of how the business thinks about how and where technology can help. Does the business respect you enough to confide in you, to commiserate with you, to invite you to brainstorm about its strategy? Who do you drink beer with?

Operations → Strategy

If you're influential, you can shape both operations and strategy. If you get operations straightened out, you can spend most of your time—with your new partners—thinking about competitive advantages, revenues, and profitability. There's no better place to work, no better way to spend your time.

Three Easy First Steps

The partnership described here can be engineered by creative, proactive, and motivated business technology professionals. Here are three steps you can take tomorrow.

- ■ Step 1: Make a list of the things that cause your business partners pain, and then rank-order them—from their perspective, not yours. Think like them. The more you do, the better the list will be. Work with your partners to

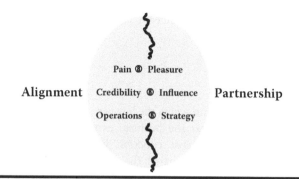

Figure 3.6   Paths to business technology partnership.

validate and improve the list. Then spend some time brainstorming about what your business partners think are the really good things that can happen for them—once their pain gets relieved.

■ Step 2: Honestly assess your credibility with the business. If it's high, then think about how to become influential. Some tips here include working through your partner's prism and then supporting the execution of your partner's plans. Once a baseline credibility is established, then transition to influencing important operational and strategic processes. But if your credibility is low, then you have to build it up slowly but surely, principally by delivering effective pain relievers.

■ Step 3: Use your new-found influence to contribute to strategic planning. The best way to do this is to initiate ideas, models, and pilots. Your partner will appreciate your skin in the game. The perfect outcome here is for your partner to rely upon your insight so much that it would be inconceivable for a new strategic initiative to launch without your fingerprints all over it.

So if you achieve this partnership, what do you give up? A little bit of yourself, a little bit of your experience, and a little bit of your credibility with your legacy peers. What's that? Yes, because true partnership means that some people get a little less of your time and interest than they used to, that you should probably no longer play cards with the data center crowd, and that you'll have to start reading all new trade publications. You might also have to buy some suits.

Leadership, Likability, and Life

Ideas are like viruses—they multiply no matter how hard we try to stop them. For decades I've wondered why there are so many books on management and leadership. I just searched www.amazon.com and found no fewer than 16,380 offerings. I then Googled "Leadership Books" and turned up 30,800,000 hits. How can there be so much wisdom on one subject? Does "leadership" change completely every week or so? That might account for all of the "new" thinking about management and leadership.

Or maybe we just have no idea what leadership is, how to develop it, or how to evaluate it. This might explain why we keep asking the same old questions about leadership, management, and people. The most recent profundity is that people like to work with likable people even if the nice people don't know very much or produce anything of much value. Isn't this insight what explains how politicians get elected? How movie stars become movie stars? How celebrity CEOs become CEOs?

The recent book—*The Likeability Factor*—by Tim Sanders and the June 2005 article in the *Harvard Business Review*—"Competent Jerks and Lovable Fools"— by Tiziana Casciaro and Miguel Sousa Lobo both suggest some really amazing, counterintuitive things: people like to work with people they like! Wow. Even likable stupid people like to work with likable stupid people. Likable smart people also like to work with other likable smart people. Everybody likes to work with likable people—even incompetent likable people. Positively shocking. This explains why some likable politicians can't lead, why some popular actors can't act, and why most celebrity CEOs don't succeed.

I don't know about you but this groundbreaking research has thrown me for a loop. Likable people succeed? Jerks fail? Wow ... I have to sit down to absorb the power of this discovery.

I bring all this up because business technology management and leadership are not exempt from the likable phenomenon. After reading the two above treatises, I sat back and thought about the business technology managers and leaders I've known over the years. How many, I asked myself, were likable? How many were competent? How many were "lovable fools"? How many were really stupid, nasty, and incompetent?

I'm matrix crazy, so I developed a picture (Figure 3.7) for us to ponder.

I then located the business technology managers and leaders that I've worked with over the years. What do you think I discovered? Well, humbly, I discovered that the likability scholars are right: most of the managers and leaders I've known over the years were more dark gray than light gray. I discovered that most of the dark gray people were closer to nice and stupid than they were to nice and smart. Stupid? Okay, that's probably an exaggeration, but I have to say that I've not been overwhelmed by the rocket science of most technology leaders over the years (technology managers are usually smarter). Leadership—fueled by intelligence, dedication, and passion—is actually pretty rare.

I can easily identify lots of technology professionals who were nicer than they were smart. They also seemed to have the knack of being extra nice to the people who promoted them (and to the people who could promote them again). I've also worked with professionals with less than "likable" personalities. Some of these people were bona fide jerks, but some of the jerks were absolutely brilliant and capable

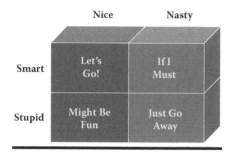

	Nice	Nasty
Smart	Let's Go!	If I Must
Stupid	Might Be Fun	Just Go Away

Figure 3.7 The people placer.

of making extraordinary contributions to their organizations and companies, but, because of their personalities, were dismissed as "difficult," "obnoxious," or just—well—*unlikable*. Many times in my career I counseled such people with the advice: "you are absolutely right … and if you persist, you will be absolutely *dead* right."

All this might also explain why there are so many consultants. Turns out we need to backfill our staffs with people who are smart, nice, and sometimes nasty (there are no stupid consultants, right?).

But much more importantly, there's a way to optimize all this (once you've completed the above matrix). Here's what I think you should do.

- Get rid of the stupid nasty people: they serve no purpose …
- Find, retain, and reward smart, nice people—as many as you can …
- Restrict the nice, stupid people to roles that exploit their talents, perhaps as communicators, facilitators, etc., though some pruning here is also necessary (how many glad handers do you really need?) …
- Work to exploit the contributions that smart—but sometimes nasty—people can make to your projects, programs, and strategies … really smart people are very hard to find …

I think these four steps equal some form of "leadership." Is there another book here?

Politics, Culture, and You

I teach an EMBA class at Villanova University on business technology optimization. The course looks at emerging business models, technologies, and technology management best practices, and ways to optimize the interrelationships across all of these areas. Something happened recently in one of my classes that I think deserves some discussion.

While wrapping up the semester's work, one of the students challenged me and the group: "Sure, all of this stuff is good—and powerful—and might even contribute to the business, but when all's said and done, politics determines what gets funded and what gets killed, what the company does, and what it doesn't do. Good arguments are nice, but they usually fall on deaf ears … I'd rather play golf with the boss than work my tail off writing the 'perfect' business case." When I failed to respond immediately, several others chimed in, agreeing that it was mostly—if not all—"political" out there, and that if you weren't a political player you were doomed.

Are these student-practitioners right? Is it all about **who** you know, not *what* you know? Does politics explain what happens—and what doesn't?

Here's what I told them. First, it's important to assess the political quotient of your company. Some companies are almost completely "political": a few people make decisions based only on what they think, who they like (and dislike), and based on what's good for them personally (which may or may not be good for the company). This is ground zero. It gets no worse than this. On the other extreme are companies that are obsessive–compulsive about data, evidence, and analysis. Sometimes they're so compulsive they fail to make any decisions at all! In the middle are most of the companies out there, with some balance between analysis and politics. Where is your company on this continuum?

It's important to locate your company accurately. It's also important to locate your own preferences, your own culture. The gap between your personal culture and your corporate culture is what will keep you sane—or drive you crazy.

The discussion with the students moved quickly toward a discussion of alternative corporate cultures and the personalities that each culture breeds. Technology decisions in analytical cultures tend to be driven by TCO and ROI calculations, but technology decisions in highly political cultures often have bad outcomes because technology decisions are frequently complicated and expensive. Industry analysts have told us for years that somewhere around 75 percent of all big technology projects fail. I suspect that if we correlated this finding with corporate culture we'd find some interesting things.

We also talked about personal preferences. What kind of culture do you like? Some of us flourish in politically charged cultures, while others thrive in analytical cultures. The key is the gap between where you live and who you are.

I ended the class with a discussion about how holistic business technology decisions really are (not with a discussion about how to neutralize political decision making or change corporate cultures). At the heart of the matter is the balance between analysis and politics or—expressed more gently—research and philosophy. For example, business technology decisions occur within a philosophical context often expressed in dictums like "we don't believe in offshore outsourcing," or "we never build applications; we always buy and integrate them." These kinds of philosophical preferences drive the decision agenda. Decisions that make the list are then approached analytically or politically, depending on the culture. Maneuvering through decision-making mazes can be challenging—or rewarding—depending on the size of your personal/corporate culture gap.

Bottom line?

If you're political but your culture is analytical—or vice versa—it may be time to move. But if you're aligned with your culture, you should prosper. The matrix looks something like Figure 3.8. As always, it's better to be dark gray than light gray. Medium gray is okay, but still not perfect. I think that highly political people in totally political cultures eventually lose their minds, but that's just my opinion, I could be wrong. What worries me most are the people and cultures that are part political and part analytical. How do they make decisions without arguing with their companies and themselves? Enough. I think everyone gets the picture. Class dismissed.

Consultants in the Hen House

Consulting training programs are everywhere. But there's a gap between generic consulting programs and programs that focus on consulting knowledge and skills leverageable within companies, on *internal consulting.*

I realize that "consulting" has a checkered image—and that's probably being kind. Many of us that hire the usual suspects—Accenture, PWC, IBM, Deloite, EDS, Bearing Point, and so on—have more tales of woe than glee. But there are definitely "good" consultants out there from whom we can learn good ol' fashioned business analysis, solid negotiation and persuasion skills, and the ability to prioritize and execute—among other skills.

Just about every company on the planet could use more good internal consultants. Yet I hear very little about importing consulting knowledge and skills into the enterprise. Most companies still appear to be more interested in hiring good (and sometimes evil) external consultants. There is a better—and cheaper—way.

Internal consultants are different from external consultants in several important ways. First, they exist within an existing and semipermanent organization with its own distinct culture. This alone distinguishes internal from external consultants. Second, internal consultants must endure the consequences of their own success or failure. Unlike external consultants, who get to leave the company when a project ends, internal consultants work within a company's organization and culture sometimes for decades. This dramatically changes the risk profile for internal consultants.

Where do internal consultants come from? They are recruited and they are grown.

Some companies recruit consultants into their companies as "change agents" or simply as an attempt to add different professionals to their ranks. Other companies grow them internally by investing in training programs that select the professionals best able to play the role of internal consultant. Growing is better than recruiting simply because internal consultants—if they are carefully selected—have credibility within the organization. They also know the company, its culture, and the business models and processes that generate the profit that keeps the whole thing going. External consultants have to earn their stripes with skeptical managers nearly every time they tee it up. Growing is also better because investments in internal consultants are likely to pay dividends for extended periods of time so the return on the training investment is generally good.

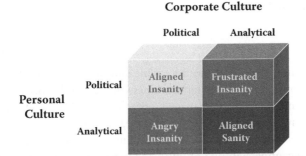

Figure 3.8   Where do you live?

So what are the skills? What might an internal consulting training program look like? First, there should be an emphasis on the consulting process followed by an emphasis on specific knowledge and skills, as suggested below.

The Consulting Process

- Identify a meaningful problem
- Assess the appetite for solutions
- Determine likely costs and risks
- Find the right sponsors
- Develop a value/cost/risk business case
- Realistically define the project
- Chunk the steps
- Execute
- Revisit the value/cost/risk business case
- Continue to conclusion and reporting

Consulting Knowledge and Skills

Knowledge of:

- The business (the business and the business)
- Multiple functional areas

Skills to:

- Listen—and translate
- Synthesize
- Communicate
- Negotiate

- Influence and persuade
- Write
- Present ...

I cannot stress enough the need for wide and deep knowledge of the business. Really good consultants understand business models and processes on all levels. They understand what keeps managers up at night and how to make managers heroes. They understand business pain and pleasure first and technology second—which is not to say that they do not understand technology widely or deeply but rather that their understanding of business models and processes drives how they leverage technology.

Why all this emphasis on internal consulting knowledge and skills? Because many technology professionals—as wonderful as they are—are unable to analyze, prioritize, or communicate as well as they should with their business partners. Some organizations have responded to this challenge by creating "Business Relationship Managers" but these professionals tend to be more glib than professionally trained. It's time to invest in formal consulting skills training in your organization if you want to really leverage technology on to business. I predict that there will be a lot of professionals interested in formal internal consulting training—many more than you might think.

Chapter 4

Acquisition and Measurement

Many Happy Returns

Let's keep return on investment (ROI) and total cost of ownership (TCO) in perspective. You cannot build a business with these hammers. Are they important? Yes. Insightful? Usually. But obsessive–compulsive TCO/ROI behavior is as unhealthy as obsessive–compulsive quality, learning, or reengineering behavior. Remember?

The ultimate argument for a technology initiative is made in the business case. But key to good business cases is quantitative *and* qualitative data about the cost of a technology project's entire life cycle *and* the strategic impact it will have on meaningful business processes. TCO is about costs and ROI is about benefits.

Let's start with costs. There are acquisition costs, operational costs, and softer costs that are by nature more difficult to quantify. TCO calculations should also include costs over the entire life cycle of a hardware or software product. Softer costs include the costs of downtime and internal consulting that comes from indirect sources and costs connected with your degree of standardization.

TCO data is an essential part of any business case that should ultimately be driven by the strategic and/or tactical return you expect to get from your investment. In other words, TCO data drives ROI data—which, like TCO data—is both hard and soft.

Is it important to ask meaningful questions about why a business technology initiative exists—and what impact it will have on the business (if it goes well)? Of course. So why is there so much disagreement about ROI? Research suggests that while lots of ROI methods are used, by far the most popular are ones that calculate cost reduction, customer satisfaction, productivity improvement, and contributions to profits and earnings. Two years is also considered by the majority of business technology executives as a reasonable time over which to measure ROI.

So What Are the Methods?

One of the easiest is based on a simple calculation that starts with the amount of money you're spending on a business technology initiative (that includes TCO and other data) and then calculates the increased revenue or reduced costs that the investment actually generates. If a project costs a million bucks but saves two million, then the ROI is healthy.

Another simple method is based on payback data—the time it takes to offset the investment of the business technology initiative through increased revenues or reduced costs. If the payback period is short—and the offsets are great—then the project is "successful."

There are also methods based on economic value analysis or value added (EVA), internal rates of return (IRR), net present value (NPV), total economic impact (TEI), rapid economic justification (REJ), information economics (IE), and real options valuation (ROV), among too many others. Do we really need this much precision? (No.)

What about soft ROI? In the mid- to late-1990s, companies developed Web sites for a variety of reasons. First-generation sites were essentially brochureware, where very few transactions took place. What was the ROI on these sites? They did not reduce costs: in fact, they increased them. Nor did they generate revenue. They were built to convince customers, Wall Street analysts, investors, and even their own employees that they "got it," that they understood that the Web was important. A significant intangible benefit? Absolutely.

Although I think that anyone who launches a business technology project without any TCO and ROI data is insane, I also appreciate the need for balance and reasonableness. This is why there's so much controversy about TCO/ROI. Lots of people think that too rigorous an application of TCO and ROI methodology will distort projects and perhaps even undermine business results. Others think that companies should know what to do instinctively and therefore shouldn't need a whole lot of data to make sound business decisions. Some think that the last thing they need to do is launch a training program to get their people up to speed on the latest and greatest approaches to TCO and ROI, that the time would be better spent just working the projects; and there are those who think that the effort to collect and analyze TCO and ROI data is disproportionate to the returns.

What to Do?

Simplicity—as usual—is our friend.

Adopt a flexible approach to TCO and ROI. TCO data should feed ROI data, which should feed the overall business cases for business technology decisions. Hard data is always better than soft data, but soft data—if it can be monetized (like generating a premium for your stock price or enhancing your brand)—should also be analyzed.

The simplest approach to TCO data collection and assessment is a template that requires the collection of specific hard and soft data, and the simplest approach to ROI data collection and assessment is based on simple metrics that measure payback over a reasonable period of time. Payback should be defined around internal metrics—like cost reduction—and external ones—like improved customer service and profitability. Not too complex—but meaningful. Some projects will pay themselves back in a year, while others may take three. Beyond three, things get too fuzzy, so I'd rethink projects with anything longer than three-year ROI tails.

TCO and ROI should not be used as clubs to bludgeon people; they should be used to inform decisions and monitor progress. (They should also play a role in the death of projects-gone-berserk.) In other words, TCO and ROI questions should always be asked, but the answers don't always need to be perfect.

Sourcing, Sourcing Everywhere

I've written about outsourcing before. But since it's growing at an incredible pace, I think we need to talk about it again—as honestly and realistically as possible.

The appeal of outsourcing is still cost savings and, increasingly, discipline in the form of elegant software documentation and improved reliability—in the case of software development and systems integration—and efficient processes and excellent customer and employee interaction—in the case of call centers. Everything's a candidate for outsourcing it seems—front office, back office, virtual office tasks are all on the list; you can always find someone to do whatever you need done—for a price, of course.

But before you leap into a short-term or (especially) long-term outsourcing agreement, you need to know some things.

First, you need to know how to craft a diagnostic outsourcing request for proposal (RFP). The most important aspect of this process is the width and depth of your understanding of the work you want to relinquish; if you don't fully understand what you want an outsourcer to do, the deal will explode. The incarnation of this understanding will be your RFP of the tasks to be performed, and the details of the service level agreement (SLA) you'll want the outsourcer to honor. These documents need to be works of art—though don't expect elegant pieces of paper to actually manage the arrangement. You'll have to do this personally.

Second, you need to know what should stay close to home and what you can export to India, the Philippines, Ireland, Russia, or wherever. Companies have outsourced technology and business processes to a variety of companies outside of the United States to save money and improve quality. When tasks are well defined and repeatable—and when you know a lot about them—they can be exported. When the outsourcing deal is with a company thousands of miles away it better be well conceived and well oiled: outsource far from home only when you understand the processes and objectives, have a mutually beneficial explicit SLA, and metrics that enable you to track performance at least quarterly (I actually prefer monthly tracking).

Third, you need to know how to develop contingency plans—and the more distant the partner, the more robust the plans should be. I understand that ubiquitous communications shrinks distance and time, but we should never underestimate the need for hands-on, face-to-face management—especially hands-on, face-to-face *crisis* management. If an offshore outsourcing effort is extremely strategic to your company, you should consider opening an office near your partner to stay close to progress and problems.

Fourth, you need to tap into insight about social and political climates in the countries and regions where you have outsourcing partners. It's obviously a volatile world, and it's possible to have great partners who find themselves held hostage to paralyzing economic, political, and military events; do you want to be the champion of outsourcing deals to countries whose economic and political systems are fragile, or whose military enemies are formidable—and close?

Fifth, be completely honest with yourself (and management) about the total cost of outsourcing. While the essential tasks—coding, answering phones, processing checks, and so on—may be much cheaper, there are all sorts of additional costs that must be calculated, costs such as additional travel, additional management, on-site presence, and performance monitoring. So-called soft costs will also kill you here. Model all the hard, soft, and other costs before you outsource, and then again during and after the outsourcing experience.

Finally, you need to keep asking tough questions about your current and anticipated core competencies. Why are you outsourcing? By this time, you should know that just saving money is sometimes a horrible reason to outsource anything. Outsourcing decisions should be driven by objective assessments about what it is you do well (and poorly), cost-effectively (and too expensively), what you think your competitive differentiators are (and will be), and what you really want your company to be (and not be) going forward. One more thing: try as hard as you can to keep the politics as quiet as possible when you're making important outsourcing decisions, especially decisions that will land a continent away.

Outsourcing can often make perfect sense. But it can sometimes result in hideous outcomes. Be careful out there.

Concepts to Clusters: The Real Technology Chasm

I was invited to the Pentagon to talk about the adoption of new technology. It was part of the government's effort to (once again) "transform" the way it does business. My role was to help them think about how to introduce new technology to old problems, processes, and decision makers. I agreed to go because I wanted to draw some distinctions among technology concepts, emerging technologies, and technology clusters. I also thought I'd get a chance to influence some heavy hitters. More on that later.

So what is grid computing? Is it a technology concept, a real technology, or a whole technology cluster? What about voice recognition technology, semantic understanding, and the Segway? Are they concepts, emerging technologies, or part of larger technology clusters?

I got to thinking about all this because I recently did a "content analysis" of a number of technology trade publications and turned up no fewer than 30 "technologies to watch." Content analysis is a technique that identifies trends by counting the frequency of mention: if something's mentioned a lot—like Web services—then it ranks high in the analysis. Lots of technologies get mentioned a lot—which is why there are 30 or so "to watch"—but let's be honest: there's no way all of them deserve our attention—or our money. What are the technologies that matter?

I segmented technologies into concepts—ideas like "real-time computing," emerging technologies, like wireless networks, and technology clusters that include real technologies plus infrastructure, applications, data, standards, a developer community, and management support. I then made the argument that technology impact was related to concepts, technologies, and clusters, that concepts are wannabes, prototype technologies have potential, and mature technology clusters are likely to have huge sustained impact on the way to do business.

I then mapped a bunch of the technologies-to-watch onto an impact chart and discovered that many of the technologies about which we're so optimistic haven't yet crossed the technology/technology cluster chasm—indicated by the thick line that separates the two in Figure 4.1. Technologies in the outer zone have proven impact; those in the middle have genuine potential, while those on the left may or may not graduate to medium or high impact technologies. The bold chasm—marked by the thick black line—is where investors manage the tipping point. Keep to the right of the line if you're conservative.

The essence of all this is that technologies will have limited impact until full clusters develop around them consisting of all of the things necessary for technologies to grow, all of the applications, data, support, standards, and developers that keep technologies alive and well over long periods of time. Figure 4.1 also suggests that it's too early to tell if many of the technologies-to-watch will become high impact technologies, that is, will cross the chasm. Real-time synchronization, business process modeling, grid and utility computing, among others, may or

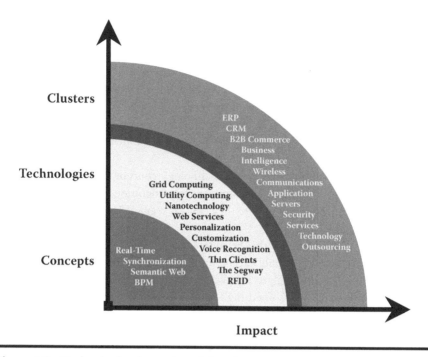

Figure 4.1   Technologies, impact, and the chasm.

may not yield successful prototypes—which may or may not evolve into full-blown clusters.

So how did I do with the heavy hitters at the Pentagon? A few of them thought I was Geoffrey Moore, the co-author of the now classic *Crossing the Chasm.* Some others thought I worked for the technology vendors who had actually crossed the chasm, and a lot of them thought that the whole notion of clusters was too restrictive, that technologies—even if they were bogus—needed nurturing. When I said that I thought such an approach could prove to be very expensive, they reminded me that their job was to invest in high-risk/high-payoff technologies, not to invest in technologies that were definitely going to work.

On the train back from Washington I finally figured out where all the money goes—and how companies can save some of the money the government spends:

- Mostly buy clusters
- Occasionally invest in prototypes
- Enjoy (but don't buy any) concepts

Or put another way, unless you're in the technology business, don't be an early adopter, a pioneer, or live on the bleeding edge. It's too expensive (unless you work for the government). Is this a good way to segment technologies? I think it helps categorize the phases technologies go through and helps us avoid investing too early in technologies that haven't proved themselves. Stay in the high impact zone; if you want to experiment a little try the medium impact zone—but if you want to gamble, enter the low impact (but potentially high impact) zone.

Vendors, Vendors Everywhere ...
Who's the Fairest of Them All?

Anne Wilms, the CIO of Rohm and Haas, a leading global chemicals company, recently hosted a luncheon on behalf of a not-for-profit organization called NPower. NPower helps other not-for-profit organizations with their technology requirements (www.NPower.org). Michael Ferreri was also at the meeting. Michael at the time was Microsoft's Philadelphia boss.

I bring all this up here because I got to thinking about Microsoft—and other vendors—during the meeting. It turns out that Microsoft has committed millions of dollars to NPower in an attempt to subsidize NPower's offerings to its nonprofit clients. This is clearly a win/win situation, but, as it turns out, there are lots of ways to think about vendor relationships. Here are a few of the major ones that we should perhaps revisit.

Vendors as Necessary Evils

Many of us see vendors as necessary evils. We need PCs or laptops so we grudgingly write an RFP to begin what we dread as an unpleasant selection process. We feel the same way about negotiating enterprise software licenses, desktop support contracts, and wireless communications. We know we need the stuff, but we really don't like the acquisition process. What's going on here?

Technologists (and their acquisition teams) who see vendors as necessary evils are short-sighted and sometimes, well, just plain lazy. The necessary evil perspective is really very 1980s and doesn't reflect even late twentieth century thinking about technology optimization. If you're in this camp, you might want to rethink your approach to acquisition, deployment, and support. If your vendors are necessary evils, then by definition you'll minimize contact with them and your interest in their offerings. You will keep them at arms' length and ultimately fail to integrate business and technology.

Vendors as Adversaries

But things could be worse. Some of us see vendors as adversaries who should be defeated every time we get the chance. Although there may be some valid reasons for hating vendors—there are always valid reasons for hating professionals with whom we contend—there are few if any valid reasons to hold grudges, lose perspective, or otherwise make emotional decisions that hurt our companies (and the vendors we hate). If you find it impossible to deal with a vendor for ethical reasons, replace the vendor, don't try to kill the vendor. The vendors-as-adversaries approach wastes way too much energy on the wrong things. About all it's good for is generating bragging rights at two o'clock in the bar.

Vendors as Partners

Vendors are not always trouble. In fact, the smart play as we move toward business technology synergism is to develop wide and deep relationships with vendors that link directly to key business metrics—like cost management, growth, and profitability. In fact, just as we think about the ROI of technology projects we should think about the tactical and strategic ROI of our vendor relationships. Do we really need the data warehouse guys who charge us an arm and a leg? How dependent are we on our ERP implementation/integration/support vendor? Heavily? Okay, then let's make that vendor a strategic partner. Let's allow that vendor "in" to participate in our strategic planning and the delivery of our products and services.

The subset of vendors who have measurable tactical and strategic value is probably smaller than you think, but the value of the group may be much greater than you realize. The vendors who make the short list should be invited into your inner circle. In return for a long-term business commitment, they will ride the highs and lows of your business. They will understand your requirements and try as hard as they possibly can not to shamelessly exploit this understanding. They will help finance your technology purchases—with favorable terms—in exchange for a long-term business commitment. Under the umbrella of professional—though not oppressive—nondisclosure agreements you will share information, insights, and plans. This will permit you to optimize their contributions to your business.

Bite the bullet and look for partners. The technology industry is consolidating. In five years there will be only several players in each major space. Already, we're essentially down to three enterprise database vendors and a few networking and communications vendors. How many ERP vendors are there likely to be in 2010? The boundaries around transaction processing are also changing. It's impossible to strategize your business around sets of discrete disconnected events—or the vendors who support them. Instead, business is becoming continuous and the vendors who support 24/7 transaction processing simply cannot be organized as a hoard of adversaries that we hope are all perfectly incentivized to do exactly what you want when you want it (at the right price). The macro trends in our industry validate the search for good partners—even if (or should I say, especially if) they're vendors.

Three Reasons More Outsourcing Is Inevitable

Time for an outsourcing reality check. Since everyone's excited about how well—or poorly—outsourcing works, let's take a look at what's likely to happen over the next few years.

Let me say first that much of the fate around outsourcing has already been sealed. How could this be? I realize that there are new reports that near- and off-shore outsourcing does not save as much money as many people assumed. Some reports suggest that quality is a continuing problem, and others complain about language barriers, competing processes, and the management challenges that especially plague many offshore outsourcing projects.

The fate may already be sealed for several reasons. First, the number of management information systems (MIS), information systems (IS), computer science (CS), and computer engineering (CE) majors has fallen so dramatically over the past few years that we're likely to lose an entire generation of replacement technologists if present trends continue—and they show every sign of doing so. Consequently, as the previous generation continues to gray, there will be precious few new technologists to keep the skills pipeline full. The obvious outcome is increased demand for the skills—wherever they happen to be.

A second trend that will fuel the demand for more outsourcing is standardization and its cousin commoditization. The industry is making increasingly less variant stuff work together. While Web services and service-oriented architectures (SOAs) represent impressive technology, they also represent freedom to those who deploy and support technology. Vendor consolidation is also fueling standardization and commoditization, and if you believe the impact that SOAs will have on software development, support, and licensing, the stage is set for the massive decentralization of cooperative software components. If this playing field truly levels itself out, the door will open even further for outsourcers who will master the new architectures (as a natural extension from where they are now in applications development and integration).

The third trend to watch is "the end of corporate computing," or the desire to buy services and rent applications rather than deploy and support them in-house. Nick Carr is at it again. In the Spring 2005 issue of the *Sloan Management Review*, he predicts the end of corporate data centers and the rise of "utility computing." Long term, I think he is absolutely right. Initially, companies will purchase transaction processing services from centralized data centers managed by large technology providers, but over time companies will rent applications developed the old-fashioned way by the same old mega software vendors. Eventually, however, as SOA proliferates, new software delivery and support models will develop from the old vendors as well as a host of new ones: "hosting" applications will yield to "assembling" applications. The appeal of "paying by the drink" is just too great to resist—especially because the alternative will still (and forever) require the care and feeding of increasingly difficult-to-find technology professionals.

If you look at these trends, there's plenty of reason to believe that down-the-street, near-shore, and offshore outsourcing will all increase over the next few years and certainly, as I believe, even more in the next decade. The recent backlash that describes failed or too-expensive outsourcing deals—while in many cases absolutely justified—will be crushed by the inevitability that the above three trends—among others—will create. Although all of these trends are important, I think the most troubling one is the technology-avoidance strategy practiced by so many undergraduates today. It's as if they've all but given up on technology careers, believing instead that they're better off studying accounting, communications, or history. At least the history majors can help us understand what happened to the U.S. technology market in the early twenty-first century.

Squeezing Willing—and Not-So-Willing—Vendors

How much do you spend with Microsoft, Oracle, IBM, SAP, or Dell? *How much?* What do you get for all that money?

If you're completely happy with these vendors, you're misguided. *What?* Why? Because if you've been a loyal customer and spend over a million bucks a year with these guys, you should get much, much more than the product or service you get in the normal transaction process. What if you spend $5M a year with a vendor? How about $10M—as many large enterprises do? What if you have mega-contracts for data center management or desktop/laptop support? What if you spend $25M a year—or more—with IBM, EDS, CSC, or Accenture—as some of us do? What kind of special treatment should you expect?

If you spend serious money with a vendor, here's what you should expect:

- **Extraordinary—Nordstrom-grade—support—even if you haven't paid for platinum service.** Long-term vendor–customer relationships should be rewarded by extremely excellent service. It should not matter that you only paid for gold service; when the heater breaks in the winter it should be fixed within hours, not days. Of course, if the heater breaks every other day, no one has the right to expect extraordinary service for less than fair and reasonable cost. But vendors should not quibble over the terms of a SLA when the pipes have burst. Nor should they provide you with a huge "I did-you-a-huge-favor" bill for such infrequent but critical services.
- **Shared risk contracts.** Shared risk relationships can be tough to manage, especially when relationships are new. But over time, relationships should be based on mutual respect: I respect your ability to deliver for me as you respect my qualifications as a customer. In fact, I am not just a customer; I am a special client. If either of us fails to fulfill our responsibilities, then we should accommodate the relationship in some meaningful way.

- **Subsidized pilots**. Let's assume that I use IBM or Oracle's database platform. Let's also assume that I spend several million dollars a year with these vendors. I am currently thinking about a data warehousing project to determine if I can better cross-sell and up-sell my products and services, but I am concerned about selling the business case to the senior management team that is notoriously cheap about such initiatives. Is it reasonable to expect IBM or Oracle to heavily subsidize the demonstration pilot project? Absolutely. In fact, the primary database vendor—who has a huge financial vested interest in the outcome of the pilot—should not only subsidize the project but pay for it entirely. The quid pro quo, of course, is additional work for the incumbent vendor if the project is successful. Is this reasonable? Yes, if the size of the additional project is substantial. Some ratios to consider: if the new project is worth $100,000, then a fully subsidized $10,000 project is reasonable; for a million dollar project, a $100,000 pilot seems right. And yes, for a $100M project, $10M is appropriate. A ratio of 10:1 is about right—if not a little light.

- **Requirements prioritization**. All vendors want us to stay with their products and services. Oracle wanted us to stay with their CRM solutions so badly they bought the industry leader. SAP wants its customers to stay with its platform so badly that it keeps introducing and improving new functional modules—CRM, BPM, and so on—to keep its customers from pursuing best-of-breed/buy-and-integrate strategies. The trouble is that the functional capabilities of some of the major database, ERP, CRM, and other vendors are often inferior to some of the more specialized vendors. This capabilities gap provides leverage to buyers—if they understand how to communicate their requirements to their primary vendors. For example, SAP needs to make its supply chain management (SCM) module as good as—if not better than—Manugistics application if it wants to keep clients from straying. This means that your supply chain planning and management requirements are especially important—or should be if communicated effectively—to your ERP vendor who will listen carefully if it is doing its job. "Fix it or else" should be what your vendor hears when you suggest what requirements need to be addressed in the next version of the application. Large clients should have a seat at the requirements table as major vendors improve, redesign, and reengineer their applications.

- **R&D partnerships**. Related to all this is a longer-term partnership that includes you in the R&D activities and plans of your key vendors. Here I am not talking about "briefing days" where your vendors get to persuade you to buy new applications or new features in old applications. Instead, a true partnership involves your vendors' sharing information about significant R&D investments they're making and plan to make and the opportunity to overlay your anticipated requirements on to those R&D plans. One way to accomplish this objective is to encourage "internships" with your vendors where your key business technologists get to spend weeks if not months with your vendors' R&D teams. If your vendors don't invite you in, invite yourself.

All of these ideas constitute advanced vendor management best practices. Remember, we buy all this stuff—over a trillion dollars a year in hardware, software, and services in the United States alone. Don't we deserve special treatment?

Guerilla Budgeting

There's never enough money. I am tired of hearing this complaint. Of course there's never enough money. Everyone wants more money—which is why there's never enough. U.S. companies are better at cutting costs than they are at growing their businesses, so there's less money in our companies to do anything meaningful. The government has already spent itself into oblivion—screwing our kids in the process—so there's no money there for essential things like healthcare and education. Many of us have huge mortgages, so we don't have enough money for even modest vacations or college tuition for the same screwed kids.

Technology budgets are always under attack. Most of these budgets have little or no discretionary room to maneuver. So when the boss says "what about that Web 2.0 stuff? What are we doing there?" most CIOs and CTOs tell the boss "we're looking at it," knowing full well that they only have enough money to put out the daily brushfires—and nothing more. Exacerbating the shortage of cash, operational technology—infrastructure, PCs, laptops, PDAs, cell phones, messaging, and the like—is expected to cost less every year. After all, everything's a commodity, isn't it? And everyone knows how flat the world is.

Let's talk about guerilla budgeting.

First, if I'm a CIO or CTO, I'm not telling anyone how my investments distribute across my operational versus strategic priorities because I can't draw a clean line myself, and because I want to make sure that I don't create a budgeting target the CFO might lock on to. In fact, I need to protect whatever discretionary latitude I have because I need to be strategically—not just operationally—responsive to the company's requirements. Because I can't draw a clean line between all of my strategic and operational projects, I will push all of the gray area projects into the strategic category. This will insulate them from the cold of commoditization and the expectation that "this-should-be-cheaper."

I will also campaign for new strategic projects with the senior management teams of the enterprise and the lines of business. This is marketing, pure and simple. I need to convince them that I can help them solve some of their most pressing problems like, of course, cost management, but also customer service, cross-selling, up-selling, and anything that leads to profitable growth. If I'm a really good salesperson, I can convince them to pay for the new initiatives as add-ons to my budget. These should be sold as special projects with pilot phases that provide enough information to determine if a major initiative makes sense. These are classic win/wins because I get more money to invest in strategic projects and the business feels good about using technology to solve major business problems.

I'm also going to squeeze my vendors so tightly that they cough up cash all over the floor—if they want to keep my business or want new business from me. The strategic pilots that I do for the lines of business should be at least partially subsidized by vendors with vested interests in the outcomes. A rule of thumb is 10 percent of the eventual project cost, where a $10M project would have a subsidy value of $1M. After the vendors stop crying, they will accept the terms. Of course, the quid pro quo is that if the project escalates to full value, the subsidizing vendor will get the deal.

I am going to create some major incentives for my people. I will develop some payback metrics that require ideas to have at least a 3× return. If one of my team can save me a ton of money in the delivery of operational technology, for example, then I will pay that person a bonus equaling one-third of the savings. The reverse equation would apply to generating revenue. This will require internal SLAs with my own people, but it could be well worth the effort. I would only pay them when the savings or revenues are realized. Try this and watch what happens.

I am also going to think about my own top line. How can I make money with technology? What can I sell? If I have excess computing and communications capacity, I might try to become a reseller. There is precedent for this. Companies have been providing services to other companies for years. Even expertise is resold, especially in the area of architecture. In a previous life, I bundled architectural and database management expertise into consulting offerings that I sold to non-competitors. Although my internal people always had lots to do, they were able to find a few days a month to consult for a share of the fees. They also learned a lot by working outside of the proverbial box.

These steps might help technology budgeting. Think about them; try them out.

Now if we could only find a way to shrink the federal and trade deficits. Does anyone know some smart people who might look at these problems?

Dissenting Opinions about Outsourcing

There have been lots of "studies" on job migration and outsourcing over the past five years that try to position outsourcing as something political: outsourcing creates jobs … outsourcing is the inevitable consequence of globalization … outsourcing will destroy the U.S. labor force. But what's really going on?

We need to level set for a moment. First, outsourcing is about (1) core competency assessments, the (2) segmentation and distribution of expertise, and (3) cost management. Nothing more, nothing less.

Many companies have decided that they no longer want to be in the IT business or the check processing business or even the R&D business. The smart ones have prioritized the tasks they should pursue as their core and decided that they really don't need to perform whole sets of tasks to remain competitive and profitable. The rise of the IT services industry is testimony to core competency (and other) analyses that companies have performed about what's core and what's not.

Expertise is also evolving. Not too many decades ago, the United States owned a relatively huge chunk of IT expertise, but over at least the past decade that expertise has become distributed across the globe. This new reality is affecting sourcing decisions on every continent.

Companies also outsource—down the street or across the ocean—to get access to expertise at a good price. If local, regional, or national expertise were at hand—and cheap—there would be no offshore outsourcing. But once a company decides about its core competencies and once it identifies the expertise it needs to satisfy its non-core requirements, then it looks for cost-effective expertise. Much of this expertise is local, regional, and national, and much if it is global.

The just released report on "Globalization and Offshoring of Software" from the ACM argues that outsourcing is "good"—if not inevitable—and, in fact, actually creates more jobs than it eliminates (http://www.acm.org/globalizationreport/). In the spirit of full disclosure, I was a member of the study team for the report contributing to the education section of the report.

Let's look at the report's major conclusions, followed by my comments.

1. *Globalization of, and offshoring within, the software industry are deeply connected and both will continue to grow. Key enablers of this growth are information technology itself, the evolution of work and business processes, education, and national policies.*

   Nothing profound here. I would have been happier had this initial finding been contextualized within the larger core competency, expertise segmentation/distribution, and cost management trends referenced above.

2. *Both anecdotal evidence and economic theory indicate that offshoring between developed and developing countries can, as a whole, benefit both, but competition is intensifying.*

   The first reaction to what is a part-anecdotal and part data-based finding is that we need to segment the nature of the jobs outsourced, in-sourced, and co-sourced before we imply that outsourcing is "okay" (because it creates more jobs than it eliminates). The technology food chain is important to assessing the effects of outsourcing. Some jobs—at the bottom of the food chain (like legacy systems maintenance programming)—are being outsourced at an accelerating rate. Others—at the top of the food chain (like architecture)—are less likely to be outsourced—at least today. What new jobs are being created as outsourcing increases? Are they at the top or the bottom of the food chain? What do careers and salaries look like for the jobs that remain? I'd also challenge government figures about job creation, loss, and trends. Aside from a healthy suspicion all of us should have about government statistics, there was real debate about the accuracy of the Bureau of Labor Statistics (BLS) technology job data and the trends that the BLS suggests will hold into the early twenty-first century. Finally, the whole notion of an invisible hand prudently allocating expertise to everyone's comparative advantage minimizes the problems connected with transition and comparative imbalance. While comparative advantage is a fact of economic life, the outcome isn't always pretty—especially if the parties involved mismanage the trends and opportunities. Does everyone, for example, believe that the U.S. government will get all this just right? (Before you answer note that the U.S. government recently cut funding in basic research in computer and information science.) Darwin—not politicians—tends to dominate discussions about comparative advantage.

3. *While offshoring will increase, determining the specifics of this increase is difficult given the current quantity, quality, and objectivity of data available. Skepticism is warranted regarding claims about the number of jobs to be offshored and the projected growth of software industries in developing nations.*

The subtext here is truly scary. Basically, the report punts: no one really knows how many jobs might be lost, but there's optimism that it will all work out fine. If ever there was an argument for better data, closer monitoring, and a robust government/industry partnership, this is it. I for one am amazed at the uncertainty and imprecision surrounding all this. If we cannot offer more definitive data, why are we presenting "findings"?

4. *Standardized jobs are more easily moved from developed to developing countries than are higher-skill jobs. These standardized jobs were the initial focus of offshoring. Today, global competition in higher-end skills, such as research, is increasing. These trends have implications for individuals, companies, and countries.*

This is also scary—especially given the problems with intellectual property (IP) that countries encounter all the time. There are countries that are not playing by the global community's IP protection rules—so why would companies trust them with their R&D? I agree that U.S. dominance in R&D is "challenged"; actually, I believe that it's much worse than just "challenged." If present trends continue, the United States will lose its dominance to a set of countries that together will move up the technology food chain and create a variety of hardware, software, and communications innovations. This will exacerbate sourcing strategies. The United States could find itself outside of the technology food chain altogether.

5. *Offshoring magnifies existing risks and creates new and often poorly understood or addressed threats to national security, business property and processes, and individuals' privacy. While it is unlikely these risks will deter the growth of offshoring, businesses and nations should employ strategies to mitigate them.*

Hard to argue with any of these findings.

6. *To stay competitive in a global IT environment and industry, countries must adopt policies that foster innovation. To this end, policies that improve a country's ability to attract, educate, and retain the best IT talent are critical. Educational policy and investment is at the core.*

The United States needs to jumpstart interest in, and support for, technology-focused education and training. At the present time, the grade I would give U.S. policymakers in this area is an "F"—and that would be a gift. In fact, the U.S. response to the trends discussed here is literally unfathomable. U.S. industry would get a generous "D." But industry's motivations here are compromised because the industry is always trying to maximize profit, shortsighted as that strategy may be.

Time will tell if outsourcing results in more technology jobs; time will tell if the jobs are at the right place in the technology food chain. I am not optimistic about the U.S. government's ability or will to respond to the challenges that comparative advantage will throw at the industry. The U.S. federal government's track record here—especially in the innovation area—is dismal. The companies that "benefit" from outsourcing on one level or another are conflicted about intentions, investments, and strategies. U.S. public companies—ever driven by quarterly pressure to achieve results—are especially conflicted, and therefore are only mediocre partners in outsourcing management or optimization. I am also worried about the educational system's ability to stay current, foster innovation, or provide leadership. A case in point: what has academia done about the huge declines in CS and MIS majors at the undergraduate level? A final comment: I am not sure at all about the ACM task force's general conclusion about job net gains, not because there may or may not be job gains (the data is way too fuzzy to predict anything definitive), but the task force's generally optimistic attitude about outsourcing trends is confusing, especially given our inability to predict empirically definitive outcomes, identify, or assess the disruptive effects of increased outsourcing, or government's horrific track record anticipating and reacting to major shifts in the national or global economy. Or, put another way, the facts don't speak for themselves.

Selling Tough Projects

Do you ever have trouble selling technology projects? Over the years I've run through a bunch of methods and approaches. But Wall Street is struggling with volatility, corporate America is under fire for its inability to tell the whole truth and nothing but the truth, and the technology capital markets—especially the liquidity markets—are awful. This last problem is especially important if you're trying to sell a technology project to a battered senior executive team that's in no mood to spend a ton of cash on a new project.

What this process is all about is the identification of real and political reasons to buy something or engage a consultant. This can be a very tricky process, because (due to the perennial competition for funds) there will always be project enemies, those just waiting to say "I told you so" when the project goes south. IT buyers—especially in large enterprises—have to make sure they've covered their flanks. The "business case" is therefore as much a "real" document as it is a political one.

Business cases are typically organized around questions designed to determine if the investment makes sense. Let's look at the key questions that you should answer before buying software, communications, or consulting services. Let me say up front that the answers to these questions should be in a ten-page document (with appendixes if you must): if you generate a long treatise on every investment, you'll never get the time or respect of busy senior executives.

Key Business Value Questions

- What business processes are impacted by the investment/application(s)? The correct answer here identifies a process that's broken, a process for which you have empirical benchmarking data. For example, if you were selling LAN (local area network) administration productivity tools, you'd have to know what you're spending now and that the costs were rising dramatically. You'd then need to know exactly what your performance target should be (e.g., reduce the costs by 25 percent).
- How pervasive is the product or service among your traditional and unconventional competitors? Many decisions about IT adoption are driven by what the competition is doing; it's always easier to sell something to a customer

whose competitors have already signed on to the product or service (of course, this assumes that your competitors are smart).

■ What competitive advantages does/will the product or service yield? In other words, why is this product or service so great and how will it help you profitably grow the business.

■ How does the new product or service interface with existing business models and processes? This is a big question, since the "wrong" answer (like: "it doesn't") will often kill a project. If deployment means ripping out or enhancing infrastructure, then you've just significantly increased the price (and given your internal enemies ammunition).

Key Technology Questions

■ How mature is the product or service? The point of these questions is to determine if the technology or service actually works—and works well. You will need quantitative data here: it won't help to tell everyone about how great your brother-in-law's company is. Additional questions concern scalability, security, modifiability, usability, and so on.

■ What share of the market does the product or service own? If the answer to the question is: "well, 1 percent," then a major explanation will be necessary.

■ How does the new product or service integrate with the existing or planned communications and computing infrastructure? This question is extremely important because it identifies any problems downstream that might occur because of decisions already made (that cannot be undone).

Key Cost/Benefit Questions

■ What are the acquisition, implementation, and support costs and benefits? Here you need to look at obvious costs, like software licenses, and less obvious ones, like training, indirect user, and help desk support, as well as the expected operational and strategic benefits like expense reduction, increased market share, improved customer service, increased cross- and up-selling, improved customer retention, and so on.

■ What are the support implications? How complex, how costly, how extensive, how timely? Support is extremely important. You need to know—empirically—what the support requirements and costs will be defined in terms of $$$, people, and time.

■ What are the migration issues? How complex, how costly, how extensive, how timely? This may or not be relevant, but if another tool was in place, you have to answer questions about how to get from one to the other.

Key Risk Questions

■ What are the technical, personnel, organizational, schedule, and other risks to be considered? What's the risk mitigation plan? The risk factors that everyone will worry about include scope creep, cost and time overruns, incompetent or irritable people, implementation problems, support inadequacies, training problems, and the like. If risks are assessed as medium or high, then a mitigation plan must be developed, a plan that either moves the risk down to the "low" category or eliminates it altogether. If the risks remain high, the project sale is dead.

The Recommendation

The recommendation is **go/no-go/we need more information**. The whole purpose of integrating a business case into the sales pilot is to avoid the "we-need-more-information-syndrome."

The business case should also identify at least two "accountable" people, people whose reputations rest to some extent on the success of the project. One should be from the technology side of the organization and one from the business side (if you can find the right hybrid). If there are no project champions, it's time to go home.

What's Your Core IT Competency? Really?

Most everyone outsources some part of their technology operation for all sorts of good—and occasionally bad—reasons. There's a reason why the IT services industry is clipping along at well over $1B per day in the United States alone. More and more companies have discovered the benefits of outsourcing relative to the recruitment and maintenance of large internal IT staffs. In the early years, we all thought outsourcing was about saving money, but then we discovered the truth: outsourcing it not only about saving money, but it's about rerouting money from non-core to core activities.

The elements of acquisition alignment appear in Figure 4.2. We'll look at the major issues in order.

Business Strategy Linkages

One of the best arguments for buying a product or service is its alignment quotient: the extent to which the infrastructure or applications investment aligns with business strategy. This of course assumes that a business strategy exists and that the fundamental infrastructure and IT investment recommendations have been made. It's now time to decide how to source them.

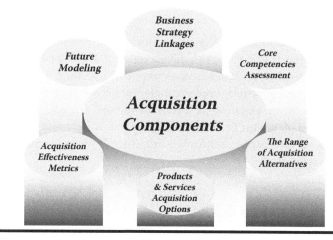

Figure 4.2 The elements of applications alignment.

Assessment of Core Competencies

This step is—when all's said and done—about whether or not you should build and maintain a large internal IT staff. All of the books, articles, and seminars about core competencies are—in the final analysis—about shedding processes. We used to call it reengineering. Now we think in terms of optimization, efficiencies, and other terms that refer to doing what we should do right (and avoiding what we shouldn't do).

The core competencies drill is critically important to acquisition alignment. As your business evolves, you need to ask tough questions about maintaining the in-house activities you've supported for all these years. Remember that the assessment is not just about cost. Here are some questions for deciding what's core and what's not:

- Does the activity support your "bottom line," defined in terms of profitability and growth?
- Can the activity be replaced with little or no threat to the bottom line?
- Can the activity be replaced with little or no additional cost, but with some measurable improvement in quality?
- Are the second-order costs to maintaining the activities measurable, growing, or shrinking (e.g., the costs to maintain in-house IT personnel should include recruiting costs, retention bonuses, and training and education costs, among others)?
- Does the reassignment of the activity dramatically reduce "distraction" costs, that is, permit your organization to focus on other, more valuable activities?

- Is the outsourcing of certain activities consistent with your vertical industry's perspective on core and non-core competencies?
- If you anticipate your primary business model and supporting processes five years out, will current in-house-supported activities still be as important to the core model and processes?

You get the idea. The key questions have to do with finding your core business purpose and then matching all of the activities to in-house versus outsourced alternatives.

Once you've determined what makes sense, it's possible to step back and assess the kinds of IT products and services that might be outsourced. But just in case you think that all roads lead to outsourcing, make sure that you objectively assess the impact outsourcing will have on specific business models and processes. It may be that certain IT activities should well stay in-house.

The Range of Acquisition Alternatives

There are all kinds of activities you can outsource. Figure 4.3 presents the range of IT services you either do in-house or might outsource. Which ones do you do in-house and which ones do you outsource? Why?

Products and Services Acquisition Options

The discussion here is about structure and form, not about whether outsourcing will play some role in your IT acquisition strategy. We're assuming that you don't have all of the talent you need in-house and that your appetite to continuously recruit, satisfy, and retrain staff is shrinking (at least a little!). If these assumptions are correct, then you have to decide how you want to outsource (of course, you may also decide that you want no part of outsourcing and decide to stay the course with your internal IT staff).

You have a number of outsourcing options:

1. Combine outside vendors with your own. Sometimes called in-sourcing or co-sourcing, this model can be very effective if structured and managed properly.
2. Completely outsource segments of your IT mission, such as data center or call center management, but keep others in-house. This option can also be effective, especially when there are clearly defined areas that you do well and those that you do poorly—and when there's no ambiguity about what's core and what's not.

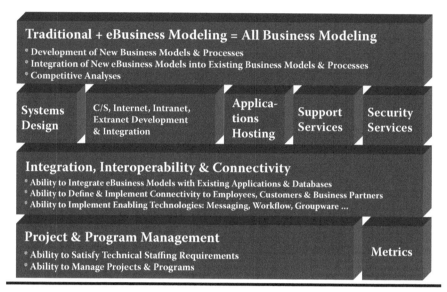

Figure 4.3   Outsourcing candidates.

3. Completely outsource everything to vendors who come on site and manage your IT resources (including machines, networks, and people).
4. Completely outsource everything to vendors who "rent" hardware and software back to you.

Of course there are variations on all of these but the four identify the primary outsourcing models you might consider.

All of these variations require that you:

■ Systematically identify requirements
■ Compare current (so-called baseline) costs with what outsourcers bid
■ Negotiate with the vendors on price and services
■ Develop clear and unambiguous service level agreements
■ Make sure that management is in place to monitor the results of the work

It's strongly suggested that you seek outside help to develop your outsourcing strategy. I realize that this may sound absurd: the recommendation is that you outsource the work necessary to outsource the work! But the fact is that outsourcing has become very complicated and there are now consulting organizations that specialize in this kind of work. These consultants have experience writing RFPs, screening the proposals and the bids, negotiating contracts, and then managing at least the initial implementation phases.

There are also some rules of thumb you might want to consider:

- Above all else, your outsourcing process should be driven by the results of your core competency assessment and your skills gap analysis. If you find that you really don't need to be in the data migration business and that you have no data migration talent in your shop, but that data migration is an important (though non-core) component of what you need to do, then obviously you need to outsource data migration (probably as part of some large applications modernization process).

- Make sure you know what you're doing. Although evolutionary experimentation is often a good way to learn about some new process (like outsourcing), it may not be prudent. Breaking off pieces of your internal IT shop to give to outsourcers to try them out may make abstract sense but in practice may be doomed to failure. Why? Because you're likely to outsource the pieces that are the most politically correct while avoiding the really hard decisions about what's core and what's not.

- Be careful with outsourcing deals intended to transfer knowledge from the outsourcer to in-house professionals. We learned in the late 1980s and early 1990s that knowledge transfer-based outsourcing deals were difficult to make work. Why? Because the outsourcer had no incentive to transfer knowledge and the in-house professionals resented the "training" forced down their throats.

- If you want to try outsourcing on for size, then partition a big piece of your IT infrastructure—like your data centers—and outsource them completely. Develop some clear SLAs and then monitor the heck out of the performance to see if (a) the outsourcer can do it more cheaply and (b) better. The implied suggestion here is to outsource what you already know how to do and fully understand, not what you don't understand. And remember that just because you understand how to, for example, run a data center, it doesn't mean that it's core to your business.

- Really think long and hard about using professionals to architect your outsourcing deals. If you're a medium-sized organization or one that has had some extraordinary IT infrastructure or applications problems over the years, you might want to take a look at using an applications service provider (ASP) who will "rent" applications to your users (who can access the applications over the Internet or through a—much more expensive—virtual private network). This kind of outsourcing is relatively new, but already the major systems integrators have begun to partner with enterprise software vendors like SAP to provide access to major applications. It's something to consider.

- The age of nonshared contracting is over. Any outsourcing deal you sign should have some shared risk built into it. If the outsourcer is unwilling to put any skin in the game, then there may be a problem with the whole deal. A confident outsourcer should welcome the opportunity to jointly develop some performance metrics and then hit the metrics to get paid. These deals can take all kinds of forms. For example, expenses can get paid but a percentage of profit may go into an escrow account to be paid as milestones and metrics are achieved. Regardless of the form, the principle is to share the best and worst aspects of outsourcing by aligning all the incentives.

■ Strongly consider owning requirements, specifications, and designs, but not implementation or support. This rule of thumb is not inviolate but will serve you well. In a sense, owning requirements, specification, and designs keeps you in control of the business/IT alignment process while freeing you from (probably) non-core implementation and support tasks.

■ Make sure that metrics are in place long before you sign any outsourcing deals (see below).

■ Do not sign any long-term outsourcing deals unless the deals have huge shared risk features.

Acquisition Effectiveness Metrics

It's critical that all of the analyses, assessments, requirements, baseline costs, new costs, shared risk assumptions—and especially performance metrics—get quantified.

Depending on what you've chosen to outsource, you should develop a set of metrics that will permit you to (a) compare what you've got now to what was the case before outsourcing and (b) determine if the outsourcer's performance is up to snuff. There should also be metrics to determine if in-house professionals are performing adequately, should you decide not to outsource.

The metrics should be rolled into formal SLAs that should form the basis for the outsourcing contracts you sign. Again, SLAs should be used to track in-house or outsourced performance.

The SLAs should also anchor your shared risk arrangements. So long as performance metrics have been quantified, the shared risk deals can be assessed. If you haven't quantified expectations, then you'll have problems with your provider.

Finally, while I've talked most about shared risk deals with outsourcers, there's no reason why they can't be applied to in-house deals as well.

Future Modeling

All this needs to be monitored closely because dramatic change is inevitable. As suggested above, one that should be especially tracked is the new movement toward applications hosting by third-party vendors. Other trends such as shared risk, premium pricing, and related incentive structures also bear close scrutiny. Eventually, we'll all have accounts with IT utilities from which we'll buy all of our IT products and services. But until that day arrives, we'll have to struggle to objectively assess our core competencies and realistic sourcing options.

Who Pays for All This Stuff?

How much are you spending on IT annually? How does it break down? Are your hardware expenses rising faster than your software expenses? Are your personnel costs rising faster than your hardware and software costs? The components of a funding strategy appear in Figure 4.4.

Figure 4.5 converts it all into a matrix that can be used to determine where you are today and where you need to go. Note that the governance issue is absolutely critical to your funding success. If governance—defined here as what is to be done and who is to do it—is mishandled, then the whole IT products and services acquisition and funding process will collapse.

Figure 4.5 can help with a current baseline assessment and with the prioritization of funding requirements. This model assumes that the enterprise—central IT—will "own" the communications networks, data centers, overall security, and the hardware and personal productivity software that runs on this infrastructure—but not the business applications that define the lines of business.

Benchmarking

You need to know where you spend your IT money and how it gets spent. You need to know what gets spent in-house and what gets spent on external consultants.

Here's a list of broad IT spending categories to get you started.

Applications
  – Applications software packages
  – Applications development (integration and deployment)
  – Applications support

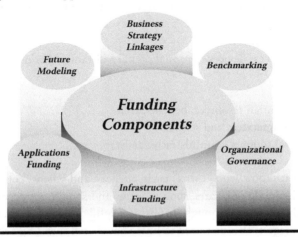

Figure 4.4   Components of a funding strategy.

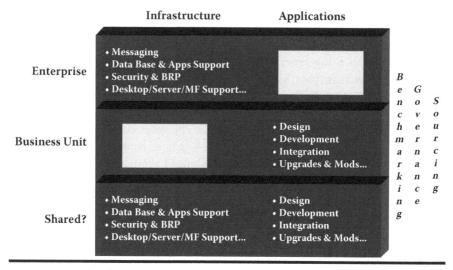

Figure 4.5   A funding requirements and planning matrix.

- Applications architecture design
- Applications architecture services and support
- Modernization and migration …

Infrastructure

- Messaging environment (e-mail, workflow, collaboration, etc.)
- Network and communications architecture design
- Network and systems management
- Voice and data services and support
- Infrastructure engineering services and support
- Data center hardware (mainframes, servers, switches, routers, etc.)
- Desktop hardware
- Laptop hardware
- Other access devices (personal digital assistants, hybrids, etc.) …

Overhead

- Staff (human resources, benefits, etc.)
- Training services and support
- General support (administrative assistants, etc.)

You also need to know who "owns" each category and where "collaborative" IT funding decision making occurs, should occur, and should not occur, given your organizational structure. Although this list is helpful, it's only the start.

Table 4.1 suggests that you need to know how much spending occurs and who owns what. This table tells us a lot. The data is drawn from an informal sampling of over 25 large (Fortune 1,000) companies that have decentralized IT organizations. First, it tells us where the money goes—relatively speaking. It also illustrates where the primary responsibilities lie in a decentralized organization. The question remains, however, which is best? Another extremely important finding is the number of jointly owned funding activities. Every time two checks appear together, there's a potential problem—which is why governance becomes so important.

Table 4.1 can also be treated as a test. Try taking it. See what you learn. Do you know the relative costs of your infrastructure, applications, and support activities? Do you know unambiguously where the responsibility lines are drawn?

Organizational Governance and Cost Allocation

Governance refers to two funding dimensions: how you fund what you buy and who funds what. There are a number of ways to fund IT products and services in the decentralized organization:

Table 4.1   Technology Funding

		Responsibility	
Categories	*Cost*	*Enterprise*	*Division/ LOB*
Applications			
Software Packages	$$	√	√
Development/Integration	$$$$		√
Support	$$$$	√	√
Architecture Design	$$	√	√
Architecture Services and Support	$$	√	√
Modernizaton and Migration	$$		√
Infrastructure			
Messaging	$$	√	
Communication/Network Design	$$$	√	√
Network and Systems Management	$$$$	√	
Infrastructure Support	$$$$	√	
Hardware Procurement	$$$	√	
Overhead			
Staff (HR, Benefits...)	$$	√	
Training	$$$$$	√	√
General Support	$$$$	√	√
Research and Development	$$	√	

1. **Allocation of Costs.** This mechanism is best applied to infrastructure invest-ments. In the decentralized organization, the enterprise—along with the lines of business—determines what the infrastructure should look like and the likely costs. The enterprise then builds the infrastructure and allocates the costs across the lines of business. Unless you want to get assassinated, allocate the costs according to usage—not equally independent of use. The problem with usage allocation, of course, is the necessary specificity about usage you must produce: you must be able to empirically "prove" that line of business "A" is using more than line of business "B" and should therefore pay more of the infrastructure allocation. Don't get cute with usage metrics. Allocate infrastructure costs according to simple ones, like the number of network connections, millions of instructions per second (MIPS) on the mainframe, amount of data storage, and so forth.

2. **Fee-for-Service.** This mechanism is challenging because in order for it to really work the lines of business should be able to look outside for the same services that a central/enterprise IT group might provide. In other words, fee-for-service works best when free market principles prevail! The obvious problem of course is that the enterprise IT group often feels like it's at a competitive disadvantage to outside vendors who can use a variety of tricks to win the business (such as fixed price/fixed schedule, loss-leader tactics, and other "best-and-final" techniques). At the same time, you might say that if the internal IT group cannot compete with outside vendors, then maybe it's time to outsource the services—and you'd have a good point. Many analysts view the fee-for-service model as a mechanism to keep the internal IT groups honest.

3. **Taxation.** This mechanism works when there are activities that fall outside of infrastructure and application costs and when there is value attached to these activities. For example, an enterprise technology group might perform analy-ses of technology or industry trends and make them available to the lines of business. A skunk works might be developed that will test new hardware and software and then share the results with the technologists in the business units. Training falls under this umbrella as well. The general administrative support of the enterprise group usually falls into this group as does the sala-ries of IT management. Finally, research and development is often taxable.

This flipside of the governance question haunts just about every company on the planet. Basically, the problem looks like this. Organizations want to make the right decisions about IT applications, infrastructure, and general support but are afraid to actually to do so. Decentralized business/IT organizations that have weak decision-making governance live in a constant state of fear, uncertainty, and doubt. No one ever knows who will actually pay for what, when, or how. Strongly gov-erned organizations publish the rules and stick by them. It's all very, very simple and very, very complicated. As always, leadership separates the organized and efficient from the chaotic and wasteful. So what kind of organization do you live in? Here's a short yes-or-no test:

1. Do you have to look pretty hard to find benchmarking data?
2. Is your organization subjected to religious wars about operating systems, databases, and other standards issues?
3. Are the religious wars allowed to continue indefinitely?
4. Does everyone have veto power over everyone else, even idiots?
5. Can infrastructure investments be made by the lines of business?
6. Can applications investments be made by the enterprise infrastructure group?
7. Do you spend hours counting MIPS?
8. When a debate breaks out, is it settled by junior people?
9. Do the senior enterprise business managers talk tough, but act like paper tigers?
10. Are allocation and taxation funding mechanisms the object of ridicule in your organization?

Okay, you guessed it: more than five "Yes's" makes your organization incompetent and pretty silly; eight or more makes it certifiable.

Table 4.2 suggests what the landscape should look like. It identifies the funding mechanisms and responsibilities that make the most sense in decentralized organizations.

Take a look at your organization with reference to this table. How does it look?

Infrastructure Funding

As Table 4.1 suggests, infrastructure funding is largely the responsibility of the enterprise. Infrastructure design and construction is funded via taxation and allocation. The design of the infrastructure benefits everyone, so it's taxable. But use of the infrastructure will vary from business unit to business unit and should therefore be funded by usage allocation.

The arguments to watch out for include:

> Business unit "A" is deploying a lot more eBusiness applications than "we" (business unit "B") ... So why should we pay for distributed security at the same rate as them? Maybe the costs should be spread across taxation, fee-for-service, and allocation funding mechanisms ... I am not willing to pay for remote access infrastructure. I don't use it today and don't expect to use it tomorrow ... Make business unit "Y" pay for it ... They're the ones sending everyone home to work...!

Table 4.2   Funding Governance Recommendations

Categories	Responsibility		
	Cost	*Enterprise*	*Division/ LOB*
Applications			
Software Packages	Fee		√
Development/Integration	Fee		√
Support	Fee		√
Architecture Design	Tax	√	
Architecture Services and Support	Fee		√
Modernizaton and Migration	Fee		√
Infrastructure			
Messaging	Allocation	√	
Communication/Network Design	Taxation	√	√
Network and Systems Management	Allocation	√	
Infrastructure Support	Allocation	√	
Hardware Procurement	Fee	√	
Overhead			
Staff (HR, Benefits...)	Taxation	√	
Training	Taxation	√	√
General Support	Taxation	√	√
Research and Development	Taxation	√	

> Tell me again why I must be taxed at the same rate as business unit "P" that requires ten times the training I require?

You get the idea. The key to the successful implementation of mixed funding mechanisms is—you guessed it—serious leadership that expresses itself in a well-defined governance policy. If arguments such as the ones listed above are allowed to infect your organization, you'll be spending as much time on resolving the arguments as you will on building and supporting your infrastructure and applications.

The simple rules should be:

Allocation = If you use it you pay for it.

Taxation = There are some things good for everyone and therefore everyone's going to pay for them—no questions, no debates, and no returns.

Fee-for-Service = There are IT decisions that the lines of business can make, decisions about applications, about desktop upgrades, and the like that they can certainly make on their own ... They have the right to look internally or externally to implement those decisions ... If they decide they want, they pay for it.

Is all this simple? No. Here's why. Much of what we're talking about in what appear to be clearly defined terms is in practice quite fuzzy. For example, when does the purchase of new laptops move from fee-for-service to allocation? If the central infrastructure organization runs the data center that houses mostly mainframe applications, but not some of the important distributed applications that reside on servers in the lines of business, where should the line be drawn between fee-for-service, allocation, and even taxation if either the mainframe or distributed applications team used a common applications architecture (developed by the enterprise group via taxes)?

What about sourcing? If the lines of business decide that they'd like to shop a bid for services internally and externally and select an external vendor, who manages that vendor if the vendor's work requires them (as it will inevitably) to interface with existing internal policies, procedures, hardware, and software? If the enterprise organization hires an outside vendor to help it perform infrastructure support for the lines of business, does the outsourcer report to the enterprise group or the line of business?

Disputes should be handled via some form of published grievance procedure. If a line of business feels it has a legitimate gripe, there should be a process that helps resolve the dispute. If you want the arbitration process to work, you will have to use external judges.

Applications Funding

Applications are the lifeblood of the lines of business—and they should pay the freight here as well (as suggested in Table 4.1). But there are some major issues surrounding applications funding that you should be aware of as you develop a funding strategy. Here are several of the most important ones:

- Applications that were initially intended to support local users who become remote users will have to be reengineered; if remote access performance is substandard, it's often assumed that the infrastructure is to blame when more often than not it's the application ...
- Applications should be reviewed by the infrastructure support team before they're built to make sure that support requirements are not prohibitively expensive ... End-to-end applications planning should become a best practice ...
- Applications integration often involves integration to back-end legacy databases, databases that are often maintained by enterprise database administrators ... Make sure that the infrastructure support team is synchronized with applications integration efforts ...

- Web-to-legacy connectivity is a common way to rapidly deploy eBusiness applications, but in order to design, develop, deploy, and support such applications, both infrastructure and applications professionals will be necessary … Make sure they are well coordinated …
- The most cost-effective way to develop applications is via an enterprise applications architecture (the specification of platforms, tools, development environments, databases, browsers, and the like) … If your organization does not have a common architecture, then you'll reinvent the wheel over and over again … The cost of a single architectural specification will be much, much lower than the costs of repetition … Of course, without a governance policy that sees that the architecture gets used (and reused), the investment will be wasted …
- Because much of the applications work will involve the implementation and integration of off-the-shelf packages, the applications architecture must evolve to accommodate these applications acquisitions practices … Make sure that the number and nature of the packaged applications coming into your environment is well understood and part of the end-to-end planning process …
- To avoid conflicts and surprises, it's a good idea to hold "integrated planning" meetings between the enterprise infrastructure team and the applications development teams in the lines of business … These meetings should be mandatory and occur at least quarterly …

Future Modeling

All this needs to be monitored closely because change is inevitable. One that should be especially tracked is the new movement toward applications hosting by third-party vendors. It's now possible, for example, to "rent" ERP and CRM applications from the major software vendors—and others—who have evolved into "application service providers" or "ASPs." Other trends such as component architectures will also significantly affect the applications development process. Infrastructure outsourcing is also likely to continue at an aggressive pace.

Who's Measuring All This Stuff?

The area of measurement is fascinating because we all think that we measure lots of things and almost no one does. We think we know what we have, who works for us, their skill sets, the applications they use, how happy our customers are, and the rate at which we're growing. But we don't. In fact, most organizations have barely inventoried their assets, their business processes, or the business and technology outcomes that should matter the most.

Here are 25 questions; see how many you can answer.

1. How many PCs/PDAs does your organization own?
2. How many PCs/PDAs has your organization purchased over the past 24 months?
3. Where are the PCs/PDAs?
4. How many applications do you support?
5. How well do they perform?
6. How many platforms are they running on?
7. How many architectures do they represent?
8. How many networks are in your organization?
9. Who owns the voice and data contracts you've recently signed?
10. How many IT professionals—including full- and part-time consultants—work for you?
11. What are their skill sets?
12. What are the knowledge and technology gaps that threaten your productivity most?
13. Who are your strategic partners?
14. How and why are they contributing to your tactical and strategic goals?
15. What are your core processes?
16. Do you routinely do risk management?
17. Do you have a standard systems analysis and design life cycle?
18. Do you have standard acquisition contracts?
19. How many procurements have you bid in the last 24 months?
20. What is your systems services quality of service?
21. Do you have service level agreements in place?
22. Who owns them?
23. Who's accountable for what's in your service organization?
24. Do you have ROI data?
25. Do you know the total cost of ownership (TCO) of your desktops, laptops, PDAs, applications, and networks?

How many could you answer?

If you can't answer these kinds of questions, you have a serious measurement problem. If you can answer most of them, you're on your way to informed IT/business alignment decision making. Unfortunately, very few IT or business professionals can answer the most common measurement questions. (A good score is 15; you're toast if your score was 10 or below and golden if you were 20 or above!)

As always, the answers must have a business purpose. The reason it's useful to know how many PCs were purchased last year is to track trends—and the trends provide insight into relationships among professionals, productivity, and PC costs. Collecting lots of data for no particular reason is silly and distorts the measurement mission. Measurement data is useful only if it's leveraged onto alignment decision making.

One of the political problems with measurement is the perceived irrelevance of the data. Some believe that the cost of collecting the data outstrips its likely value. This section does two things that speak to these issues. First, it identifies—in true "book of lists" fashion—what the measurement issues are, and second, it offers sets of "if/then" rules for inferring the significance of the measurement data. The hope is that the information provided here will jumpstart your measurement efforts and address some of the political challenges you'll inevitably face.

Perhaps a navigational note is in order here. I hope you've gotten a good feel for the practical-over-pretty approach I've generally taken to business/IT alignment. I've avoided complex processes in favor of straightforward, nonbureaucratic ones. Measurement presents an interesting challenge to this philosophy. Because measurement is almost cerebral (compared to middleware or standards decisions, for example), it's important that you approach the subject from the proper perspective. Measurement is not about forms, templates, sheets, or databases. Nor is it about process for its own sake. Nor should it be methodologically driven, that is, assessed according to the elegance of the data collection and measurement tools and techniques versus the insights the data provides and the subsequent decisions enabled by the data. In other words, I'm not advocating the creation of yet another organization—complete with people, offices, desks, computers, support, and—of course—a budget; rather, the hope is that measurement—however you get it done—leads to alignment. Previous sections all focused on a specific alignment area (such as applications, communications, or standards). Measurement is essential to all of them, since it's impossible to modernize your applications portfolio without knowing what's in the existing one, or determine if you have enough bandwidth if you don't know how much is enough, or define and enforce standards if you're unsure about the variation in your environment. Measurement is key to all of the alignment processes, but the effort to measure should not exceed its benefit. This "heads-up" is to those who may have heard that measurement can only be accomplished from the cockpit of a Gulfstream V or the front seat of an S-Class Mercedes. Piper Cubs and Chevies can also get the job done.

Components of Measurement Alignment

The elements of a measurement alignment strategy appear in Figure 4.6. We'll look at them in order.

Business Strategy Linkages

The meaningfulness of your measurement strategy and results is completely dependent on your business models and processes. If they're unclear or ambiguous, your measurement efforts will fail. Why? Because the essence of measurement is clarification through analysis which, in turn, triggers decisions. Another way of say-

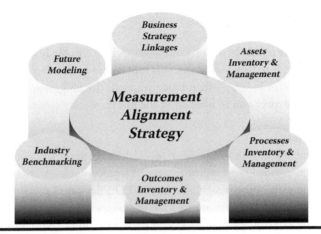

Figure 4.6   The elements of measurement alignment.

ing all this is to acknowledge that it's pointless to measure ill-defined models or processes—or the assets, processes, or outcomes that support the efficacy of those models and processes—unless there's some reason to do so!

For example, you need to know if you're spending too much or too little on bandwidth. But unless you can answer questions about the need for bandwidth, the purpose of more or less bandwidth, and how bandwidth relates to sales, customer service, growth, and profitability—among other business metrics—it's—literally—an impossible question to answer.

The ultimate metrics are the business metrics, not the technology ones, though the latter should be derived from the former. This means that technology metrics—like the cost per MIPS (millions of instructions per second) is only meaningful with reference to throughput and cost/benefit requirements. Similarly, knowing how often you upgrade desktop or laptop PCs only matters if you're (a) significantly out of line with your industry's best practices or (b) you cannot determine why you're upgrading machines at all! Although there may be some very good reasons why you're upgrading at a much faster rate than your competitors, you really need to know what they are before you continue spending.

Assets, Processes, and Outcomes

Figure 4.7 can help with a current baseline assessment and with the prioritization of measurement requirements. Let's start with assets and let's define them very broadly. As with the other two measurement areas—processes and outcomes—we'll focus on relatively "hard" and "soft" metrics. For example, hard assets include PCs and servers, whereas soft ones include relationships and brands. The purpose of this distinction is to sensitize you to the not-so-obvious assets (processes and outcomes) that populate your environment.

Here's the list of hard assets you should measure (most—though not all—will apply to you).

(**Note:** If you're in a large organization—especially a publicly owned one—your auditors may be able to help you gather this information … If they don't have it and haven't asked you for it—yet—then brace yourself: the judgment day is approaching when they'll expect you to have all of the numbers …)

"Hard" Assets

- Number/location/assignment/age of desktop personal computers
- Number /location/assignment/age of laptop/notebook computers
- Number/location/assignment/age of PDA devices
- Number/location/assignment/age of servers
- Number/assignment of local area networks under your control
- Number/assignment of wide area networks under your control
- Number/assignment of virtual private networks under your control
- Description of network topologies in your organization and under your control
- Number/location/assignment/age of midrange computers
- Number/location/assignment/age of mainframe computers
- Number/location/assignment/age of storage devices
- Number/location/assignment of desktop/laptop/PDA applications and licenses
- Number/location/assignment of utility applications (such as change management, configuration management, requirements management, maintenance, testing, and related applications across all your computing environments)

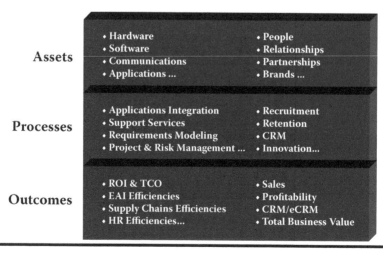

Figure 4.7   A measurement requirements and planning matrix.

- The original equipment manufacturer (OEM) brands of your hardware suppliers; the percentages across vendors
- The distribution of software vendors in your software asset/license pool
- The number/location/ownership/age of applications by platform: mainframe, minicomputer, client/server, desktop ...
- The number/location/ownership/age of applications by architecture: single-tier, two-tier, three-tier, multitier, *n*-tier ...

"Soft" Assets
- Number of people in your organization
- Their educational backgrounds and professional experiences
- Their current applicable skill sets
- The mapping of those skill sets onto your requirements; skill set gap analyses
- The salaries and bonuses (and other parts of compensation packages) of your professionals and support staffs
- The intracorporate relationships and partnerships
- Your external alliances and partnerships
- Your brand(s)
- Your goodwill
- Your professional reputation ...

Some Hard and Soft Asset "Rules"

Measurement is pointless without purpose. Here are some of the high-level rules of thumb that extend from asset measurement data. Although the list below is by no means exhaustive, it's representative of the kinds of decisions you can make from the assets you measure.

■ Data about the age and configuration of your desktops should inform your desktop upgrading strategy; over time, you will learn about optimal holding periods for PCs (and other devices) that will permit you to only upgrade when necessary (and thereby avoid the costly churning from PC to PC for no empirical reason).

Rule: *If* your need for newer versions of primary desktop applications and the platforms they run on is minimal or manageable, *then* institute a 24- to 36-month "holding period" for desktops, laptops, and PDAs.

■ Data about the number, age, architecture, and platform base of your applications will provide insight into the support necessary to keep them going; if you discover a lot of different architectures, lots of different platforms, and as many old applications as newer ones, then you're probably paying too much for support; the data would suggest the cost-effectiveness of reducing the platform/architecture variation in your applications portfolio.

Rule: *If* your applications platforms and architectures are highly varied, *and* your goal is to reduce support costs, *then* reduce the variation in your computing and communications environment.

■ The rates of adoption of new computing devices will tell you a lot about where your business processes are going. For example, if you find that you're adopting laptops and notebooks at a much faster rate than desktop PCs, then you're probably moving toward a more distributed workforce and customer/supplier network that will stress your remote access, security, and data storage capabilities.

Rule: *If* the rate of laptop adoption outstrips desktop PC deployment by 1.5:1, *then* check your remote access and security services capabilities and prepare for additional investment in distributed remote access, security, and ongoing support.

These "rules" suggest how to convert dry, dead data into serious cost savings. The conversion is key to the success of your asset measurement alignment strategy. Insight into your hard and soft assets can lead to all sorts of discoveries, such as huge gaps between what you need to do (like integrate applications) and your existing skill sets (you have no applications integrators!). You might find that your brand and external image is inconsistent with your new business models and process, or that your partners (suppliers and distributors) are confused about where your business model ends and theirs begins. All sorts of great and horrible news about your assets is just waiting to be discovered!

Processes represent a special kind of measurement challenge, because they're so often extremely soft and often even ambiguous. The processes you should be concerned about include—at a minimum—the following (again, we draw a "hard" and "soft" distinction):

"Hard" Processes
- Your systems analysis and design processes (your life cycle methodology)
- Your requirements management processes
- Your risk management processes
- Your project management processes
- Your process adoption/sustainment rates
- Your SLAs and success rates

- Your hardware and software acquisition processes
- Your hardware disposition processes
- Your asset management processes
- Your network and systems management processes
- Your vendor management processes
- Your vendor selection and management processes
- Your help desk processes
- Your security authentication processes
- Your security authorization processes
- Your security administration processes
- Your disaster recovery and business resumption processes
- Your database administration processes
- Your knowledge management processes
- Your standards setting processes
- Your standards governance processes
- Your IT audit processes …

"Soft" Processes

- Your human recruitment processes
- How effective has it been (measured by number of recruits and the percentage that have stayed over time)?
- Your employee performance review processes
- Your jobs/opportunities description/classification/posting processes
- Your benefits administration processes
- What are the processes that "touch" your customers?
- How effective have they been (measured by customer service data)?
- What processes have you implemented to stay technologically current? Are there internal R&D/innovation processes? How many internal proposals have you received? How many have been funded? And how many have been successfully concluded…?

Innovation represents a very, very special process. Given the pace of technology change and the pressure everyone's under to keep costs down (creating a schizophrenic monster—which may be you!), you'll need to define and implement a process designed to keep your organization current and cost-effective.

Begin with the positioning of the value of an R&D/innovation process—complete with candidate investment areas. We then offer a draft memorandum that describes the process and offers mechanisms for participation. The memorandum is one that you might actually use to "sell" the benefits of an R&D/innovation process in your organization. At the same time, the whole package can be extended to other process areas, such as risk management, systems analysis and design, architecture design processes, and the like.

Industry Benchmarking

It makes sense to benchmark your experiences with others in your industry. Given how vertical industries are converging, it might also make sense to look at vertical industries close to your own for insight into assets, processes, outcomes, trends, and best practices. Investments here are well worth the money.

Make sure someone is responsible for modeling the future in the form of extrapolations, that is, insights and inferences only possible through the collection and analysis of measurement data. It's always valuable to illustrate the kind of insights and cost-effective decisions that will accrue from investments in a measurement strategy.

Security Solutions Outsourcing: It's Time

Many companies have "piecemealed" their security capabilities. Large enterprises have been hammered by auditors who love to prepare letters chastising their lack of internal and external security. Smaller organizations are scared to death of viruses and worms, while small dot.coms are painfully aware of their need to make sure that Internet-based transaction processing is secure. As business-to-business (B2B) eBusiness picks up, organizations will have no choice but to deploy digital signature, public key infrastructure (PKI), and perhaps even biometric authentication technologies. This stuff is getting very complicated very fast.

So how should organizations migrate from where they are today to where they'll inevitably need to go?

There are three watchwords that we ignore at our own peril: integration, interoperability, and solutions. Take a look at Figure 4.8. Look at all of the pieces to the security puzzle and how deployment is dependent on the integration and interoperability of a ton of technologies, products, and services. Some of these technologies, products, and services your in-house IT professionals can handle, but some are well beyond their capabilities. Who owns integration? Who makes sure that all the technologies, products, and services interoperate? Key here is the development of a comprehensive security policy that defines a security architecture that describes how authentication, authorization, administration, and recovery will occur inside and outside of the corporate firewall. But who should own the pieces of what should become your security *solution*?

Regardless of how many disparate security pieces you have today, you probably have too many. If you have more than one redundant or overlapping security SLA, you have too many. And if you've distributed security accountability across your organization, your security efforts are diffuse at best—and dangerous at worst.

Here's the deal. Because just about every business on the planet will have to integrate its traditional business models with models that exploit Internet connectivity and soon, pervasive computing, bulletproof security will become a transaction pre-

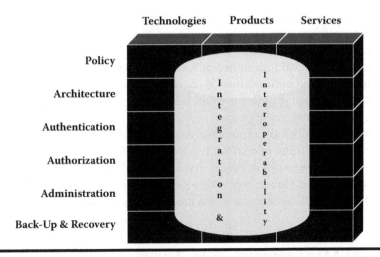

Figure 4.8 Security requirements—and sourcing candidates.

requisite. Because just about every business has underspent on security, additional resources will have to be found to solve the inevitable problems that distributed business models will create. All the authentication, authorization, administration, and recovery problems will have to be solved by stitching together a variety of technologies wrapped in products and services. What will these technologies be? What products will you use? How will you support them? Can internal IT staff cope with all of the changes?

Some advice. Unless you're a security products or consulting company, get out of the security business. (If you doubt the wisdom of this advice, stare at Figure 4.8 for five minutes. Can you cover every cell in the security matrix?) It's time to consider outsourcing security to vendors who can provide reliable, integrated, interoperable solutions. But this advice does not extend to the specification of security requirements or the development of security policies. It's always prudent to own requirements and specifications—strategy—and optimize the implementation and support of that strategy—tactics. In other words, it makes sense to in-source strategy and outsource tactics.

Finally, remember that success here is defined only around *solutions*—the integration of technologies, products, and services that work together as seamlessly and efficiently as possible. You need a single point of accountability that really gets your business. You need killer security requirements analysts who can specify security policies and architectures, and you need professionals who can manage the implementation of those requirements through the creative synthesis of security technologies, products, and services.

Your solution will be a hybrid that integrates some existing technologies and processes with a new set of technologies, products, and services that will span the above matrix. The technology architecture must be flexible and scalable enough to integrate new technologies—like PKI, smart cards, and biometrics—and reliable, inspiring confidence among your employees, customers, and suppliers. In addition to the myriad technologies, products, and services that support authentication, authorization, and administration, there are steps you'll need to take to make sure that you can resume business if you're temporarily hacked into nonexistence. Business resumption planning is yours, but recovery tools, techniques, and services belong to your outsourcing partner.

It's time to realistically assess what you can and should do to satisfy an increasingly complicated suite of security requirements. Unless you're really special and very lucky, it's time to call in the cavalry. Find a solid security solutions vendor and stop worrying. The phrase "stay with your core competencies" didn't semantically infiltrate the IT lexicon because it was pretty; it's there because it's meaningful.

Project Management—Yes, Again ...

This one's been around for a long, long time. It's actually masqueraded under lots of aliases over the years including total quality management (TQM), capability maturity, statistical quality control, and balanced scorecards, among other attempts to better organize us at work. Of course, all these movements have their gurus and disciples, and all of them are different in their own important ways, but by and large they're about professional discipline—which, of course, very few of us actually have—which is why these movements come and go.

Project Management Is Different

But project management *is* different because it's never really achieved star status. It just keeps on rolling along. Maybe that's why it never makes the top five initiatives we need to worry about this month, but *always* makes the top ten we're worrying about this year. It's a real discipline that we don't practice very well, and therefore always need to improve; we're told by industry analysts that it's 75 percent likely that our mega technology projects will fail, so I guess we need help.

At the outset, let's stipulate that discipline—like adhering to technology standards or hiring only smart, hard-working, ethical people—is hard, primarily because it means that we have to control our impulses. And we hate that. But discipline works: it makes money. And project management should be a core discipline in every company in the world.

The first thing we need to do is declare project management an important thing. Then we need declare this very publicly. If you're in a big company, then you need to organize a serious off-site to raise consciousness; if you're a medium-sized company, then you need to speak to all of the employees and incentivize the change agents. But the real key to this is consistency and persistence. Initiatives fail because companies roll out programs, processes, and policies that vary from group to group or organization to organization, or because they lose interest over time, something that employees can smell long before the plug is officially pulled. I well remember sitting in audiences listening to senior executives talking about the company's major new initiative only to hear the lifers muttering "this too shall pass." The "been there/done that" problem is a big one, especially if your track record is weak. Lots of long-term employees have adapted to management's lukewarm commitment to major initiatives and have learned to drag their participatory feet for as long as they can (or until management loses steam).

Five Not So Easy Pieces

Enough politics. What should your project management expertise look like? What skills do you need—really? Here are five:

1. **The ability to assess a project's likely success or failure**. Note that this assessment comes after the business case has been filed—and approved. Can the project be successful? What are the risks? Who's the best person to lead the project? Is a good team available? What are the immediate problems we have to solve? Honesty is of course the best policy here.

2. **The ability to keep the business case front-and-center as the project unfolds**. Once approved, the business case is the blueprint developed by well-dressed, well-meaning architects; the project is all about construction—schedules, subcontractors, screw-ups, miscommunication, and so on. You know, reality. Companies need to continuously link project progress to the business case that gave birth to the project in the first place. This means that the business case also needs to be reassessed on a regular basis, especially if the project is a big, long one. Measure the distance between the business case and project progress on a regular basis; if they start to drift away from each other then it's time to take action.

3. **The ability to execute project fundamentals, such as milestones, deliverables, schedules, cost management, reviews**. These skills are not necessarily resident in your company. You might consider getting a number of your good project managers certified in the latest thinking, processes and tools. The Project Management Institute (www.pmi.org) is a good place to start.

4. **The ability to kill bad projects; the ability to determine if a project is hopeless or salvageable**. How do you kill projects? There are at least three reasons to kill a project: (1) The business case and project are drifting far apart; the business assumptions about the importance of the project are no longer valid; (2) project execution is way off track; the project is overbudget, behind schedule, and so on; and (3) the probability of recovery is low for all sorts of empirical reasons.

5. **The ability to "see" your projects together to assess your overall project situation**. How do you "see" all of your projects? Some companies have

weekly project meetings, some have monthly ones, and others only do it informally, privately. What you need is a *dashboard* that immediately shows you which projects are on track and which are underperforming—and which are candidates for capital punishment.

Dashboards are not hard to build; they're even easier to buy. Microsoft Project can be used to feed off-the-shelf reporting applications, or you can customize one to show projects as red, yellow, or green, as well as the trends. You should standardize on both the project management and dashboard application. You should also make sure that accurate information gets into the dashboard. Some of these tools—like The Project Control Panel (developed by the Software Program Managers Network; www.spmn.com/pcpanel.html)—extract data from Microsoft Project and inject it into a Microsoft Excel tool that displays project status. Other tools, like Portfolio Edge from Pacific Edge Software, enable you to track multiple projects at the same time.

Project management discipline is a not-so-glamorous discipline that we all need to practice well. Maybe it's time to revisit project management requirements. I know there are several projects I wish I could reexecute. If I saw them on a dashboard, I'd kill them instantly.

What to Do? Triangulating on Requirements

We all need a repeatable requirements management methodology to manage the pace of business and technology change that every organization is experiencing. We need a methodology that provides insight into project requirements *before* we spend serious money.

Over the years I've developed a very, very simple way to size business/technology projects. Some of you may think it's too simplistic, but it's worked pretty well for some pretty complex projects. The methodology is generic enough to be flexible but specific enough to help solve a lot of business/technology alignment problems.

A Requirements Management Methodology

Here's the methodology in an outline:

    1.0   The Request
        1.1   Discretionary/Nondiscretionary Analysis
        1.2   Business Linkage
        1.3   Technology Linkage
    2.0   Requirements Definition
        2.1   Purposeful Requirements
        2.2   Functional Requirements

Let's look at each of the steps in a little detail.

Request Analysis

Request analysis asks the simple question: what's the project all about? It also asks the analyst and his or her business partner to decide whether the project is "aligned" with the business and technology strategies. The key here is to determine—as early as possible—whether the request is "discretionary" (nice to have) or "nondiscretionary" (must have).

Requirements Definition

To analyze and model requirements it's necessary to *define* requirements. There are three kinds of requirements: "purposeful," "functional," and "nonfunctional" (or design) requirements.

User profiles are essential to cost-effective design. If users are inexperienced, it creates all sorts of problems for the designers and developers of information and software systems. The key is to understand the challenges that the users present to the design and development team *before* major design and development decisions are made.

Requirements Analysis

Requirements analysis looks at the interrelationships among requirements, the relative importance of requirements, implementation costs, and the risks associated with satisfying each of the purposeful, functional, and nonfunctional requirements. Once requirements have been assessed with reference to costs and risk, it's possible to rank-order them. The drill here requires you to assess whether the requirements are of high, medium, or low importance. Figure 4.9 describes it graphically.

Requirements Modeling

Once requirements have been defined and analyzed (in terms of importance, costs, and risk), it's possible to model them. We model because we need to communicate. Good designs emerge from the understanding that results from good communication. We use narratives to communicate, we use simple outlines, we use data flow diagrams, entity relationship diagrams, and hierarchical models. We also use static screen displays and interactive prototypes.

Requirements Change Management and the Requirements Agreement

The change management process is straightforward. All it requires is an agreement among all of the stakeholders that new requirements will be assessed according to their expected impact on the existing schedule and budget. If there's evidence to suggest that the impact will be substantial (more than 5 percent), then the requirements definition, analysis, and modeling process should be rerun.

All we have to do now is write it all down. Yes, and in spite of any visceral objections, we all have to sign an agreement, a kind of baseline contract about what the project's all about. The fact is that we need a baseline document that describes what the understanding—at a particular point in time—is about: what will and will not be done. The agreement itself is part symbolic and part organizational; it commits the stakeholders to an initial course of action and allows the assignment of resources to initial tasks.

A Requirements Management Case Study

Let's look briefly at some decisions around the deployment of a simulated data warehouse project. The requirements analysis here, however, suggested that the project should be killed! The risks are way too high *and the percentage of effort adds up to 180 percent of the resources allocated to complete the project.*

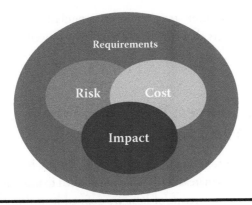

Figure 4.9   Triangulating on requirements.

How Many of Your Projects Should Have Been Killed?

The worst outcome of the analysis is tons of requirements that are highly important, very risky, and very expensive. Too many of these and the project is automatically a death march. On the other hand, it's great when you identify lots of highly important, low-risk, cheap ones, or low importance, high-risk, expensive requirements, the ones that can be immediately eliminated from the project.

Obviously not all projects should be killed. But the requirements management methodology described here can help make crazy project assumptions explicit and identify the landmines you'll have to avoid to survive a major (or minor) business/ technology project.

	Functional requirements	*Impact*	*Risk*	*Cost*
1.0	Database conversion/integration	H	H	30 percent
2.0	Database centralization	M	M	10 percent
3.0	Anytime/anyplace data mining	H	H	30 percent
4.0	Reporting	H	M	5 percent
Total: 75 percent				
	Nonfunctional requirements	*Impact*	*Risk*	*Cost*
1.0	Modifiability	M	M	20 percent
2.0	Usability	H	H	10 percent
3.0	Reliability	H	H	20 percent
4.0	Survivability	H	M	10 percent
5.0	Remote access	H	H	25 percent
6.0	Security	H	H	20 percent

Total: 105 percent

Total functional and nonfunctional requirements = 180 percent

You might try this simple requirements triangulation methodology. It might help you identify projects that simply can't get done as well as ones that will actually work.

Sourcing the Sources: Who Does What Today? Who Wins Tomorrow?

If we look at sourcing trends, it's pretty obvious that the back end of the systems development life cycle is increasingly being outsourced to near- or offshore partners. Programming—at least in terms of how we defined it in the 1990s—has already been commoditized. Maintenance has been commoditized. Lots of customization has been commoditized. What about other business technology activities? What are the sourcing trends? What *should* the sourcing trends look like?

But while everyone frets about who's sourcing what and where, there's another sourcing issue that we need to confront: education and training. Or, put another way, are we producing the right minds?

I've used five layers to describe business technology activity in the past. The same layers will serve us well here as we look at in-sourcing, outsourcing, education, and training trends.

The five layers include:

■ Business strategy
■ Strategic business applications
■ Enterprise business technology architecture
■ Infrastructure
■ Support

Each layer assumes a set of activities, as suggested below:

Business Technology Strategy

■ Business modeling around collaboration, customization, and personalization
■ Supply chain planning and management
■ Competitor intelligence
■ Business process management
■ Enterprise performance management
■ Business requirements modeling
■ Overall business technology strategy

Strategic Business Applications

- Application selection
- Application design (for new applications)
- Application optimization
- Business applications management
- Business analytics
- Application development (for new and customized existing)
- Application integration (for off-the-shelf, packaged)

Enterprise Business Technology Architecture

- Application architecture design
- Communication architecture design
- Data architecture design
- Security architecture design
- Enterprise architecture design

Infrastructure

- Messaging/workflow/calendaring implementation
- Automation
- Database/content/knowledge management and analysis
- Integration and interoperability

Support

- Desktop/laptop/PDA support
- Data center operations
- Server farm design and maintenance
- Network design and support
- Security and privacy
- Procurement management
- Asset management
- RFP and SLA development
- Metrics management

The interesting sourcing questions around these activities and layers are both descriptive and prescriptive: what's happening—and what *should* be happening?

Answers to the second question in part at least depend on where one sits. From the perspective of U.S. companies—and education and training organizations—

there's been an uncomfortable shift in the location of expertise over the past five years. But from the perspective of technology organizations in India, China, the Philippines, Russia, Canada, Mexico, and some eastern European countries, the reallocation and distribution of global technology expertise is more than appropriate. Without rehashing all of the arguments around the advantages and disadvantages of outsourcing—depending on your perspective—it is safe to say that changes have occurred and will continue to occur as the world settles into at least a sourcing process, if not an outcome.

Let me examine the situation first from the perspective of a U.S. company. Figure 4.10 describes and prescribes with reference to the activities and layers listed above. Note that "strategic," "analytical," and "managerial" activities are currently "owned" primarily by U.S. companies. As suggested earlier, the front end of the general life cycle is still largely in U.S. hands, while the back end—with some exceptions—is moving more and more to near- and offshore outsourcing partners. But note also the education and training imperatives in Figure 4.10. In order for the United States to maintain its current position as owner of strategic, analytical, and managerial activities, it must educate and train in these areas. Just as importantly, the United States cannot continue to yield activities and layers.

Now let's look at the situation from a non-U.S. perspective. There's no question that more and more activities will become fair game over the next few years and beyond. In fact, Figure 4.10 suggests that everything's fair game! While today we tend to think about outsourcing as mostly involving the development, implementation, maintenance, and support, there's no reason why in three to five years—and certainly over a longer period of time—more and more activities and layers can be added to the list of competitive sourcing contracts.

So what's really going on? Simply speaking, there's a war going on for control of the overall technology life cycle. For the past five years or so the United States has been losing more and more layers and activities. What happens over the next five years? Where will the new global centers of excellence be? Will the United States perhaps "own" new architectures—like service-oriented and event-driven architectures—or will its global competitors grab an ever larger share of the life cycle? Will non-U.S. technology providers become as proficient with architectures (and new business models, business performance management, and technology acquisition) as the United States? Who will do what?

Ultimately, the war will rage on but the outcome will be decided according to three primary metrics: quality, cost, and risk.

Just as the United States has suffered recently because of the availability of high-quality and low-cost technology providers outside of its borders, what might happen to some of those providers over time? Will Indian technologists remain the best, brightest, and cheapest? Or will they yield some of their market share to the Chinese, or some other competitor who provides high-quality, cost-effective technology services? And what about risk? How will the world manage the risk of distributed technology provisioning?

We have a lot to learn—and adapt to. The law of competitive advantage is alive and well—and directing a lot of global technology traffic. What's happened in the U.S. sourcing world is by no means stagnant: lots more will change over time—and not just in the United States. It's likely that an integrated technology supply chain will surface that will distribute technology expertise across centers of excellence that will—like all market providers—emerge, prosper, and redefine themselves over time. What this means to all of the technology providers is that cost-effective, high-quality expertise will travel the globe over time. Today India is excellent at the development and maintenance of code; the United States is excellent at architecture and modeling. But will these countries maintain their leads in these areas or will other players threaten them over time? Perhaps the best way to stay ahead of the competition is through education and training. Figure 4.10 suggests what the United States should be doing in the education and training areas—today. But what should the learning agenda look like over time in the United States—and elsewhere? Can this war be won? Or is it just a moving target?

Strategy, Applications, and Architecture Sourcing: Where There Are Still Competitive Advantages

Emerging Acquisition Strategies

It's no secret that outsourcing is increasing. Infrastructure support outsourcing, for example, is just about inevitable. Although it remains to be seen just how far outsourcing trends will go, one thing is for sure: companies need acquisition strategies anchored in their understanding of commoditization trends and the knowledge and skills necessary to satisfy their business technology requirements—regardless of whether they satisfy those requirements in-house or with outsourcing partners.

This section looks at the emerging structure of the business technology industry, outsourcing trends, educational and training gaps (given the structure and trends), and where companies should invest to remain competitive in the early twenty-first century.

The Business Technology Landscape

Let's begin with a familiar mapping of business technology. Figure 4.11 presents five layers of knowledge and skills that all companies have to address as they align their business and technology strategies. These layers can be used to identify not only what we need but also where outsourcing trends are going. The line in Figure 4.11 provides a clue about how the industry is bifurcating into "operational" and "strategy" business technology.

Activity \ Action	In-Source	Out-Source	Educate	Train
<u>Business Technology Strategy</u>				
Business Modeling around Collaboration, Customization & Personalization	✓		✓	
Supply Chain Planning & Management	✓		✓	
Competitor Intelligence	✓		✓	
Business Process Management	✓		✓	
Enterprise Performance Management	✓		✓	
Business Requirements Modeling	✓		✓	
Overall Business-Technology Strategy	✓		✓	
<u>Strategic Business Applications</u>				
Application Selection	✓		✓	
Application Design (for New)	✓		✓	
Application Optimization	✓		✓	
Business Applications Management	✓		✓	
Business Analytics	✓		✓	
Application Development (for New & Customized Existing)		✓		✓
Application Integration (for COTS)		✓		✓

Figure 4.10 Sourcing, education, and training (continued).

Figure 4.12 takes the layers and combines them with three specific objectives: creating technology, applying technology, and servicing technology (or consulting). It also identifies the relevance that applies to each cell in the matrix.

Figure 4.12 suggests, for example, that those who create technology are pretty far removed from those who develop business strategies. The cell thus suggests that the relevance of this intersection is "low." But note that relevance is "high" for business applications/apply, business applications/consult, architecture/apply, and architecture/consult.

Action Activity	In-Source	Out-Source	Educate	Train
Enterprise Business Technology Architecture Layer				
Application Architecture Design	✓		✓	
Communication Architecture Design	✓		✓	
Data Architecture Design	✓		✓	
Security Architecture Design	✓		✓	
Enterprise Architecture Design	✓		✓	
Infrastructure Layer				
Messaging/Workflow/Calendaring Implementation		✓		✓
Automation		✓		✓
DataBase/Content/Knowledge Management & Analysis		✓		✓
Integration & Interoperability		✓		✓

Figure 4.10 Sourcing, education, and training.

This matrix is important because it helps us prioritize what we need to learn to perform better. Wherever the matrix points to "high" relevance is where you need to focus most of your energy (depending, of course, on your role as a creator, applier, or consultant).

But what kind of job are we doing? Are we educating and training the right people? Are our education and training strategies aligned with the relevance matrix?

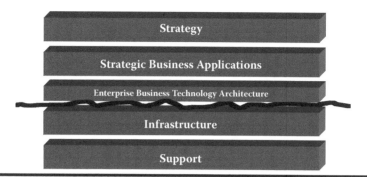

Figure 4.11   Five business technology layers.

	Create Technology	Apply Technology	Consult/Service Technology
Strategy	Low Relevance	High Relevance	High Relevance
Strategic Business Applications	High Relevance	High Relevance	High Relevance
Enterprise Architecture	High Relevance	High Relevance	High Relevance
Infrastructure	Low Relevance	Medium Relevance	Medium Relevance
Support	Low Relevance	Medium Relevance	Medium Relevance

Figure 4.12   Layers, activities, and relevance.

Education and Training Gaps

Figure 4.13 suggests that there are problems.

There are too many large gaps between what needs to be done and what we're teaching. Is this a failure of the educational and training organizations that service the business technology area? Pretty much. Some programs are better than others, of course, but by and large university programs focus much more on theory than they do on practice, and many of the training organizations focus much more on specific products and certifications than on architecture or application optimization. The gaps are real—and growing. Much of the training that occurs out there is customized for specific customers by outside providers or created in-house by companies that need the creation of very specific knowledge and skills.

	Create Technology (Education & Training Programs)	Apply Technology (Education & Training Programs)	Consult/Service Technology (Education & Training Programs)
Strategy	Large Gaps	Medium Gaps	Medium Gaps
Strategic Business Applications	Medium Gaps	Medium Gaps	Medium Gaps
Enterprise Architecture	Medium Gaps	Large Gaps	Large Gaps
Infrastructure	Large Gaps	Large Gaps	Large Gaps
Support	Large Gaps	Large Gaps	Large Gaps

Figure 4.13 Layers, activities, and education/training gaps.

Outsourcing Trends

The next step is to identify outsourcing trends. Figure 4.14 describes what's going on out there.

There's little or no technology outsourcing going on in the create technology/business strategy cell, but there's lots of outsourcing in the infrastructure and support cells.

What to Do

What does all this mean? Figure 4.15 provides some guidance. Essentially, it recommends that we yield the low ground—"below the line" operational technology—to down-the-street, near-shore, and offshore outsourcers. There are lots of large education and training gaps here, as well as a lot of outsourcing already. Relevance is low to medium: if you're sitting in a U.S. company, you've already pretty well lost this world.

The high-priority areas are those where the education/training gaps are not huge, relevance is high, and there's relatively little outsourcing going on. These are the salvageable areas, the areas where companies can still—through in-sourcing—exert major influence on the business technology relationship.

	Create Technology	Apply Technology	Consult/Service Technology
Strategy	Little or No Outsourcing	Little or No Outsourcing	Little or No Outsourcing
Strategic Business Applications	Little or No Outsourcing	Little or No Outsourcing	Little or No Outsourcing
Enterprise Architecture	Little or No Outsourcing	Little Outsourcing	Little Outsourcing
Infrastructure	Some Outsourcing	Lots of Outsourcing	Lots of Outsourcing
Support	Some Outsourcing	Lots of Outsourcing	Lots of Outsourcing

Figure 4.14   Outsourcing trends.

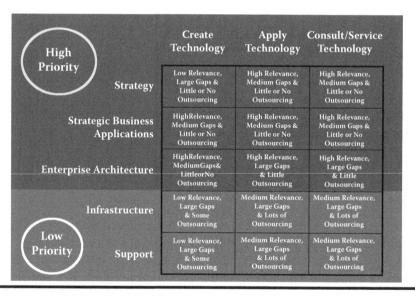

Figure 4.15   Priorities

Longer term, this may be where the United States draws the line. Regardless, it suggests that while there's a "clear and present danger" of forever losing control of our infrastructures, there are also opportunities to reinvest in business strategy, business applications, and architecture.

So who should you hire? Who should you educate and train? *How* should they be educated and trained? What should you outsource? What should you "own"?

This journey—from layers and activities → relevance → education and training gaps → outsourcing—suggests that we're not optimally positioned to deploy or support technology infrastructures. Much of it is already out the outsourcing door, and the educational and training programs in our industry don't focus directly enough on infrastructure or support. This leaves enterprise architecture, business applications, and strategy for the taking. But even here there are large education/training gaps (in architecture), and medium gaps in many of the other areas. But there's still time to refocus our efforts: there's not all that much outsourcing occurring here so there's time to capture—at least for a while—some key business technology areas.

Advanced Vendor Management: A Graduate Course in the Optimization of Vendor Relationships

Let's talk about specialty offices, one of which is the vendor management office (VMO).

VMOs became popular at about the same rate as outsourcing increased. More and more companies realized that they needed special expertise to manage their vendors, that the development of RFPs and the development of comprehensive SLAs were just as important as removing latency from their communications networks. The challenge here, however, was newer—and therefore less understood—than either project or process management. Companies are still struggling with vendor management, especially as the nature and depth of outsourcing activities increase. VMOs will become even more important as the field continues to bifurcate into "operational" and "strategic" layers where the former is likely to eventually be completely outsourced. The expertise necessary to optimize the client/vendor relationship is still very much in development; best practices here are changing as the nature of outsourced offerings change.

This discussion is about advanced vendor management, or how to "squeeze" vendors to your advantage—especially if you spend big bucks with multiple hardware, software, and services vendors. Some of you are already pursuing these suggestions, but some others may not be availing yourselves of some of the ideas discussed here.

Big Spenders

How much do you spend with Microsoft, Oracle, IBM, SAP, or Dell (or some other major vendors)? If you don't know, you should find out as soon as possible so you can join the ranks of what your vendors consider their "big spenders." Knowing your place in their hierarchy of customers is essential to leveraging your financial clout.

Regardless of where you sit in the hierarchy, if you're completely happy with these vendors, you're misguided. **Why?** Because if you've been a loyal customer and spend over a million dollars a year with these guys you should get much, much more than the product or service you get in the normal transaction process. What if you spend $5M a year with a vendor? How about $10M—as many large enterprises do. What if you have mega-contracts for data center management or desktop/laptop support? What if you spend $25M a year—or more—with IBM, EDS, CSC, or Accenture—as many of us do? What kind of special treatment should you expect?

So what are you—a big, medium, or small spender? The answer is important for optimal vendor management.

Advanced Vendor Management Best Practices

If you spend serious money with a vendor, here are five things, as suggested above, that you should expect:

- **Extraordinary—Nordstrom grade—support—even if you haven't paid for platinum service.** Long-term vendor/customer relationships should be rewarded by extremely excellent service. It should not matter that you only paid for gold service; when the heater breaks in the winter it should be fixed within hours, not days. Of course, if the heater breaks every other day no one has the right to expect extraordinary service for less than fair and reasonable cost. But vendors should not quibble over the terms of a SLA when the pipes burst. Nor should they provide you with a huge "I did-you-a-huge-favor" bill for such infrequent but critical services.
- **Shared risk contracts.** Shared risk relationships can be tough to manage, especially when relationships are new. But over time, relationships should be based on mutual respect: I respect your ability to deliver for me as you respect my qualifications as a customer and my willingness and ability to pay for your services. In fact, I am not just a customer; I am a special client. If either of us fail to fulfill our responsibilities, then we should accommodate the relationship in some meaningful way—or terminate it altogether. Vendors unwilling to share performance risks are not partners. Vendors that quibble over performance metrics are not long-term business associates.

■ **Subsidized pilots.** Let's assume that I use IBM or Oracle's database plat-form. Let's also assume that I spend several million dollars a year with these vendors. I am currently thinking about a data warehousing project to deter-mine if I can better cross-sell and up-sell my products and services, but I am concerned about selling the business case to the senior management team that is notoriously cheap about such initiatives. Is it reasonable to expect IBM or Oracle to heavily subsidize the demonstration pilot project? Absolutely. In fact, the primary database vendor—who has a huge vested financial interest in the outcome of the pilot—should not only subsidize the project but pay for it entirely. The quid pro quo, of course, is additional work for the incumbent vendor, if the project is successful. Is this reasonable? Yes, if the size of the additional project is substantial. Some ratios to consider: if the new project is worth $100,000, then a fully subsidized $10,000 project is reasonable; for a million dollar project, a $100,000 pilot sees right. 10:1 is about right. Does this strike you as excessive? How about a $100M project? Shouldn't the ven-dor spend 10 percent of the amount to actually get the project? Obviously, smaller vendors do not have deep enough pockets to heavily subsidize dem-onstration pilot projects. But the top 25 technology vendors definitely have pockets wide and deep enough to completely subsidize pilot projects whose outcomes benefit them directly.

■ **Requirements prioritization**. All vendors want us to stay with their prod-ucts and services. Oracle wanted us to stay with its CRM solutions so badly it bought the industry leader. SAP wants its customers to stay with its platform so badly that it keeps introducing and improving new functional modules— CRM, BPM, and so on—to keep its customers from pursuing best-of-breed buy-and-integrate strategies. The trouble is that the functional capabilities of some of the major database, ERP, CRM, and other vendors are often inferior to some of the more specialized vendors. This capabilities gap provides lever-age to buyers—if they understand how to communicate their requirements to their primary vendors. For example, SAP needs to make its supply chain management (SCM) module as good as—if not better than—Manugistics' application if it wants to keep clients from straying. This means that your supply chain planning and management requirements are especially impor-tant—or should be if communicated effectively—to your ERP vendor who will listen carefully if it is doing its job. "Fix it or else" should be what your vendor hears when you suggest what requirements need to be addressed in the next version of the application. Is this unreasonable? Absolutely not: in fact, your major vendors should appreciate your requirements insight as they improve the functionality of their applications. If they resist your suggestions, then there's a larger problem—not unlike when politicians ignore their con-stituents and do whatever they feel like doing. Over time, you will vote the politician (and vendor) out of (your) office.

■ **R&D partnerships.** Related to all this is a longer-term partnership that includes you in the R&D activities and plans of your key vendors. Here I am not talking about "briefing days" where your vendors get to persuade you to buy new applications or new features in old applications. Instead, a true partnership involves your vendors' sharing information about significant R&D investments they're making and the opportunity to overlay your anticipated requirements on to those R&D plans. A perfect example of this is SAP's decision to invest in its Netweaver platform, software that supports greater integration and interoperability among software applications. A truly significant investment, Netweaver caught some SAP clients a little by surprise. Ideally, important R&D investment plans are shared with customers from the outset so major users of the product or service will be able to anticipate the functionality and integrate it into their business technology strategic planning. One way to accomplish this objective is to encourage "internships" with your vendors where your key business technologists get to spend weeks if not months with your vendors' R&D teams.

Tomorrow's Assignment

All these ideas constitute advanced vendor management best practices. Remember, we buy all this stuff—well over a trillion dollars a year in hardware, software, and services in the United States alone. Don't we demand special treatment?

Examine your major vendor relationships. Look for opportunities to leverage your dollars to take the relationships to the next level. There's an excellent chance that you're leaving some leverage on the table.

Project Management Rigor (or Rigor Mortis)

We've all had a chance to think about project management discipline and how project management offices are doing. For about a decade now, many companies have implemented formal PMOs to help them deal with project inefficiencies usually defined as "late and overbudget." But where are we now? Have PMOs been "successful" or have they just added another bureaucratic layer to our projects? Has project management discipline taken hold or is it more about paying lip service to what lots of people think makes sense?

Project management is a discipline and like all disciplines needs to be applied judiciously. Over the past few years we've seen PMOs and project managers run the discipline gamut where some PMOs comprise overzealous professionals who sometimes lose sight of their primary mission—and some professionals who barely apply PM discipline, working only to very loosely consult on the project management process.

So what are the options? What makes sense—and what doesn't?

Discipline

At the outset of this discussion, let's stipulate that discipline—like adhering to technology standards or hiring only smart, hard-working, ethical people—is difficult, primarily because it means that we have to control our impulses. But discipline makes money, and some degree of project management should be a core discipline in every company in the world.

The key to discipline is consistency and persistence. Initiatives fail because companies roll out programs, processes, and policies that vary from group to group or organization to organization, or because they lose interest over time, something that employees can smell long before the plug is officially pulled. Lots of long-term employees have adapted to management's lukewarm commitment to major initiatives and have learned to drag their feet for as long as they can (or until management loses steam). The other key is to identify and consistently apply the right amount of discipline.

So what are the basic skills we need to practice bare bones project management discipline?

- **Enough organizational governance to get everyone to take the rules seriously.** The "rules" in this case pertain to the origins, processes, and outcomes of business technology projects. These rules need to be defined, communicated, and understood. If they are not, then the overall discipline will fail.
- **The ability to develop an informed business case about a possible project.** This skill requires that evidence be brought to bear on the strengths, weaknesses, opportunities, and threats to the prospective project. Objectivity should rule here, but obviously there are occasions where corporate politics will enter into the analysis. The key skill here is to manage the ratio between evidence and politics.
- **The ability to assess a project's likely success or failure.** Note that this assessment comes after the business case has been filed—and approved. Can the project be successful? What are the risks? Who's the best person to lead the project? Is a good team available? What are the immediate problems we have to solve?
- **The ability to keep the business case front-and-center as the project unfolds.** Once approved, the business case is the blueprint developed by well-dressed, well-meaning architects; the project is all about execution. Companies need to continuously link project progress to the business case that gave birth to the project in the first place. Measure the distance between the business case and project progress on a regular basis; if they start to drift away from each other then it's time to take action.
- **The ability to execute project management fundamentals, such as identifying milestones, tracking deliverables, managing schedules and cost, conducting project reviews, and so on.** The Project Management Institute

(www.pmi.org) can certainly help here, though there are tons of companies that will help you perfect the basics.

◼ **The ability to kill bad projects; the ability to determine if a project is hopeless or salvageable**. There are several reasons to kill a project: the business case and project are drifting far apart; the business assumptions about the importance of the project are no longer valid; project execution is way off track; the project is overbudget or behind schedule, etc.; and the probability of project recovery is low or nonexistent.

Rigor

If we assume the basics, then how should they be applied? There are major choices here. Should the PMO and its professional project managers "own" projects? Should they "control" project management processes? Should they have veto power over project decisions? How should they interact with project sponsors and the project team?

These questions suggest a balance between project management discipline and project execution. Project management discipline should not become a hammer we use to hit project teams over the head; instead, project management discipline should behave more like a repository of consulting best practices. In other words, in much the same way seasoned consultants influence their clients in the right direction, project management professionals should behave more like consultants than storm troopers.

This is a controversial recommendation. Many companies create PMOs because their project execution records are dismal. They believe that project management discipline will save them, so they often empower their project managers with whatever they need to succeed. This often means that project managers are free to do whatever they want to get projects and project teams in line. Governance may even extend to the PMO where project management discipline becomes something that everyone must subscribe to—regardless of the implications. The controversy occurs when companies that have a history of failed projects think about project management discipline as the way to quickly right the ship and then impose tough project management standards—standards so tough that they actually undermine project success. The line between rigorous and rigor mortis is thin.

Rigor Mortis

Rigor mortis sets in when project managers take off the gloves and under the air cover of project management governance impose draconian practices on business technology projects. This is an extremely dangerous trend. Well-meaning executives may believe that the only way to get their projects on track is to impose a no-exceptions discipline that everyone practices—or else. They are almost always wrong.

The draconian approach has become popular in tightly governed organizations where the corporate culture is "can do." But the risks here are huge. Project teams are often held captive by process Nazis who define project success around compliance to project management rules—not overall business value. The overzealous adherence to the rules can cripple projects and directly threaten the business impact the project is expected to have.

Appropriate Discipline

Appropriate project management discipline, like appropriate technology, is just enough discipline to increase the probability of project success. But, to achieve appropriate discipline status, several things must be true:

■ Governance that tilts much more toward consultative project management services than no-exceptions-based rigor mortis.
■ The codification of just enough project management rules; no one needs to adhere to every single project management principle, best practice, and so on. "Just enough" discipline will be defined around your corporate culture.
■ Project management "consultants" with deep consultative skills (not disgruntled project team members who want to change their roles in the company).
■ "Value" defined as project impact, not as adherence to project management discipline for its own sake.
■ Project management training that directly addresses the "just enough" and consultative principles.

The take-away here is to inspect your PMO and its project managers to determine where they are on the rigor → rigor mortis continuum. Once you locate them, you can decide what makes sense for your company. But remember that rigor mortis is what sets in after death! Try to keep an open mind about long-term success. It's much easier to gradually increase discipline (still way short of rigor mortis, of course), than to decrease it abruptly because of complaints about storm troopers wreaking havoc with otherwise solid projects.

Chapter 5

Operational Effectiveness

Thin Is Beautiful

Thin is still beautiful. It was beautiful when it was a concept, and it's even prettier now that it's a reality. Opening shot: "Are you happy with the fat client architecture that runs your life today, with the ever-more-powerful PCs that require more and more support?"

Let's step way back.

About ten years ago Larry Ellison appeared on the Oprah Winfrey show to discuss "network computers." This was when a lot of ahead-of-their-time ideas were out there, like Apple's Newton and IBM's voice recognition applications. Larry was wrong then because our networks weren't reliable, secure, or ubiquitous enough to support "thin client" architectures. Never mind that the devices themselves were also a little weird and way too proprietary. But if Larry reprised his appearance on Oprah tomorrow, he'd be dead right. The concept was always right.

Let's look at several trends that point to why "thinfrastructure" makes sense. First, we've segmented our users into classes based on their frequency and depth of use: some people use very expensive and hard-to-support laptops pretty much for e-mail. We've begun to deploy a bunch of devices—like PDAs, cell phones, and pagers—that are converging. Many of these devices are pretty dumb, but that's okay because we don't ask much of them. Multiple device synchronization is, however, difficult and expensive. Desktops and laptops are way overpowered for the vast majority of users (as is the software that powers them). Enterprise software licensing is getting nasty (if you don't renew your Microsoft software every three years, you get punished). Desktop/laptop support is still complicated and expensive; large enterprises—even if they have network and systems management applications—still struggle with updates, software distribution, and version controls—and the larger the organization, the greater the struggle.

Network access is ubiquitous today: we use desktops, laptops, PDAs, thin clients, and a host of multifunctional converged devices, such as integrated pagers, cell phones, and PDAs to access local area networks, wide area networks, virtual private networks, the Internet, hosted applications on these networks, as well as applications that run locally on these devices. These networks work. You can be on if you want to be on.

Many companies provide multiple access devices to their employees, and employees often ask their companies to make personal devices (like PDAs) compatible with their networks. All this is made even more complicated with the introduction of wireless networks that make employees more independent and mobile (though less secure). The cost to acquire, install, and support all of these devices is out of control. What if I told you that the annual support cost for each wireless PDA in your company was more than $4,000? You'd either laugh at me or run and hide. Run and hide.

How should companies approach the network access device problem? What are the viable alternatives—today—and three to five years from now? Should companies prepare to support multiple devices and access strategies for each employee? Should we standardize on one device? Should we skinny it all down?

We should think about thinfrastructure.

Small, cheap, reliable devices that rely on always-on networks make sense. Shifting computing power from desktops and laptops to professionally managed server farms makes sense. Moving storage from local drives to remote storage area networks makes sense. Fat clients should lose some weight—as we bulk up our already able servers. The total-cost-of-ownership (TCO)—not to mention the return-on-investment (ROI)—of skinny client/fat server architectures is compelling (to put it mildly). Is this about control? Is it about reliability? How about security? Yes. Since we all agree that timing is everything, given all of the new devices appearing and how many of them are converging into wholes greater than the sum of their parts, isn't this a great time to think thin? If you don't, then the only people you'll make happy are the vendors you have to hire to keep all the toys humming. If you get control of the servers, you control everything that plays on every access device; and if you skinny down the access devices, you get control, flexibility, standardization, reliability, and scalability for your users. No more software conflicts, instant software upgrades, quick and easy new application deployment. Sound too good to be true?

Think about thin.

Vinfrastructure

Let's challenge vendors to develop simple, cost-effective solutions to vertical industry problems with horizontal technology that's customized for specific industries. For decades vendors have offered one-size-fits-all infrastructure technology that gets "tuned" by in-house or outside consultants after it's deployed. Applications vendors have offered specific solutions to several industries for years. Manufacturing, financial services, and healthcare all have their technology leaders, but they tend to be on the applications—not the infrastructure—side.

Let's challenge the vendors not only to develop customized infrastructure solutions, but also to develop *simple* infrastructure technologies that satisfy specific industry requirements—without the overkill that characterizes just about every infrastructure technology out there.

What am I talking about? Three things:

■ The documentation of vertical industry requirements
■ Vertically customized infrastructure technology
■ Simplicity

Vertical Industry Requirements

Vertical industries have mature relationships with information technology. It's not like we're still trying to figure out how banks should use IT to solve their problems. Vanguard—the giant financial services company outside of Philadelphia—knows exactly how to leverage IT on to old and new business models and processes. But it does almost all of it in-house. Like many companies, Vanguard has served itself with wide and deep vertical expertise. It has customized off-the-shelf software to satisfy its financial services requirements. But why couldn't the vendors customize it for them? I realize of course that one can always hire an army of consultants to do whatever is necessary, but why bloat the process with more overhead than necessary? Besides, consultants are really, really expensive and once they've become part of the furniture, well, they've become part of the furniture. Aren't the financial services, pharmaceutical, and chemical industries—among others—big enough to justify their own infrastructure requirements—and solutions?

Just about all of the major vertical industries have sets of requirements that are generalizable across the companies within that industry. Are Fidelity's requirements all that different from Vanguard's? Are DuPont's all that different from Rohm and Haas'? What happens when RFID really takes off? How many flavors will there be? Why wouldn't there by one primary flavor for each vertical industry?

Customized Infrastructures

I'd love to see the primary vendors of hardware, software, and communications infrastructure develop full vertical suites complete with all of the bells, whistles, and hooks that make it possible to transact business across any number of vertical industries. Issues like privacy, compliance, reporting, business-to-business (B2B) transaction processing, data representation, and security, among others, are approached differently by different vertical industries. Why can't we get some help here to at least create some intraindustry infrastructure standards?

The chemical industry is a case in point. Just about all of the major companies have standardized on SAP as their ERP application. This means that infrastructure providers (without the consulting middleman) can optimize their solutions to back office and front office SAP application modules. How easy is that? Vendors who provide communications, workflow, groupware, knowledge management, messaging, content management, security, and database management, among other capabilities, can tailor their offerings to SAP and the chemical industry.

Simplicity

Are you tired of buying, deploying, and supporting capabilities that you seldom, if ever, use? Human factors experts have told us for years that we use about 10 percent of the capabilities of Microsoft Office, but, of course, pay for 100 percent. Every time I use the term "bloatware" in a speech, the audience loves it. CFOs really hate the whole concept of "shelfware," where bloated applications never even get installed—even though they were purchased as part of the enterprise licensing agreement.

One of the most interesting opportunities for open source providers is the possibility of simplifying hardware and (especially) software architectures. It's unlikely that the major proprietary vendors will travel down this path, but the Linux desktop crowd could move in this direction pretty easily.

But the real leverage still lies with the optimization of proprietary legacy infrastructure technology. Although the open source community wants to simplify its offerings, real progress could be made if the proprietary vendors would *lighten and verticalize* their applications: we really don't need all the bells and whistles they shrink-wrap; instead, we need applications stripped down—and juiced up—to optimally support specific vertical industries.

Marching Orders

Let's push these people to customize and simplify our vertical worlds. Vertical industry infrastructure requirements are far from mysterious. Why can't they make our vertical lives easier?

Another Look at Open Source Software

One of my graduate student teams recently pitched me on the virtues of open source software. The leader of that pack works for a not-for-profit corporation, so you know what his bias was. The rest of them worked for companies that lived for profit—and you probably know what their biases were. We analyzed some open source alternatives to Microsoft Office, Siebel Systems CRM, and other proprietary applications and even some database management software, and concluded that while they were all impressive, they were still not quite the real thing. Nor, we concluded, would they offer the cost savings that everyone had been lobbied to expect. I then took the analysis to our CIO Advisory Council, 25 or so CIOs from the greater Philadelphia area, and asked them straight up: "What are you doing about open source software in your companies?" Note that the companies in the room included Rohm and Haas, Unisys, Johnson & Johnson, Sunoco, Wawa, Vanguard, Aramark, Sungard, the Philadelphia Stock Exchange, Cigna, and Wyeth-Ayerst, among other prominent companies. My back-of-the-envelope calculation indicated that the people taking that ad hoc survey spent about $5 billion a year on technology—surely they'd be interested in something that might save them some serious money.

What do you think that they said?

Nearly all of them were anything but enthusiastic about open source software—aside from the use of ("not on *my* desktop") Linux and Apache. Several of them indicated that the cost savings they might enjoy from migration would be eaten alive by the migration cost itself, not to mention the hassle and weirdo factors. (Many of the CIOs were far more concerned about cell phone bills than the cost of Microsoft Office licenses.)

Sun Microsystems and Google recently announced a partnership whereby Google would distribute Sun's software including its competitor to Microsoft Office, OpenOffice. If you look at the list of open source alternatives to the proprietary systems that we buy, deploy, and support, the list is getting longer and longer—and the features richer and richer. The not-for-profit and for-profit open source support community is also getting much more sophisticated and professional. More importantly, many of the largest technology vendors long ago embraced open source software.

So are we there yet?

We're getting closer—and it's not the features and compatibility of open source software that are getting us there (though it certainly helps the open source cause). It's the structure and mechanics of the software industry that's making open source more attractive to increasing numbers of small, medium, and even large companies.

Yes, I know I already said that my CIO Advisory Council rejected open source software and that my graduate students made a less-than-convincing case against the proprietary software giants. But there are some trends that bear very close watching over the next few years—trends that might very well change their minds.

The first is pricing. At some point, technology managers are going to resist the sheer cost of buying—and maintaining—enterprise software. Although I realize that there are always "deals" out there, enterprise software is incredibly expensive (and there are human factors experts out there telling us over and over again that most users barely use 10 percent of the features embedded in large software suites, and then there's the "shelfware" issue).

The second trend is hosting. Many companies are looking seriously at renting software instead of buying, deploying, and supporting complex applications. As the hosting/renting trend continues, companies will revisit how they spend their technology dollars in some creative ways. The evolution of thin client architectures is part of this trend.

Third, the new software architectures based largely on Web services standards will enable whole new service-oriented and event-driven architectures that will challenge traditional software distribution and pricing models (this is part of the Sun/Google long-term strategy).

These three trends will place tremendous pressure on the large proprietary software vendors to rethink their pricing strategies. If they fail to adjust their prices, more and more companies will defect to alternative software acquisition and support approaches. Some will rent, some will move toward new architectures, and some will strongly consider open source alternatives.

This will all play out over the next three to five years—not in a decade or two. The major software vendors can influence the direction all this takes, but the only way they can guarantee market share is to reduce their profits. Regardless of how proactive the major vendors become, the three pressure points described above will accelerate changes in how software is designed, acquired, distributed, supported—and priced.

Does this mean that open source software will become more popular over time? It depends on how the software market shakes out. Here are some scenarios that will influence the adoption of open source software:

- If the large proprietary software vendors fail to radically alter their pricing policies, then more and more companies will look to open source alternatives ...
- If the expected trends toward hosting and renting fail to continue and the large proprietary software vendors fail to radically alter their pricing policies, the adoption of open source software will dramatically increase ...
- If whole new software architectures fail to evolve, expected trends toward hosting and renting fail to continue, and the large proprietary software vendors fail to radically alter their pricing policies, the adoption of open source could become as popular—if not more so—than proprietary software ...

- Let's also acknowledge the role that open source software might play in renting/hosting and the new architectures that could be based on open source applications and open source components ...

One thing is for sure: the open source movement is gaining momentum and serious technology managers are beginning to rethink how they might participate in the open source movement. So what would you say if I asked you straight up: "What are you doing about open source software in your companies?"

Commodities: Where Premiums Meet Payments

A friend of mine runs a company that provides remote backup and recovery. It's very nice little company that makes money and provides a valuable service to its customers. About a year ago it piloted its technology at my university. The results were great. They quoted us a price of around $14 per month per user for automatic, almost limitless backup with guaranteed recovery of any file within hours. Good stuff. But just last month the university signed a deal with a competitor for around $2 per month per user for pretty much the same services. In one short year the price had fallen from $14 to $2! How is that possible? Was the $2 vendor making money on the deal? Yes. How is that possible? Well, just like so many other things in our business, remote backup and recovery just simply got commoditized.

Here's a better (true) story. In 1999, I worked with a company that built Web sites for Fortune 500 clients. Actually, in those days companies that built Web sites were often referred to as "agencies," as they liked to combine eBusiness marketing strategy with Web site development. Many of these engagements resulted in the exchange of millions of dollars for 100-page Web sites—and a marketing strategy, of course. Today anyone can hire some freelancers to build a 100-page transactional Web site in Dreamweaver or some such tool for well under $5K. Even better, one can post an RFP on the Web and receive bids for site development from all parts of the world. I bet you could get the same 100-page site for less than $3K through this bidding and negotiating process. (I'm confident because a friend of mine just did it with some Eastern European Web developers.)

What else is getting commoditized? PCs and servers have already become commodities. So have a variety of services, like desktop and laptop support, legacy system maintenance, and even data center management. What's next? Ah, this is the challenge—predicting the next wave of commoditization (especially as you're negotiating for the services as though they were still specialized).

What do you think? Here's a list of things that may or may not be true in a year or two. You be the judge.

- Backup and disaster recovery will be fully commoditized by the end of 2008. The cost of storage and storage area network (SAN) technology has fallen so dramatically that security and/or SAN companies may well give backup and disaster recovery services away for free—in exchange, of course, for some other higher margin services like the development of security architectures.

■ PCs, laptops, and especially thin client prices will fall dramatically over the next year or two. The age of the $200 to $300 PC is almost upon us—again, in exchange for higher margin services (in fact, many companies and organizations are working on $100 PCs and throwaway thin clients).

■ Database platforms will become commoditized in exchange for long-term deals for data warehousing, business intelligence, and data mining, which is where the money is today (and likely to be tomorrow). I'd gladly give away a DBMS in exchange for a long-term data warehousing (DW)/business intelligence (BI)/master data management (DM) deal. Wouldn't you?

■ The same fate will commoditize ERP applications that will eventually give way—after a period of software-as-a-service delivery—to full commoditization where all sorts of services will be added on, a la carte, to the "free" platforms. This one will take more than a year or two, but certainly within five years there will be very few—if any—companies willing to pay $100M to $300M (or more) for an SAP or Oracle implementation. Would you?

What do you think? What else will become commoditized?

Just don't sign any long-term deals for hardware, software, or services that might just turn into tomatoes.

Who Needs PCs?

There's not much one can't find, analyze, or purchase on the Web. The past ten years has seen the evolution of the Web from a passive repository of information to a proactive pusher of user-generated content and an enabler of personal and professional transactions. Educational curricula, music, films, surveys, customer service portals, travel planning, job placement boards, and personal matchmaking services are all on the Web. For some, the Web is woven so deeply into the fabric of their lives that it's impossible for them to imagine a disconnected world. (I think I may become one of these vagrants living as much in digital as in physical space. This year, for example, I am working on giving up paper.)

Let's argue that the Internet is the ultimate virtual server and all that anyone needs to access its content and transaction capabilities is a very thin, throwaway client. The argument obviously is that we should focus much more on the virtual server than on the device used to access it. In fact, given communications technologies and trends, it makes sense to invest in the server much more than in the client. (There's also the digital divide issue: the cheaper the access device, the more people can participate in the digital revolution.)

Let's look at several trends that point to why this approach makes sense. By now I believe that in addition to helping companies compute more cost-effectively, thin clients can help everyone exploit the Web—regardless of their lot in life.

First, network access is essentially complete: we use desktops, laptops, PDAs, thin clients, and a host of multifunctional converged devices, such as integrated pagers, cell phones, and PDAs to access local area networks, wide area networks, virtual private networks, and metropolitan networks. The networks work! Are they perfectly secure and 100 percent reliable? Not quite, but we're getting there. And for those who worry about the collapse of the Internet, there's enough redundancy and reconstitutability in the technology to let us sleep well—if not perfectly—at night.

Small, cheap, reliable devices that rely on always-on networks make sense. Shifting computing power from desktops and laptops to professionally managed servers makes sense. Moving storage from local drives to remote storage area networks makes sense. Fat clients should lose some weight—a lot of weight—as we bulk up our already able, underutilized servers.

One way to approach this is to begin with what the ideal converged device might look like and then strip it down to make it as thin and cost-effective as possible—while still allowing it to be functional. Some of the characteristics of today's "fat clients" include:

- Small (pocketable; about the size of a larger PDA on the market today) with as large a screen as possible within the given form factor
- Touch screen
- Expandable memory
- GSM or CDMA cellular phone service with broadband (EV-DO or EDGE)
- Address/phonebook
- Mp3 playback (via broadband or memory)
- Video playback (via broadband or memory)
- Web browsing with full Java support
- Popular OS allowing a wide range of programs
- Camera with video capabilities
- GPS with full mapping capabilities
- Bluetooth (file transfer, keyboard, headset, etc. compatibility)
- Wi-Fi

The cost for such devices is in the $500 to $700 range. Over time, we can certainly expect the cost to drop, but the ongoing maintenance and replacement costs for such devices will remain substantial.

What if there was another way to exploit all of that content and transaction processing capability? What if we could develop devices so thin and cheap that everyone could afford one? Here are some of the characteristics they might have:

- Even smaller form factor (comfortably pocketable; about the size of a nonflip mobile phone), as large a screen as possible or preferable in that form factor
- Touch screen
- GSM or CDMA mobile phone service with Internet with broadband
- Web browsing with full Java (or any open standard) support that makes e-mail client, word processor, audio/video playback, and so on available without installing applications, which can be accessed directly from the Web

The technology is here to make these devices in these form factors, so long as they remain "open." Wide area wireless network technologies, such as WiMAX, have the potential to drastically reduce the price of such devices. With WiMAX, companies (or municipal governments—as they are now beginning to do) could blanket entire cities with Wi-Fi-like broadband Internet service. This would not only enhance the "always-on" nature of devices, but could potentially render the entire mobile phone industry obsolete due to VoIP services. Devices would need only the Internet.

Over time the cost for ultrathin devices will be less than $100 (they might even be free as new pricing models emerge for Web-based transaction processing). Thin Web clients will become throwaways, eliminating completely the break-and-fix/replacement cycle that plagues so many IT shops and frustrates so many not-so-tech-savvy users. Pricing trends will also make the devices affordable to just about everyone.

There's great appeal in stepping away from managing any aspect of the communications infrastructure or content management on fat devices that require substantial care and feeding. When the industry first started thinking about thin clients—even before Larry Ellison's appearance on Oprah Winfrey's show over a decade ago—everyone understood the network and transaction processing implications of thin client architecture. In those days there was a lot of uncertainty about just how to power the transactions that a 24/7 network would deliver. But more recently, architectures have developed that suggest just how a thin client/fat host might work. New service oriented architectures (SOA) will make it possible for transaction power—and flexibility—to reside on distributed servers capable of communicating and fabricating transactions at a moment's notice. SOA combined with AJAX (asynchronous JavaScript and XML) will make it possible for consumers to use incredibly skinny devices to accomplish all sorts of Web-based activities. What this all means in practice is that our ability to extend distributed computing is growing dramatically and that new architectures will make it possible to imagine all sorts of seamless, instant communications from all sorts of devices—including ultrathin ones. What a wonderful world it will be.

So the next time you think you need a PC, look at what thin clients can do for you. I suspect that you may not need to lug all that capacity around—that you can get pretty much what you want for a whole lot less money, pounds, and hassle.

Where Does Software Come From?

The textbooks tell us that requirements analyses help us understand business problems. This understanding is then converted into technology solutions comprising hardware, software, and services. It seems to me that we have a pretty good read on where hardware and services will come from over the next ten years or so, but a lot of alternatives when it comes to software.

Hardware will be produced by a small number of vendors that will fight over increasingly shrinking profit margins. Services will be provided by the same silver-tongued devils that provide them now. Software will confuse the heck out of everyone.

In the old days we wrote code. Then we installed it. Then we rented it. Eventually we'll assemble it. But code still doesn't like other code, in spite of all of the progress we've made with interoperability and integration. Although we've made progress with standards, there's still a lot left to do.

But let's assume that we'll get it right, that software will work together reasonably well. How will we acquire and deploy it?

Over the past few months I've asked a number of CIOs and CTOs if they had a technology do-over would they still install their enterprise applications. Not one of them said they would. Why not? Because it took them all years to get the software to work and—in some cases—the projects cost hundreds of millions of dollars. Some of these CIOs got fired when they exceeded budgets and schedules; others struggled to realize the benefits everyone promised when they signed the contracts.

Some of the same CIOs and CTOs told me that they weren't interested in open source software because it was too flaky and they didn't want to be associated with the open source crowd. What?

Some of them don't trust Web services and think that SOAs are still ideas, not reliable software architectures.

Some don't trust Mark Benioff or IBM's on-demand guys.

So here's how it will go:

- Big time CIOs will not launch multiyear, multimillion dollar software implementations. There's too much time, money, and politics involved, and many of the biggest projects haven't delivered the goods. Only CIOs in the last year of their employment contracts will attempt multiyear software projects.
- If at all possible, CIOs will rent versus buy-and-install major software applications. They're all secretly hoping that ASP 2.0 is successful. They really don't want to get back into the enterprise software acquisition, deployment, or support business. Most of them are really bad at it, and they just don't have the stomach for technology marathons anymore.
- CIOs will pilot as many SOA implementations as possible to determine where the price/pain/performance ratios lie. They really want all this stuff to

work—they need software-as-a-service (SaaS) to become a reality (but they'll be happy to sit on hosted applications for as long as they can—as long as someone else is hosting them).

■ SaaS will take much longer to evolve than anyone thinks, but eventually it will mature to the ultimate mix-and-match software architecture.

■ The major software vendors will have to decide when they're willing to cannibalize their own business models. Now they make tons of cash through enterprise licensing and generous maintenance fees, but as more and more vendors offer alternative software acquisition models the big proprietary ones will have to completely change their fee structures to accommodate the move away from installed software. Even Microsoft is hosting software these days. Within just a few years, they will be hosting their own software and encouraging third-party providers to host and resell the very same applications. What a world.

■ Open source software will penetrate the most inner sanctums of the enterprise because it will meld increasingly easily with proprietary software and the new SOA architectures. In fact, the gap between open and proprietary software will dramatically narrow over time.

■ No one will expect software to be "free," but, like hardware, it will definitely commoditize.

■ Innovation will come from small entrepreneurs running small companies, just as it always has.

So when someone asks "where does software come from?" you can tell them from big vendors with creative partners who have finally figured out that their customers would rather pay by the drink at someone else's bar and grill.

Everyone to the Woodshed

I'm angry about our inability to police ourselves against self-inflicted wounds. I've been at this for a lot of years, and I cannot believe how often the same problems repeat themselves and how otherwise impressive companies find it impossible to get the most basic things right. Why is the business technology learning curve so flat?

Not long ago I visited a large company that had 11 ERP systems and 19 instances of them. Shortly after that I found myself talking with technology executives about their failed attempts to standardize their hardware, and right after that I helped a company think about how it should train its business technology professionals to think more about the business value of technology. I then found myself talking with some CIOs about whether they should think about outsourcing desktop support and their help desks.

Is it me, or are these issues like 20 years old? Where has everyone been, and why is it still so hard to practice discipline in the acquisition, deployment, and support of technology?

I told the CIO of the company with the 11/19 ERP problem that I could guarantee $250M to the company's bottom line if he'd agree to practice some discipline. I know, I know, you think that $250M is an exaggeration; I assure you that it is not. The company in question has an annual global IT budget of more than $2B and is wasting a ton of money on the installation, support, and maintenance of unnecessary hardware and software. I can guarantee a $250M savings if the company commits to a disciplined approach to standardization and deployment that would forbid the deployment of redundant applications. I even offered to forgo a consulting fee to make it happen, offering instead to take a percentage of the savings that was actually achieved—a completely risk-free deal. They declined.

Why?

Why do companies continue to make the same mistakes year after year? Well, the answer is almost too simple—and equally exasperating: they just can't bring themselves to tell people things they don't want to hear. Reducing the number of ERP applications might upset some people—I was actually told. Standardization makes people angry. People don't like being told what to do, I've been told a million times. Of course, these same people complain all the time about the cost of technology, arguing that IT should be cheaper every year because, after all, IT's all been commoditized.

Enough of this stupidity. We all learn early in life that we can't have it both ways. Either we adhere to best practices or we pay the price. I really resent management's insistence that technology costs be reduced when it fails to discipline the acquisition, deployment, or support processes. I really resent the CIOs and CTOs who don't have the courage to make the tough political calls when their corporate cultures might support these calls. There's no excuse for the lack of discipline that is sometimes avoided just to avoid tough conversations with the boys—who I guess might not tell the bearer of bad news about Saturday's tee time. An even more serious concern is among the shareholders of public companies that waste millions and in some cases billions of dollars on perfectly avoidable technology mistakes. Who is accountable to them?

It's epidemic. Too many companies have too many applications, too many servers, and too many laptops. Too many CIOs are afraid to make anyone mad. Too many CEOs fail to demand discipline from their technology executives—yet still complain about technology costs. Much of the "technology-is-hard" crowd doesn't pay enough attention to the lack of discipline that makes IT so hard. It's not about performance, reliability, or even security. These are solvable problems. The really tough problems are exacerbated by lack of will, poor discipline, our need to be liked, our tendency to avoid conflict, just about everyone's desire to take the easy way out, and our desire to dodge accountability whenever we can.

No one thinks he or she will end up in a woodshed. Maybe we should bring it back.

What You Need to Know about Pervasive Analytical Computing

What is "pervasive computing" and why should you care?

The challenge is to reassess your computing and communications environment, this time with reference to pervasive computing. Figure 5.1 describes the various computing eras in a little detail; as you can see, we entered the pervasive computing era around 2000. The analytical computing era began around 2005.

Let's look at pervasive analytical computing through the multiple lenses of software, services, and communications. What I've done here is develop a checklist you can use to prepare yourself for the inevitable connectivity that will change the way we all do business.

A Pervasive Computing Checklist

- **Software**

  - **Enterprise Application Integration (EAI)/Exchange Integration**
  "If your applications were fully integrated, how would integration accelerate your business?"
  "Have you piloted or deployed any of the major exchange engines?" "With good or poor results?" "What went right; what went wrong?"
  "What's your company's overall integration quotient?"
  "How much have you invested in service-oriented or event-driven architectures?"
  - **Transaction Platform Development**
  "Have you piloted or deployed any of the major transaction platforms?"
  "Do you have a standard internal applications architecture?"
  "Have you piloted E-payment or storage area management platforms?"
  - **Supply Chain Connectivity**
  "What aspects of your business would be more productive and profitable if your supply chains were integrated?"
  "Have you piloted any supply chain management software?"
  "Do you have an integrated supply chain strategy?"
  "How optimized is your supply chain?"
  - **Personalization and Customization/Business Intelligence**
  "Is there a mass customization strategy for your company?"
  "Is your sales and marketing team part of your customization/personalization strategy?"

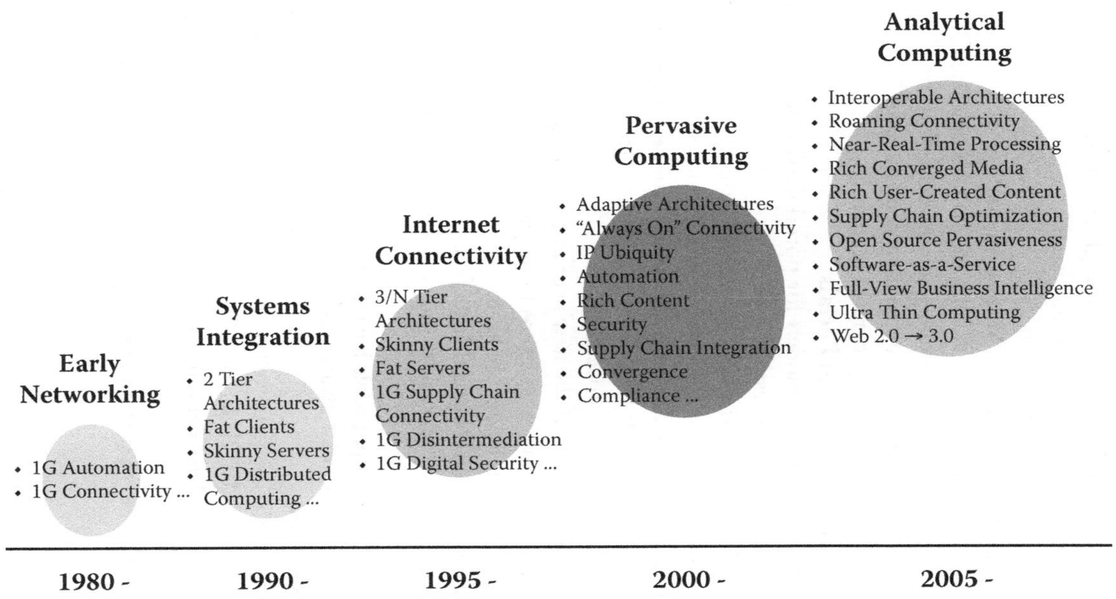

Analytical Computing

- Interoperable Architectures
- Roaming Connectivity
- Near-Real-Time Processing
- Rich Converged Media
- Rich User-Created Content
- Supply Chain Optimization
- Open Source Pervasiveness
- Software-as-a-Service
- Full-View Business Intelligence
- Ultra Thin Computing
- Web 2.0 → 3.0

2005 –

Pervasive Computing

- Adaptive Architectures
- "Always On" Connectivity
- IP Ubiquity
- Automation
- Rich Content
- Security
- Supply Chain Integration
- Convergence
- Compliance …

2000 –

Internet Connectivity

- 3/N Tier Architectures
- Skinny Clients
- Fat Servers
- 1G Supply Chain Connectivity
- 1G Disintermediation
- 1G Digital Security …

1995 –

Systems Integration

- 2 Tier Architectures
- Fat Clients
- Skinny Servers
- 1G Distributed Computing …

1990 –

Early Networking

- 1G Automation
- 1G Connectivity …

1980 –

Figure 5.1   Major computing eras and pervasive computing.

"What personalization/customization/business intelligence software have you piloted?"

"What's the plan for comprehensive BI?"

– Automation

"What 'manual' transactions in your organization could be automated?"

"What efficiencies could be gained through automation?"

"Have you piloted any automation software?"

"What are your plans for Web 3.0?"

– Rich Content Aggregation/Management

"How will your content evolve? What parts will become 'rich'?"

"Have you piloted any of the content management platforms?"

"How will you store and distribute content continuously?"

"How are you leveraging user-generated content?"

– Personal and Professional Portals

"Have you run cost-benefit models for portal deployment to improve data/ application/network access?"

"Have you piloted any of the leading portal platforms?"

"Is there an 'owner' of your company's portal strategy?"

– Architectures: Embedded Applications and Peer-to-Peer Computing

"What applications in your portfolio would benefit from continuous, peer-to-peer connectivity, and processing?"

"Have you looked at any of the new peer-to-peer products?"

"How are you leveraging Web 2.0 technology?"

"Do you have API and widget repositories?"

– Voice Recognition/Natural Interfaces

"What applications in your portfolio would benefit from voice connectivity?"

"What voice input/output tools have you piloted?"

"Is there high or low voice awareness in your company?"

– Web Services

"Is the 'Web services' concept well or poorly understood in your company?"

"Have you discussed Web services with your primary service providers?"

"Have they offered to demonstrate their capabilities and measure their impact?"

"How have Web Services standards penetrated your company?"

■ Services

– Outsourced Service Providers (ASPs, TSPs, CSPs, MSPs ...)

"Are you currently renting any applications?"

"Have you piloted a hosting arrangement with an ASP/TSP/CSP/MSP/VSP?"

"Have you benchmarked your currently in-house hosting versus outsourced hosting requirements and capabilities?"

    – **Application Integration Service Providers**

"Are you outsourcing your EAI/IAI requirements?"

"Have you measured the effectiveness of the outsourcing?"

"Have you developed any important partnerships or alliances with integration service providers?"

"Who are your SOA partners?"

    – **Rich Content Management Service Providers**

"Are you outsourcing your content management service requirements?"

"Have you measured the effectiveness of the outsourcing?"

"Have you developed any important partnerships or alliances with content management service providers?"

"Who are your media partners?"

    – **Development Services**

"Are you outsourcing your application development requirements?"

"Have you developed any important partnerships or alliances with application development service providers?"

"Have you assessed open versus proprietary opportunities?"

"Have you piloted Linux and other open systems?"

    – **Infrastructure Engineering Services → Solutions**

"Are you outsourcing your infrastructure engineering requirements?"

"Have you measured the effectiveness of the outsourcing?"

"Have you developed any important partnerships or alliances with infrastructure engineering service providers?"

"How virtualized are you?"

■ **Communications**

    – **Wireless Applications**

"How would widespread wireless applications affect your industry, your competition, your company?"

"What wireless standards have you adopted?"

"What are your plans for third- and fourth-generation (3G/4G) networking?"

"What's the plan for ubiquitous mobile computing?"

"What is your Wi-Fi strategy?"

    – **Network Security Solutions**

"Have you assessed your security vulnerabilities in light of always-on, continuous transaction processing?"

"How will you protect the privacy of your customers in an automated environment?"

"Have you explored alternative connectivity options, such as the public Internet, WANs, and VPNs?"

"How will you authenticate users of your applications and networks?"

"What authentication techniques—beyond encryption and passwords—have you deployed?"

- **Bandwidth Management and Optimization**

"How much bandwidth do you have; how much will you need when ubiquity hits?"

"How will you ensure its quality and reliability?"

"How will you optimize bandwidth when continuous commerce and fully integrated supply chains emerge?"

"How have you augmented your bandwidth requirements with service providers?"

- **Telecom**

"Have you explored the potential of voice-over-IP (VoIP)?" "What has been the impact?"

"Which of your telecom providers are the most aggressive moving toward a completely packet backbone infrastructure?"

- **Broadband**

"Have you evaluated broadband options, including hybrids?"

"Are you tracking the implications of fiber to the consumer's curb?"

"How will FIOS and other fiber offerings change the game?"

- **Network Applications and Services**

"Are you exploring the implications of the integration of IP voice and data?"

"How would unified messaging affect your business models and processes?"

"Have you piloted any of the network and systems management frameworks or are you still relying on point solutions?"

"Have you considered how you would support a large wireless environment?"

- **Optical Networking**

"Have you assessed the impact that a ubiquitous optical mesh network would have on your business?" "And on your competitors' business?"

- **Touch Technologies**

"How might your call centers change if commerce becomes continuous and automated?"

"Can your Web site support continuous commerce?"

Five years from now we'll wonder why we didn't prepare better for pervasive analytical computing. Perhaps the questions here can get us off to a good start—while we ponder the next major era in computing and communications technology.

Ten Things You Can Do Tomorrow to Improve Biz/IT Convergence

Every once in a while it's therapeutic to step back and look at the forest. Then after you feel a little better, it's fun to target some trees. Here are ten things you can do to improve the relationship between business and technology. Some of them are a little draconian, some pretty obvious, some edgy, and some really nasty. If you're change challenged, this is the time to stop reading and go do something else. Here we go.

1. **Reward the good, fire the bad, punish the costly (and give up on the reluctant):** Everyone knows that success depends on people. But how many of your people really know what they're doing? Do you watch them for clues? Do they ask for training? And then more training? Are they competitive? If they're technologists, are they always trying to learn more about the business? If they're on the business side, do they make an effort to learn about technology? You be the judge. Line 'em up.

2. **Disband large teams:** I realize that we've been talking about teams, bonding, and collaboration for years. But how many of us really enjoy those offsites intended to get us to relate to each other (while the senior guys play golf)? Look, the more people working on a project, the more likely it is to fail. At the very least, it will cost a ton of money, much of which goes for meeting coordination. Keep it small; keep it manageable. Big projects can be broken up in small pieces. According to industry research, more than 75 percent of all uber-projects fail, so there's reason to rethink how we do things.

3. **Kill flat management structures:** Whose idea was it to empower everyone? If we take this to its logical conclusion, it means that everyone gets veto power over everything. Successful experience should rule the day. The last thing you want to do is empower idiots. You know who they are and where they live. Keep them away from all the important discussions. And rethink the way you manage generally: I still like high-access hierarchical structures, where smart, experienced professionals make the big decisions after listening to (just about) everyone.

4. **Hire only partners:** Some of my best friends are consultants, but before hiring them you really have to make sure you know *precisely* what you want them to do and you understand the structure of their direct and indirect vested interests in the outcome of the work they do. Sounds like fox and hen house stuff, right? One of the best acquisition practices you can adopt is shared risk: if your vendors won't share risk, then you shouldn't share your money with them. It's also usually a good idea to hire honest brokers to look over the shoulders of the mainstream consultants and vendors you use, honest brokers who, regardless of the advice they provide, cannot make a dime after their gig is over.

5. **Get requirements right:** It's like a nightmare that you have every night: We don't understand the requirements! Who owns the requirements? Are they valid? Does everyone agree about which ones are important and which ones are expendable? Requirements are hierarchical: there are strategic, tactical, and operational requirements. Who owns them in your company? If you get these requirements right, a lot of good things happen. But keep in mind that strategic business and tactical technology requirements are intertwined and ideally seamless bedfellows.

6. **Stop building, start buying:** Off-the-shelf software—as an alternative to building stuff from the ground up—has made sense now for about a decade. Why do you still build when you could buy and integrate? Yes, nothing's perfect, but it makes more sense to customize a packaged enterprise application than to build one from scratch. Do you really need all those Java programmers? Do you really need to spend an extra 90 percent to get an extra 5 percent of "custom" features?

7. **Measure everything:** You have to measure everything. I really hate this. It's almost like exercise: we do it because we have to, not because we like to. But if you don't measure things—like assets, processes, people—then you have no way of knowing how you're doing and no way to benchmark yourself against your competition. Without empirical data, you fly blind.

8. **Best of breed:** This one will breed lots of controversy, but it makes more sense to commit to a few hardware and software vendors than to anything more than several of them. Yes, this is an argument against best of breed in strong favor of single- or double-sourcing strategies. Why? Because of the complexity of our computing and communications environments and because emerging business requirements call for scalability and agility, we have to increase the chances for the successful integration and interoperability that reduces complexity and fosters agility. Look around your company to see just how much variation you're paying for and how much money you're leaving on the table. Okay, so nobody's perfect, but do you really want to have three database management environments just to prove a point about independence?

9. **Look good:** While it's easy to criticize people who spend way too much time grooming their personal and professional selves, it's nonetheless important to keep "form" and "content," "style" and "substance" in perspective. If you develop a killer business case for a major enterprise technology project but it looks and reads like it was written while you were on vacation, your case will fail. If you're presenting to the senior management team and your folks are in jeans and t-shirts, the team will be treated accordingly. Training materials, documentation, office signs, business cards, Web sites, and people all need to look and feel professional. Not cool, professional.

10. **Rethink relationships:** I know, here we go again. But this time there are some major differences in the maturity of both business modeling and technology effectiveness. Ten years ago business models were linear and sequen-

tial; now they're dynamic and continuous. Twenty years ago most computing and communications technology barely worked. We're now at a very different business technology place. If we're now talking about collaborative, integrated, and continuous business, then we're no longer talking about business requirements thrown over the fence to eager or not-so-eager technology professionals who have to interpret what the requirements mean, but rather a holistic approach to business technology convergence that renders most of today's reporting relationships obsolete. Very simply, if your business gurus are at arm's length from your technology gurus, and your organizational structure endorses the distance, then you have a fundamental problem in how you do business. It's time to rethink everything.

Some Final Thoughts (from the Bunker)

Change never occurs in a vacuum. The ten things you can do to achieve business technology convergence—to get to collaborative, continuous transaction processing—are not simple extrapolative changes you can make a little at a time. They're much more dramatic and therefore much less likely to happen. But hope springs eternal: maybe once we get ahead of the curve. Good luck—and don't e-mail me if you're angry … only if you like the ten things!

Killer Apps

There's a pretty good chance that your applications portfolio is not what it should be. It's probably got a hodgepodge of applications developed over the past 20 years or so that require some form of life support to exist. You've probably got applications that are mainframe based, some client/server applications, and some Internet applications that are driving your eBusiness strategy. You support some of them in-house and outsource support for others—most likely your eBusiness applications.

Time for an applications health check.

eBusiness requirements will define an enterprise applications strategy that will marry back-office applications with front- and virtual-office ones. You'll need to connect your employees with your customers and suppliers—and you'll need to retain enough flexibility in your environment to accommodate enhancements and whole new strategies—as you juggle mobility requirements.

The applications end-game consists of a set of interrelated, interoperable back-office, front-office, virtual-office, desktop, and personal digital assistant (PDA and other thin client) applications that support your business strategy. These applications should be standardized applications that support activities, processes, employees, customers, and suppliers regardless of where they physically sit or how mobile they are. All your applications should be reviewed to determine their compatibility with this goal.

Elements of Applications Alignment

The elements of an applications alignment strategy appear in Figure 5.2. Let's look at them in order.

Business Strategy Linkages

Make sure that you understand what the business wants to accomplish with the applications you buy, build, and support. If you can't put your finger on "purpose," then your applications portfolio will—by definition—perform suboptimally. All applications should be deployed based on their measurable contribution to business results.

Applications Portfolio Assessment

Look at your applications objectively. Which ones contribute *measurably* to your business? Which ones require disproportionate support? It's essential that you assess your applications with reference to your business strategy and the relative contribution they're making to the company's business processes and profitability. If the outcome of that assessment is clear, then decisions should be made to decommission applications (in the case of expensive applications that contribute little to the business) or transfer functionality to other, less-expensive-to-maintain systems (in the case of older systems with limited, but still valuable contributions to the business).

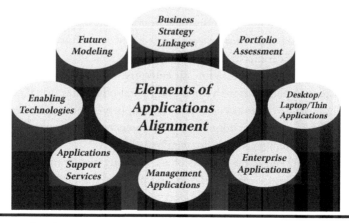

Figure 5.2   The elements of applications alignment.

You need to assess the variation in your applications portfolio. How many architectures are you supporting? What's the distribution of functionality and architecture type? Do you have your most important applications on the oldest, most-expensive-to-maintain platforms? You need a standard applications architecture. If you keep buying and integrating different host-based, client/server, Internet, hybrid architectures, your support costs will rise as rapidly as your reliability declines. You need to think about the range of applications in your portfolio, how you procure them, how you support them, and how you replace or modernize them. A framework that might suit your purposes here is shown in Figure 5.3.

Desktop/Laptop/Thin Applications

Stay as standard as possible here. Go with the mainstream vendor—Microsoft—and stay within primary standards with non-Microsoft applications. The primary desktop and laptop applications include the office suite running on a Windows platform. Although some of us may find this ubiquity disconcerting, it makes the world compatible.

Watch the upgrade treadmill. Upgrading hundreds or thousands of desktops to get access to a few cool features makes no sense at all. Skip versions whenever possible.

	Corporate	*Personal*
PDAs/ Thin Clients	• *E-mail & Groupware* • *Calendaring* • *Browsers …*	• *E-mail & Calendaring* • *Personal Transactions* • *Instant Messaging …*
Desktop/ Laptop	• *Word Processing* • *Presentation Graphics* • *Browsers …*	• *Financial Management* • *Communications* • *Knowledge Management*
Enterprise	• *Legacy* • *Packaged ERP* • *Internet, Intranet …*	• *Training & Education* • *Productivity Tools* • *Knowledge Management*
Management	• *Network & Systems Management* • *Applications Management*	• *Project Management* • *Program Management* • *Workflow …*
Services	• *End-to-End Services* • *Vorizontal Services* • *Hertical Services …*	• *Information Management* • *Searching* • *Configuration …*
Enabling Technologies	• *Middleware* • *Artificial Intelligence* • *Components …*	• *Voice Recognition* • *Fingerprint Recognition* • *Artificial Intelligence …*

Figure 5.3 An applications assessment and planning framework.

PDA applications are still evolving. We're a couple of years away from serious skinny applications that run on robust handheld operating systems. Until then, synchronization will provide integration with a suite of desktop and laptop messaging and calendaring applications.

Enterprise Applications

Decisions here can make or break your company. If you really need to get out from under myriad home-grown applications, your culture can sustain a long implementation process, your business can adapt to the business models embedded in ERP applications, and the value of standardizing on processes, reporting, and management is very high, then consider an ERP application. But be careful. If any part of the organization bails on the effort, the whole thrust will crash and burn. Migrating to an ERP application must also provide necessary impetus to your eBusiness strategy. In other words, a project of such momentous proportions must look forward not backward.

Management Applications

Beyond ERP applications are network and systems management enterprise applications that can also add value—or pain—to your organization. The same decision criteria above apply here as well, but in addition, the sheer size of your organization has to justify a robust management suite. Regardless, you'll need to manage your distributed applications via different tools and processes than you're now using to support your mainframe applications.

Other enterprise management options include enterprisewide project and program management training. Strongly consider instituting programs here to get your staff up to speed. Enterprisewide training initiatives are also a good idea, especially when there are significant skill-set gaps in your organization.

Applications Services

You really need to evaluate your ability to design, develop, integrate, support, and modify your applications. If you have a large, well-trained internal staff capable of supporting all varieties of applications and applications architectures, then you might want to stay where you are; but if the variation of your applications portfolio is high—and you're moving faster and faster toward distributed eBusiness applications—then you might strongly consider outsourcing. Since the 1990s and beyond you need a better reason not to outsource than to keep it all in house, the direct opposite of the decision-making process popular in the late 1980s.

Enabling Technologies

Keep an eye on those enabling technologies most likely to affect your applications performance and costs. Access devices—like biometric fingerprint authentication tools—can help a lot, enabling single-sign-on and reducing security administration costs.

Other technologies, like component technologies, can help your applications support and modification processes. They should be watched.

Other human–computer interface (HCI) technologies should be monitored as well, as speech input/output—as one example—will revolutionize applications performance.

Middleware will continue to be a critical applications technology. Don't leave it to the geeks! As the glue that makes the applications work together, it's important that you understand your overall middleware strategy.

Finally, artificial intelligence will remain hot for some time to come. Track progress here closely, especially as it's used to beef up applications monitoring and performance, in particular automated transaction processing.

Future Modeling

Institutionalize a process that reviews—at least twice a year—the whole applications strategy (driven—ideally—by new business models). Track key applications technology to determine what your migration plans might look like.

Ownership and Communication

You need to own the applications technology strategy (driven by a jointly owned business strategy). Communications need to be clear and couched in meaningful costs (what it will cost to implement and support recommended applications technology and any lost opportunities if the technologies are not implemented) and benefits (defined in terms of business benefits, like increased customer satisfaction, retention, cross-selling, and the like).

Communications

If we've learned anything over the past few years, it's the importance of pervasive, secure, and reliable communications. It not just about the Internet. It's about communications inside and outside of your firewalls, and it's about mobile communications.

It's no exaggeration to say that communications technology will make or break your ability to compete. There are all sorts of issues, problems, and challenges that

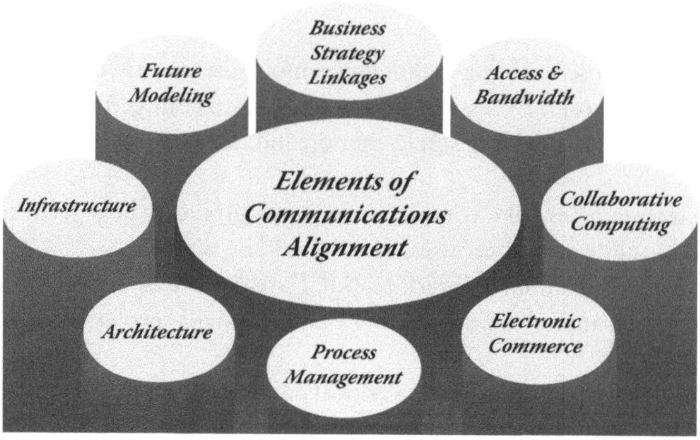

Figure 5.4 Elements of communications.

face your organization as it wrestles with its business strategy, its communications response, and its ability to adapt quickly to unpredictable events. Figure 5.4 identifies the elements of communications alignment. Some advice in each of the areas follows.

Business Modeling

■ Make sure that the new business models are developed and that they speak to communications requirements. Some of the communications requirements will be obvious, but others will be subtle, for example, like the ratio of in-house versus mobile users now and three years from now ...

Communications Strategy

■ Proceed holistically. Make sure that decisions about communications technology are linked. Tilt toward a standardized environment and away from a best-of-breed one: you don't have time to deal with the endless integration and interoperability problems (unless you've already decided to outsource the whole infrastructure) ...

■ Identify the change drivers that pertain most to your situation. Identify the drivers—like the number of mobile users you'll be expected to support, the amount of disintermediation and reintermediation occurring in your industry, and to what extent your business will go virtual ... rank-order these drivers in terms of their importance and probability of occurrence ...

■ Summarize your change-driven communications requirements: calibrate your current bandwidth and estimate future requirements (for bandwidth and bandwidth management), identify your security needs (as the number of remote users increases), identify the number and nature of the remote access points you'll need to provide and support, and plan for the new architecture's infrastructure processes and ongoing maintenance …

Access and Bandwidth

- Measure your current bandwidth against current and anticipated requirements to determine the bandwidth (and bandwidth management) "gap" …
- Build usage scenarios to validate the bandwidth and bandwidth management you'll need—*and then up the estimate by 25 percent* …
- From the top down, think about your access and connectivity architecture and infrastructure and—objectively—estimate its ongoing design and support costs: try to develop a TCO model per employee for your communications technology …
- Against a suite of requirements—like speed, availability, security, adaptability, and configurability—baseline your current communications performance and then project effectiveness against anticipated new requirements. Use the gap data to drive the new architecture, which will move you to (re)consider wireless communications, fiber-optic connectivity, and fast → gigabit Ethernet network connectivity. Given the complexity of this kind of migration, consider outsourcing the migration and support of the new architecture, but not the design …
- Devote very special attention to your network topology. Much of action here by the major vendors is now providing switching and routing options that didn't exist a year ago, and the move toward bandwidth management (versus providing more and more raw bandwidth) is real. It may be that you can save a lot of money by better managing what you have instead of spending more to add more!
- Look into optimizing your network and communications architecture for your applications. Many vendors are offering tools that allow you to optimize traffic for one or another application. If you've deployed an ERP application, you might be able to increase its efficiency dramatically via bandwidth allocation and management …

Collaborative Computing

- Calibrate your collaborative appetite. Do it internally and externally. If your business model calls for lots of action/reaction/threaded communications, you're moving toward collaboration. Internally, collaboration takes time and effort: you might already have a gregarious culture that likes to "share," but if not you'll be faced with some stiff challenges if you try to force-feed sharing …

- Many businesses will need to (externally) collaborate. If that's the case for you, stay mainstream with the standards and tools. This leaves you—essentially— with two choices for your primary platform: Microsoft or Lotus/IBM ...
- Consider migrating toward unified messaging where all forms of communications occur via a single application and device. Eventually, it will be commonplace to receive faxes where you receive e-mail and where you receive voicemail. Plan now for the infrastructure to support unified messaging ...

Electronic Commerce

- Your eCommerce business models must be clear yet adaptive (because you'll be changing them often). You also need to think about the applications you'll need, connectivity to legacy systems (because you're not likely to throw out all your legacy data), project and program management, support and metrics to measure your eCommerce efficiency ...
- Evolution is the key here. The idea is to evolve your Web site from an information repository about your company to a bona fide transaction processing platform. But doing so quickly—given the volatility of the business model and Web technology areas—is unwise. A smarter strategy is to evolve from one transaction processing level to another ...
- It's also important to rethink your customer relationships. While that's always good advice, the Web makes it imperative because (a) your competition will certainly be doing the same thing and (b) the anytime/anyplace possibilities of virtual connectivity must be assessed from whole new strategic vantage points. It's now possible, for example, to sell, service, sell again, service, crosssell, service, up-sell service—and then sell the data surrounding all of that activity to affinity marketers! Make sure to follow the products in the CRM and eCRM areas ...

Process Management

- Well-defined, understood, communicated, and approved processes will sustain your investments in communications technology. Without process buy-in, your technology investments will not pay dividends—and whoever is responsible for those investments will suffer politically ...
- A process guru—not an entire process organization—is necessary to make sure that the processes stay synchronized with the technology investments. Processes are essential to implementation and support. If you build a great infrastructure via an elegant architecture but fail to define and implement the operational processes, you will fail ...

Architecture

- Your overall communications architecture—the access/technology and transaction processing technologies that you implement—must be integrated ...
- Bottom-up design—or continuously patching an existing architecture—will not yield the results necessary to support your virtual enterprise. Top-down design of the architecture should yield better, more integrated, and supportable results. Err on the side of standardized architectures versus those that require massive amounts of customization and integration ...

Infrastructure

- Make sure that whatever applications you select and whatever communications architecture you design can be cost-effectively supported by current or outsourced staffed ...

Future Modeling

- Institutionalize a process that reviews—at least a couple of times a year—the whole communications strategy (driven—ideally—by new business models) ...
- Track key communications technology to determine what your migration plans might look like sooner rather than later ...

Ownership and Communication

- Communications need to be clear and couched in meaningful costs (what it will cost to implement and support recommended communications technology and any lost opportunities if the technologies are not implemented) and benefits (defined in terms of business benefits, such as increased customer satisfaction, retention, cross-selling, and the like) ...

These are the minimum prerequisites to success.

Data's Still King

But now we call it information, knowledge, and even content. Whatever you call it, it's the lifeblood of your applications and your plans to link employees, customers, and suppliers in a virtual world. We now think beyond database administration and about intelligent decision support, online analytical processing, data warehousing, data mining, metadata, and universal data access. Or at least we should.

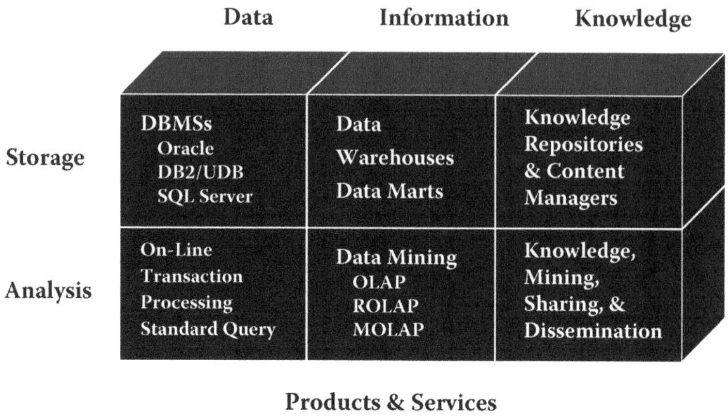

	Data	Information	Knowledge
Storage	DBMSs Oracle DB2/UDB SQL Server	Data Warehouses Data Marts	Knowledge Repositories & Content Managers
Analysis	On-Line Transaction Processing Standard Query	Data Mining OLAP ROLAP MOLAP	Knowledge, Mining, Sharing, & Dissemination

Products & Services

Figure 5.5 A data, information, and knowledge requirements matrix.

Data Alignment

The elements of data alignment appear in Figure 5.5, which should help define your data/information/knowledge strategy and prioritize requirements.

Data Storage

Not long ago the list of viable database vendors included five or six major players, but now for all practical purposes there are three. In addition to the core DBMS applications are the hardware storage solutions you'll need to balance against expected data/information/knowledge processing requirements. Another major trend is the movement from hierarchical to relational database management systems and the migration from relational to object-oriented database management. The more distributed your applications—and the greater your need for flexibility— the more you'll want to move to an object data architecture. Avoid supporting even two database environments: if it's at all possible, select one.

Information Storage

Information storage options—data warehouses, data marts, and special-purpose hybrids—require some serious thinking about where you think you'll ultimately end up, how much money's available for the construction of these artifacts, what users will require and—relatedly—what the data mining tools will look like.

So what should you spend money on?

If you're a DB2/UDB or Oracle shop but your business model calls for data warehousing with some front-end analysis tools, you may need to implement an entire blueprint, but if your needs are more modest, then you can pick and choose.

A note of caution, however. It all needs to work together. If you don't have cracker-jack data architects on your staff, then go out and get some. If you fail to implement your strategy holistically, you'll spend orders of magnitude more than you have to.

If you've implemented an ERP application (like SAP R/3 or Oracle Financials), then you have additional integration and interoperability requirements to satisfy.

Knowledge Storage

Knowledge storage is akin to dressing for a party to which you have no directions. Or—if you prefer—investing in a solution in search of a problem. The "knowledge management" (KM) business is just that, but the serious (read: measurable) pain it's intended to relieve is better described by the consultant doctors than by the victims (you). Nevertheless, you'll have to think about how to store unconventional, unstructured "knowledge" to play the KM game (once you figure out what the problems are). Here's some food for thought. Rather than be flip about the young field, let's look at some of the assumptions. First, KM assumes there is knowledge to manage, that you've somehow codified the collective wisdom of your industry's and company's experiences. Second, it assumes that your culture and processes are sharing centric, that is, capable of exploiting codified knowledge. Next, it assumes that you have—or are willing to invest in—the tools to make all this happen. Some vertical industries will be in better positions than others to exploit KM. But some industries will have little or no need for what the consultants are assuring us is the next great revolution in database management technology. Look at your industry, your culture, your processes, and your current and planned data infrastructure. If everything looks green, then do a KM pilot to validate your expectations.

On the other hand, there's lots of opportunity to exploit content management tools and applications. At some point, you'll need to move to a serious content management platform from vendors like Interwoven and Vignette. But make sure your requirements justify the investment to acquire and support these platforms.

Data Analysis

Storage is essential to analysis. So what's all this online transaction processing (OLTP) and online analytical processing (OLAP) stuff? Online transaction processing is what everyone's been doing for a long, long time. Online analytical processing—especially when coupled with data warehousing technology—is how data, information, and knowledge get usefully exploited.

OLTP is the mother of all analysis. It provides insight into current internal data, especially as it applies to operations and real-time transactions. OLAP provides insight when the focus is strategic, when the need is for reports and analyses, and when access is unstructured.

It's easy to see why OLAP has fans: it provides flexible querying of data that is relatively untapped by OLTP. In fact, OLAP provides a gateway to "information analysis."

Information Analysis

Information analysis requirements extend from OLAP capabilities to desktop OLAP (DOLAP), relational OLAP (ROLAP), and multidimensional OLAP (MOLAP). DOLAP includes PC-based tools that support the analysis of data marts and warehouses; ROLAP includes server applications that support analyses cubed from a RDBMS or a data warehouse; MOLAP exploits predeveloped data cubes.

Knowledge Analysis

Knowledge analysis and management is the end game of database management, data warehousing, OLAP, and data mining. It's also at the heart of a learning organization. But it suffers from an identify crisis and should be pursued only when the criteria described in the Knowledge Storage section above are satisfied.

And the Holy Grail ...

So where's all this leading? Everyone's working on universal data access (UDA) from all tethered and untethered devices. Eventually, structured, unstructured, hierarchical, relational, object-oriented data, information, and knowledge will be ubiquitously accessible. Although we're a few years away from all this, it's helpful to understand the Holy Grail and to adapt your business models in the general direction of UDA. Microsoft, IBM, and Oracle all have plans to provide UDA. It's important to stay abreast of their progress—and the implications to your business models and processes.

Don't Forget the Plumbing

To make cost-effective infrastructure investments, several things should be true:

■ You have to know what you have in your infrastructure: the laptops, the desktops, the servers, the PDAs, the minicomputers, the mainframes, the communications network, the routers, the switches, the business applications, the messaging applications—all of it (and if you don't have an enterprisewide asset management system, now might be a good time to think about getting one) ...

- You have to know what the skill sets in your organization are for supporting and transforming your infrastructure ...
- You have to know what your organization's plans are for eBusiness and enterprise applications, since chances are there's an "infrastructure gap" at your company ...
- You have to know what it costs to run your infrastructure; you have to know the return on your infrastructure investments and your total cost of ownership of infrastructure gear ...
- You have to know what processes define your infrastructure support; how you acquire hardware and software, how you administer passwords, when you upgrade software, who works the help desk, and how applications are tested prior to deployment ...
- And finally you have to know who pays the bills, what you have centrally funded and what you expect your end users to pay ...

This is a partial list, but you get the idea: in order to improve your infrastructure you have to baseline your current infrastructure assets and their performance.

But you also have to know what your infrastructure is expected to do. Are you primarily a back-office, legacy applications shop maintaining aging applications in centralized data centers(!), or are you distributing your applications and making them accessible to remote customers, suppliers, and employees? Depending on the answer, you'll need two very different infrastructures. Most likely, you'll need both: the former while you continue to support your legacy applications and the latter as you migrate to your future.

It's also likely that you have an infrastructure gap on your hands. Part of the reason is of course cost. No one wants to keep buying new stuff all the time, and you're probably no exception: it's been easier for you to invest in new applications linked directly to business processes than *infrastructure* that everyone finds hard to define or appreciate.

You can support the databases and applications in-house or you can outsource support, but one way or another you have to get the trains to run on time. Interestingly, many IT organizations have already segmented their infrastructure requirements from their application development requirements. In "decentralized" environments, infrastructure usually stays with the enterprise while the applications development professionals move directly into the business units. In these organizations, the CIO is actually the "chief infrastructure officer," as his or her responsibilities begin and end with the company's computing and communications infrastructure—the plumbing.

Companies can influence the effectiveness of their infrastructures through the organizational decisions they make; companies that separate infrastructure from applications often do so because they want the focus that segmentation creates. Unfortunately, in weakly governed organizations, they also often set up conflict between those who build applications and those who support them. The reality?

Make sure that applications and infrastructures integrate and interoperate—and that the planning for both is synchronized.

Elements of Infrastructure Alignment

The elements of an infrastructure alignment strategy appear in Figure 5.6. Let's look at them in order.

Business Strategy Linkages

■ All decisions must be passed through the business model(s) filters. If none exists, and you can't get the organization to make the investments in business modeling necessary to optimize infrastructure investments, then make minimally acceptable investments until the business strategy clarifies.

Governance Policy

■ Who owns what? You need to determine where the lines of responsibility and governance are drawn between the infrastructure and the applications and how decisions on both sides of the line are made. For example, is there a common applications architecture—so you can be sure that applications that are developed will efficiently run on the existing infrastructure? Fights here will paralyze your business.

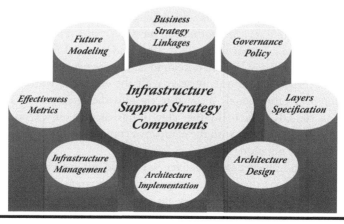

Figure 5.6   The elements of infrastructure support alignment.

Layers Specification

Many IT professionals think about infrastructure as computing and communications layers. Here are three to focus on:

- The *access layer* includes the desktops, laptops, browsers, PDAs, and other devices that permit access to your data, applications, communications, messaging, workflow, and groupware capabilities. You need to profile your current access "assets," including your desktops, laptops, PDAs, and other devices used to access your applications and databases. You need to determine how skinny or fat your access devices need to be. You need to standardize on browsers and on an applications architecture that uses the browser as the common applications interface, that is, the primary way users (employees, suppliers, and customers) access applications and databases through your communications networks. You need an asset management tool at the very least to identify what you have. You need to plan for an environment that will support an increasing number of skinnier clients and one that uses all computing devices as remote access devices.

- The *coordination layer* includes the query, messaging, directory, security, and privacy services that comprise your infrastructure. It also includes the transactions, applications, and Web servers that permit you to support your applications portfolio. You may also invest in the tools and processes necessary to coordinate access and management. The most obvious tools are the network and systems management point solutions and frameworks—and make sure you track developments in Web services. Lots of vendors will be offering comprehensive eBusiness applications support in the coming months. Even though perfect standardization seldom works, the goal should be to standardize on as few directory services, messaging systems, applications servers, and the like that make your eBusiness and enterprise applications work. Standardization can be vendor specific or best of breed. Increasingly, large enterprises are moving away from best of breed and toward a more vendor-specific standardization strategy. You'll need a network and systems management strategy that can be based on individual point solutions or on an integrated framework. Point solutions work best in smaller environments where network and systems management processes are hard to define and govern; frameworks work best in large organizations where governance is strong enough to define and sustain processes. The implementation of network and systems management frameworks is complex and expensive. Be careful—and make sure you develop some effectiveness metrics for your network and systems management processes and tools.

- The *resource layer* includes the applications themselves, as well as the applications management services necessary to keep transactions humming. It also includes the data/information/knowledge/content/metadata resources necessary to support transactions and applications. Your data centers reside in the resource layer of your infrastructure. But data centers will evolve to distributed data centers that (virtually) house distributed applications and data/information/knowledge/content as well as legacy applications and databases that all must coexist in the same infrastructure.

Architecture Design

■ Applications and communications architectures need to be designed and supported. Make sure that these designs are done holistically and with reference to the layers described above. Here's where business strategy requirements are converted into technology designs that support business transactions. Integrated design is complex; make sure that you ask enough smart people to help design your communications and applications architectures.

Architecture Implementation

■ Planning is tough, but too often execution is nearly impossible. Architecture involves hardware, software, and processes, and the discipline to faithfully convert strategic architecture requirements into robust, reliable, secure, and scalable infrastructures. Take the long view here. Build an infrastructure that can adapt to evolving strategic requirements.

Infrastructure Management

■ It's difficult to find professionals who can support heterogeneous environments. Make sure that your in-house personnel are up to the task. If they're not, then consider outsourcing to a company that has the right mix of skills and experience. Although there may be some reluctance to outsource your data centers, for example, remember that legacy data centers have been outsourced for years. As the number of deployed eBusiness and enterprise applications rises, it's likely that legacy data center management processes will have to be substantially modified to integrate and support the newer applications. All this may make outsourcing the smart move. If you can manage your infrastructure cost-effectively with in-house people, and infrastructure support is on your core competencies list, then go for it; but if you're in over your head, look for outside help.

Effectiveness Metrics

■ What works—and what doesn't? Just as it's essential to track your infrastructure assets, it's also important to track their effectiveness. Without obsessing over return-on-investment (ROI) modeling, you should develop quantitative and qualitative effectiveness metrics that will permit objective performance assessments. Business cases should be developed prior to any significant infrastructure investments—and be prepared to pull the plug if the data looks bad.

Future Modeling

■ Make someone accountable for developing infrastructure scenarios that recognize the likelihood of more eBusiness and enterprise applications working alongside legacy applications. Access, coordination, and resource infrastructure support requirements will rise in number and complexity as your (eBusiness and enterprise) applications environment becomes more heterogeneous. Track what the competition is doing and inject it into your business modeling and infrastructure requirements analyses. Develop an infrastructure tiger team to continuously look for infrastructure gaps.

Standards Now or (Lots of) Cash Later

The whole area of standards is fraught with emotion. Nearly everyone in your organization will have an opinion about what the company should do about operating systems, applications, hardware, software acquisition, services, and even system development life cycles. Everyone, even the people who have nothing to do with maintaining your computing and communications environment, will have strong opinions about when everyone should move to the next version of Microsoft Office. In fact, discussions about standards often take on epic proportions with otherwise sane professionals threatening to fall on their swords if the organization doesn't move to the newest version of Windows (or Notes, or Exchange—or whatever).

It's likely you've heard references to ROI and the TCO every time the subject of standards comes up. Lest there be no misunderstanding here, there is no question that environments with less-rather-than-more variation will save money. Or put another way, you have some choices here. You can aspire to be sane or insane.

What does business management really want here? Standards are a second-order business driver. Most businesses don't associate standards setting with business models, processes, profits, or losses. Whether the environment has 1, 5, or 20 word processing systems has probably seldom been associated with business performance: it's hard to link homogeneity with sales! But the fact remains that expenses are clearly related to sales, and standards are closely related to expenses. Herein lies the subtlety of standards and alignment.

What else does business management want? It wants flexibility—and here lies the real argument against standards. If your environment doesn't support the business computing or communications processes the business feels it needs to compete, there will be loud complaints. Business managers want to compute and communicate competitively. Standards are often perceived as obstacles, not enablers.

Try out these standards questions:

- How varied is your current environment? How do you know?
- Do you know what it's costing you to support a highly varied environment?
- What is your organization's tolerance for governance of any kind? For standards governance?
- Who's in charge of standards in your organization? Who's not?
- Is there business buy-in to the concept of standards and to the cost-effectiveness of standards?
- Has your organization been audited for its compliance to standards? The result?
- Do you have standard desktops, laptops, and PDAs?
- Do you have a standard communications architecture?
- Do you have a standard applications architecture?
- Do you have standard hardware and software acquisition practices?
- Do you have standard design, development, and project management standards?

The answers you give to these kinds of questions will reveal a lot about your attitudes about standards, standards responsibility, authority, and accountability—and whether or not your chances of standardization are high, low, or miserable.

If we've learned anything over the past few decades, it's that standards are as much about organizational structures, processes, and cultures as they are about technology. The ability to actually control computing and communications environments through thoughtful governance policies and procedures will determine to a great extent how standardized organizations become. We've also learned that the more you succeed the less you'll pay.

Elements of Standards Alignment

The elements of a standards alignment strategy appear in Figure 5.7.

As always, everything needs to sync with your business strategy—assuming one exists. If none exists, then make sure that you cover your political you-know-what. The real key here is governance and the processes that make standards management effective. Without serious support for a standardized environment, you're toast.

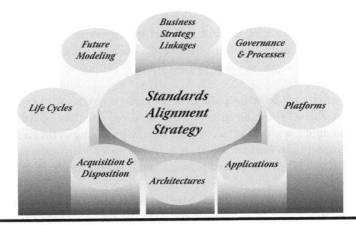

Figure 5.7   The elements of standards alignment.

Clearly, less variation in your platforms, applications, architectures, acquisition and disposition practices, and life cycles will reduce your costs. And as always, you need to focus on what the environment should look like in the next two to three years.

Figure 5.8 will help you implement your standards strategy. It offers cells in a matrix that you can use to identify, define, and prioritize requirements.

Note the distinction between the enterprise and the business division or units. This is a killer distinction because it determines ultimately whether you succeed or fail in your quest to reduce variation in your environment. If you're in a strong centralized organization, then your chances for success are much, much higher than they are if you're in a decentralized organization with a weak enterprise group

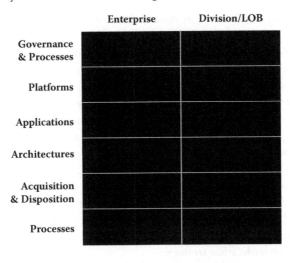

Figure 5.8   A standards requirements and planning matrix.

responsible for infrastructure. Put another way, it you're in an organization that has a central CIO whose job is really a "Chief Infrastructure Officer" and whose charter is full of authority holes, then you're not likely to reduce variation in your environment. In fact, you're likely to find yourself suiting up for one standards crusade after another.

The organizational structures that have the greatest chance of success are either a strong centralized IT organization or a decentralized one that has unambiguous separation of duties, with the infrastructure usually belonging to the central group. This latter model only works when there is buy-in to standardization, and when buy-in begins to weaken, the central management is willing to step in to reestablish standards authority.

The figure can help with a current baseline assessment and with the prioritization of standards requirements. This assessment should be focused on today and tomorrow. An assessment of current variation in each of the areas should be made followed by a strategy for reducing variation over some reasonable period of time.

The figure requires you to look at your governance and processes, your platforms, your primary software applications, your architectures, your acquisition and disposition standards, as well as your life cycles. The objective of these assessments is to reduce variation as a means to save money and preserve flexibility. The figure also requires you to realistically determine your organizational structure's relationship to standards setting. If you're decentralized, then you have some serious governance work to do; if you're centralized, then you'll have fewer religious wars over standards. The figure asks you to think about the enterprise versus the divisions or business units and proceed accordingly.

Here are some standards recommendations:

■ You need to standardize on your desktop, laptop, and PDA devices. Get a couple of vendors to bid, but select one and stay with it until there are too many good reasons to switch! Without a truckload of reasons, stay with the single vendor, avoiding best-of-breed approaches (that complicate your integration and interoperability requirements).

■ You need to standardize on browsers and on an applications architecture that uses the browser as the common applications interface, that is, the primary way users (employees, suppliers, and customers) access applications and databases. One way to do this is to designate a standard portal application.

■ Although perfect standardization seldom works, the goal should be to standardize on as few word processors, messaging systems, spreadsheets, databases, and the like that make your company work.

■ Standardization can be vendor specific or best of breed. Increasingly, large enterprises are moving away from best of breed and toward a more vendor-specific standardization strategy.

■ Architectures often fall through the cracks. You need to identify at least the communications, applications, and security architectures and standardize them as much as you can. Move to a single messaging system if at all possible and standardize on groupware, workflow, imaging, and related applications.

■ The way you build applications—if you're still building applications—and the way you configure your off-the-shelf applications will save you or cost you lots of money. Standardize your applications architecture so you can support your environment as it grows without bankrupting the whole company. Make sure you standardize on a single security architecture as well.

■ Standardize on the processes by which you acquire hardware and software: one individual or organization in your company should have the necessary responsibility and authority to purchase hardware, software, and services for your entire organization. Don't let vendors divide and conquer you.

■ Life cycles come in many shapes and sizes. Focus on three: requirements management, development/integration capabilities, and end-to-end systems design, development, deployment, and support.

■ Make someone accountable for developing standards scenarios that calculate the quantitative costs and benefits of standardization. Check out what the competition is doing to gain insight into these numbers. Project what might happen over time if your organization refuses to standardize.

Because standardization does not generate direct impact to the bottom line, you'll have to communicate why it makes sense to standardize. Use industry benchmarks to communicate why you should standardize and how the process might work.

If you're lucky, you'll avoid a few religious wars over standardization.

Should You Buy or Rent?

I was talking to a CIO recently who successfully deployed a monster ERP system across three continents. It all went amazingly well—but it cost an arm and a leg. I then asked another CIO friend of mine about how his CRM application deployment went and the results were not as successful. In fact, it was a nightmare. I needed a tiebreaker, so I called yet another CIO and asked about how her network and systems management framework implementation was going but she hedged, claiming that it was too early to tell, that in a year or so she'd have a better idea about whether or not it was working. I scored that as a miss.

I then found myself talking to some graduate students about the challenges of enterprisewide application deployment and support and one of them wondered why anyone would begin a $100 million project without some guarantees that it would result in a measurable contribution to the business. The discussion expanded from applications to databases to infrastructure. Everyone wanted to know why—if it's so hard to acquire, deploy, and support all this stuff—companies continue to take the path most traveled, to spend hundreds of millions of dollars on enterprise software behemoths.

"What's the alternative?" one of the students asked. "Well," I said, "you don't have to always buy; you can rent."

Five years ago application service providers (ASPs) were all the rage. Lots of companies emerged to host dot.com Web sites and facilitate B2B and B2C transactions. There was talk about extending the idea to all kinds of hosting, but before they could launch the next wave, the dot.com bubble burst. The large enterprise software vendors breathed a sigh of relief: they were safe for a while at least. But little by little the ASPs—like zombies—came back from the dead. Worse, the software vendors themselves broke ranks and began to host their own applications for customers who were too small or scared to implement the software in-house. Up until now, this trend has been relatively slow to mature. But now even Siebel Systems has decided—again—to host its CRM software. SAP is also doing it. What's going on?

Research in the field tells us that the probability of a successful enterprise software implementation is somewhere around 0.25. We know that unless you've got Houdini working for you, it's almost impossible to decipher enterprise software licenses. Unless you're blessed with internal "competency groups" (and the deep pockets necessary to keep them happy), you'll need consultants to help you implement and support the application (and even deeper pockets to keep *them* happy). But much more importantly, unless your company adopts the processes that underlie the application—that is, unless your company has, for example, a customer-centric culture with supporting models and processes—you're unlikely to ever recoup your technology investment in, for example, a CRM application. Need more logic? Compute the (real) TCO and ROI of a major enterprise application and see if the numbers make sense over some reasonable period of time. There are also some risk calculations we could walk through.

There's a quiet trend toward renting. Salesforce.com, the premier CRM ASP, has gone public. Siebel Systems (now part of Oracle) is offering hosting services, as is Microsoft, SAP, IBM, and others. In fact, when we step back and look at a variety of trends in the industry, we see even more evidence that hosting will expand with a vengeance. Web services, utility computing, thin client architectures, and even the semantic Web are all conceptually consistent with the hosting trend.

Are we sliding toward to new implementation standard? Are large-scale enterprise application projects dinosaurs? Will paying-by-the-drink become the new revenue model for enterprise software vendors?

Given your odds of success, given the uncertainties around TCO and ROI, and given other supporting trends, should you buy or rent?

Don't Crack the Box

During a recent class of executive MBA students where we looked at a bunch of successful and unsuccessful technology implementation projects, someone asked why so many large-scale enterprise software projects fail. Because the class was full of student-executives from more than 30 companies, we were able to explore the question with the benefit of multiple, real-world perspectives.

After about an hour's discussion about the usual suspects—bad project management, poor contract negotiations, and inaccurate cost estimates—a trend emerged: way too many of us are customizing enterprise software packages.

Let's step back a bit. How many times have we read the disclaimer about consumer electronics (CE) warranties warning not to attempt repairs on our own—to not crack open the box. If we do, the disclaimer makes clear, we'll invalidate the warranty. Interestingly, although there are some CE vendors who would like us to crack the box—and invalidate the warranty—most of them would prefer that we left repairs to experts. Owing to the complexity of most products—take cars as an example—it makes no sense to attempt repairs on our own. Smart companies create disincentives—like disclaimers—to keep us out of the engines of their products.

Carry this notion to enterprise software packages, like ERP, CRM, or even network and systems management software. What's the conventional wisdom around cracking ERP or CRM boxes?

ERP and CRM vendors are schizophrenic about customization. On the one hand, they like the idea of their enterprise platforms serving as enterprise anchors, that their platforms can solve all sorts of back-office and front-office problems. But on the other hand, the more that customers customize their applications, the more likely they are to fail—and the more likely customers will throw the baby (the core platform) out with the bathwater (the customized software that fails). The consultants that both install and customize big enterprise software packages win either way: they make a ton of money installing packages and then even more customizing them. They therefore have little incentive to talk their clients out of cracking the box (since it keeps their revenue streams going).

What's the answer? Quite simply, don't crack the box. ERP and CRM applications are far from perfect, but they're more rather than less likely to satisfy the lion's share of your real requirements. Resist the temptation to violate one of the more significant of Murphy's laws: the last 10 percent of a project will consume the last 90 percent of the resources. Although I have never been a huge fan of embedded-software-processes-should-define-business-processes arguments, I'd look long and hard at proposals to reroute data or redefine functions by poking around with ERP or CRM engines—which are finicky at best and downright inexplicable at worst. Not only will customization often result in conventional software failures, but it will unnecessarily complicate your integration and interoperability challenges, spike the cost, make it hard to measure performance, and otherwise thrust you into the role of packaged enterprise software architect, a role that you're probably unprepared to perform.

If you're not intimidated by Murphy laws or the law of unintended consequences, have a ton of extra money, and believe that you always know best, then by all means crack open the box and have some fun. But if you're prudent and disciplined, post "Keep Out" signs all over the office—and send engraved versions to the vendors who would just love you to crack open the box, take the engine all apart, add some custom parts, and then try to put it all back together again, good as new, except better. Right.

Data Information and Decision Making: Platforms, Analysis, and Real-Time Management

A few weeks ago I had the pleasure of meeting with Raj Gupta, the chairman and CEO of Rohm and Haas, a global specialty chemicals company that had recently—and successfully—implemented the SAP R/3 ERP platform. After I picked his brain about how he pulled off a monster project on time and within budget, I asked him about benefits realization. "If you could have one thing from all of the time, effort, and money you spent on the R/3 implementation," I asked, "what would it be?" Without hesitation he said: "friendly data." "Friendly data," I said, "what do you mean by that?" "Simple," he said, "accurate data that's in a form that's easy to access and understand, and therefore the basis for good decision making."

We spend trillions of dollars a year globally on technology. Some companies spend billions every year. All the CEO wants is "friendly data." Can we provide it? What steps should we take to ensure that we comply with his—and lots of other similar—requests.

Data lies at the heart of the new collaborative business models; without data it's impossible to customize, personalize, up-sell, cross-sell, automate, or gather business intelligence in real time. But to achieve these capabilities, data, information, content, and even "knowledge" all need to integrate—and be secure, accurate, and accessible.

Getting the Platforms Ready

Collaborative business models drive data integration. We can't become collaborative unless data (information, knowledge, and content) are integrated. Over the years, we've deployed lots of different database management systems and lots of applications that had specific data requirements. Consequently, depending on the amount of data variation in your company, you may be exquisitely ill-positioned for collaboration. Or, if you've had some discipline along the way and only have one or two database platforms, you're in a pretty good position to collaborate.

Data integration efforts complement application integration work. Some of the enterprise application integration (EAI) tools include (data) extraction, translation, and loading (ETL), and vice versa. Investments in integration technologies should be driven by the results of strategic planning exercises that position companies within the collaboration space. These scenarios will determine what applications are needed and the extent to which the applications and data must be integrated. But regardless of where you find yourself in the collaboration space, you'll need to invest in data (and application) integration technologies.

If you have lots of different kinds of data in different places, then you need to develop a data integration strategy, which may involve building some kind of data warehouse. Once you build a warehouse, you can conduct all kinds of analyses— analyses that facilitate collaboration. Over time, you need to reduce the need for all this integration by moving to fewer data platforms and standardizing the analysis tools—the tools you use to mine the data for collaborative insights and models.

Getting Ready for Analysis

Data warehouses, data marts, and special-purpose hybrids require some serious thinking about where you think you'll ultimately end up, how much money's available for the construction of these artifacts, what users will require, and—relatedly—what the data mining tools will look like.

As I said earlier in this chapter, OLTP is what everyone's been doing for a long, long time. OLAP—especially when coupled with data warehousing technology— is how data, information, and knowledge get usefully exploited. It's the link to business intelligence and business analytics.

OLTP is the mother of all analysis. It provides insight into current internal data, especially as it applies to operations and real-time transactions. OLAP provides insight when the focus is strategic, when the need is for reports and analyses, when access is unstructured, and when optimization is an objective.

Information analysis requirements extend from OLAP capabilities to desktop OLAP (DOLAP), relational OLAP (ROLAP), and multidimensional OLAP (MOLAP). DOLAP includes PC-based tools that support the analysis of data marts and warehouses; ROLAP includes server applications that support analyses cubed from a RDBMS or a data warehouse; while MOLAP exploits predeveloped data cubes.

Decision making and management is the end game of database management, data warehousing, OLAP, and data mining—all in the context of collaborative business.

Everyone's got data in one place or another. Some of it's in Oracle databases, some in IBM/DB2 databases, and some still in Sybase databases. This operational data—especially if it's in different forms—often needs to get translated into a form where it can be used by any number of people in your company to perform all sorts of analyses. "Translation" results in the development of data warehouses and smaller data marts that support all varieties of online analysis and ultimately "data mining," the ability to ask all kinds of questions about your employees, customers, suppliers, and partners.

All this means that it's wise to invest in the right data mining tools once your database platform will support the kinds of analyses that business collaboration requires.

One of the interesting trends to watch is database/data mining optimization around specific application platforms. IBM, for example, just announced that it will optimize its DB2 database for SAP applications. Optimization, according to the announcement, means that IBM will develop a customized version of DB2 to optimize the performance of SAP applications. Other database and data mining vendors will no doubt do the same. This means that the path to mining and analysis may well be mapped by large vendors who continue to drive industry consolidation. Over time, if present trends continue, there will be a relatively small number of vendors working to optimize each other's products.

Getting Ready for Real-Time Management

Everyone's working on UDA from all tethered and untethered devices. Eventually, structured, unstructured, hierarchical, relational, object-oriented data, information, and knowledge will be ubiquitously accessible. Although we're a few years away from all this, it's helpful to understand the Holy Grail and to adapt your business models in the general direction of this capability. Microsoft, IBM and Oracle all have plans to provide UDA. It's important to stay abreast of their progress—and the implications to your business models and processes. Collaboration will require UDA, and integration is the short-term path to that goal. Longer-term, if acquisition decisions are made properly, there should be less need to integrate disparate databases.

Ultimately, all of this is about real-time transaction processing. Companies should begin to rearchitecture their data → information → decision-making strategies with real-time transaction processing in mind. This means that they should begin to consolidate their data, identify mainstream database management, analysis, and mining applications, and extend the collaborative business processes enabled by integrated data and real-time analysis.

Put another way, all of this is about satisfying requests for "friendly data." If we keep decision makers happy with timely, accurate, and diagnostic data and information that supports decision making, we'll succeed. Along the way, it appears we'll be able to leverage the efforts of several major software vendors to accelerate progress.

Open Source Software Redux

Last year, one of my graduate student teams pitched me on the virtues of open source software. Earlier in this chapter, we analyzed some open source alternatives to Microsoft Office, Siebel Systems CRM, and other proprietary applications and even some database management software, and concluded that while they were all impressive, they were still not quite the real thing. Nor, we concluded, would they offer the cost savings that everyone had been lobbied to expect. I then took the analysis to our CIO Advisory Council, 25 or so CIOs from the Greater Philadelphia area, and asked them straight up: "What are you doing about open source software in your companies?" Note that the companies in the room included Rohm and Haas, Unisys, Johnson & Johnson, Sunoco, Wawa, Vanguard, Aramark, Sungard, the Philadelphia Stock Exchange, Cigna, and Wyeth-Ayerst, among other prominent companies. The people taking that ad hoc survey spent about $5 billion a year on technology—surely they'd be interested in something that might save them some serious money.

What do you think that they said?

Nearly all of them were anything but enthusiastic about open source software (aside from the use of "not on *my* desktop" Linux and Apache). Several of them indicated that the cost savings they might enjoy from migration would be eaten alive by the migration cost itself, not to mention the hassle and weirdo factors. But that was a year ago.

Sun Microsystems and Google recently announced a partnership whereby Google would distribute Sun's software including its competitor to Microsoft Office, OpenOffice. If you look at the list of open source alternatives to the proprietary systems that we buy, deploy, and support, the list is getting longer and longer—and the features richer and richer. The not-for-profit and for-profit open source support community is also getting much more sophisticated and professional. More importantly, many of the largest technology vendors long ago embraced open source software.

Are we there yet?

We're getting closer—and it's not the features and compatibility of open source software that are getting us there (though it certainly helps the open source cause). It's the structure and mechanics of the software industry that's making open source more attractive to increasing numbers of small, medium, and even large companies.

Yes, I know I already said that my CIO Advisory Council rejected open source software and that my graduate students made a less-than-convincing case against the proprietary software giants. But that was last year and there are now some trends that bear very close watching over the next few years—trends that might very well change everyone's minds.

The first is pricing. At some point, technology managers are going to resist the sheer cost of buying—and maintaining—enterprise software. Although I realize that there are always "deals" out there, enterprise software is incredibly expensive (and there are human factors experts out there telling us over and over again that most users use barely 10 percent of the features embedded in large software suites—and then there's the "shelfware" issue).

The second trend is hosting. Many companies are looking seriously at renting software instead of buying, deploying, and supporting complex applications. As the hosting/renting trend continues, companies will revisit how they spend their technology dollars in some creative ways. The evolution of thin client architectures is part of this trend.

Third, the new software architectures based largely on Web services standards will enable whole new service-oriented and event-driven architectures that will challenge traditional software distribution and pricing models (this is part of the Sun/Google long-term strategy).

These three trends will place tremendous pressure on the large proprietary software vendors to rethink their pricing strategies. If they fail to adjust their prices, more and more companies will defect to alternative software acquisition and support approaches. Some will rent, some will move toward new architectures, and some will strongly consider open source alternatives.

This will all play out over the next three to five years—not in a decade or two. The major software vendors can influence the direction all this takes, but the only way they can guarantee market share is to reduce their profits. Regardless of how proactive the major vendors become, the three pressure points described above will accelerate changes in how software is designed, acquired, distributed, supported—and priced.

Does this mean that open source software will become more popular over time? It depends on how the software market shakes out. Here are some scenarios that will influence the adoption of open source software:

- If the large proprietary software vendors fail to radically alter their pricing policies, then more and more companies will look to open source alternatives ...
- If the expected trends toward hosting and renting fail to continue and the large proprietary software vendors fail to radically alter their pricing policies, the adoption of open source software will dramatically increase ...
- If whole new software architectures fail to evolve, expected trends toward hosting and renting fail to continue, and the large proprietary software vendors fail to radically alter their pricing policies, the adoption of open source could become as popular—if not more so—than proprietary software ...
- Let's also acknowledge the role that open source software might play in renting/hosting and the new architectures that could be based on open source applications and open source components ...

In addition to the scenarios described above, there are other drivers of open source software adoption as well. Many start-up technology companies have deployed open source software as part of their initial technology platforms. They have done so because of cost and because of flexibility. This trend is significant because some start-ups will have a disproportionate influence on software adoption trends, especially if the start-up business model is to extend open source software!

One thing is for sure: the open source movement is gaining momentum and serious technology managers are beginning to rethink how they might participate in the open source movement. So what would you say if I asked you straight up: "What are you doing about open source software in your company?" The answer is probably something like "looking at it." The problem with this perspective is that it fails to appreciate the potential sea change that could occur in the near-term future. If this sea change occurs, there will be all kinds of scrambling around to determine what an optimal software acquisition strategy should be. How many companies will just throw up their hands and scream "outsource it all—I am tired of dealing with all this nonsense!?" How many will try to mix-and-match software deployment strategies, only ending up with a hodge-podge of proprietary and open source software? How many will stay the proprietary course? How many will aggressively tilt toward open source software solutions?

Three years ago I was unimpressed with open source software. Now I have reconsidered its functionality, support, cost-effectiveness, and adoption prospects. I am influenced most by changing software delivery models. It is very unlikely that the status quo will persist for very long. Open source software will play a large role in what develops over the next few years. It's time to start reassessing your approach to open source software and how you plan to acquire, deploy, and support enterprise software in the next few years.

Chapter 6

Strategic Effectiveness

Appropriate CRM

Let's talk about customer relationship management (CRM) and what I'll call the price/value/service ratio and its relationship to the CRM process and technology investments.

But before we get to that, let's agree that CRM is not technology, software, or "architecture": CRM is a state of mind, a philosophy, and a business strategy. I cannot believe the number of companies I see—still—that believe that a CRM (in-house or hosted) application is the answer to their customer relationship problems. Successful CRM software applications that we buy (from Siebel) or rent (from Salesforce.com) assume a variety of things to be true before implementation (though the vendors tend to hide many of them in fine print). Newsflash: If your company isn't customer friendly, technology will not change a thing (except the technology budget).

CRM—*the philosophy*—versus CRM—*the technology*—regards customers as life-long clients whose personal and professional lives can be monetized through the proactive management of the client's needs, values, and ability and desire to pay. CRM *the technology* is about applications that leverage customer data, supplier data, company data, and even vertical industry data into actionable information. The disconnect that sometimes occurs is between the corporate and technology views of customers, not different perspectives on how software applications should be acquired and deployed. There are also disconnects among what companies sell, what they charge, and what customers are willing to pay.

Customer-centered companies have wide and deep protocols around customer care. They also have specific protocols around the acquisition of new customers. Nordstrom department stores get it; Ritz-Carlton hotels get it; Lexus car dealers get it. While far from "perfect," these and other vendors understand that the extra profit they embed in their products and services better be offset by the quality of the service they provide. Many customers are quite willing to pay more than they should in return for over-the-top service. High-end vendors have always understood this and manage their customers accordingly. Many middle-end vendors also treat their customers elegantly; while some others offer alternative value propositions to their customers—like low prices—as a trade-off to mediocre or downright poor service.

The CRM danger zone is reached when companies misjudge the product/value/customer service relationship ratio of customer care and investment. Some companies, for example, are in the middle of the price/value hierarchy but provide horrible service. Other companies are at the very top and provide marginal service. (Any company at the top of the price/value hierarchy that provides horrible service is unlikely to stay there.) The CRM success zone is reached when a company synchronizes its price/value/service ratios with investments in CRM processes and technology.

Where is your company in the price/value/service space? If all your customers care about is low prices, then why invest in elaborate CRM processes or technologies? All it will do is increase your costs, lower your margins—and eventually require you to raise prices—which will alienate your price-obsessed clientele. If you are on the higher end of the price vector—or aspire to climb the price/value hierarchy—then you need to make sure that your prices, value, and service are synchronized.

The decision to invest in CRM *technology* comes much later. Companies need to understand who they are, where they are, and what they want to be when they grow up before talking to a CRM software sales rep. Figure 6.1 suggests where CRM technology investments make the most sense (the dark gray zone) and where it might make sense to keep CRM process and technology investments to a minimum (the light gray zone). The medium gray zone is where the real CRM action is, where CRM management gurus and technology vendors can make real money. Dark gray zone companies will spend on process and technology because they understand the price/value/service ratios well (and because they can pass the costs on to their loyal, accepting customers anyway). Light gray zone companies should underinvest in CRM processes and technology because their customers already have low service expectations. The medium gray zone companies are really not sure what to do. Clever CRM vendors can excite them about climbing into the dark gray zone—where they will spend big bucks on CRM. Or they might be convinced that they have no hope of ever behaving (or charging) like Nordstrom, so they might as well fall into the light gray zone and kill all CRM investments. Or, with just a little

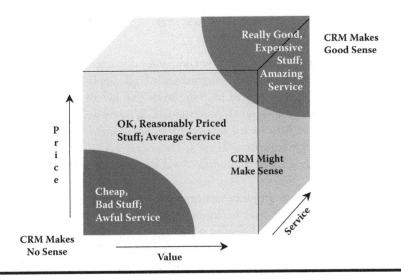

Figure 6.1   Price/value/service ratios and likely CRM investment payback.

investment in CRM, they can maintain their medium gray zone positions and even make some more money along the way. You decide.

Web 2.0 and the Enterprise

Well, it's all the rage. Publications like *Business 2.0, Fast Company,* and even *Business Week* are all writing about Web 2.0, the new net and the next digital gold rush. What the hell is going on now? Is this another bubble? Will Web 2.0 companies crash and burn like their parents?

I thought a lot about this over the past couple of years and really wanted to stay almost neutral on the rise of wikis, blogs, podcasts, RSS filters, mashups, crowd-sourcing, and service-oriented architecture (SOA) and the impact they would have on us all, especially the enterprise. Initially I thought that these technologies were destined to support social networking in all its glory. But after thinking about it some more I realized that important changes were occurring, changes that would affect the entire computing and communications spectrum.

I hate to say this. I was in the very heart of the dot.com bubble when I guided Safeguard Scientifics, Inc. into one Internet investment after another. We took lots of companies public in those days. Only a few survived. Many of the companies in the Safeguard family crashed and burned and lots of good people suffered. Is anything that different now? I find myself muttering phrases like "sea change," "game over," and "killer apps" way too often. I really thought I was cured.

So is this a sea change? I am pained to say yes.

Here's only some of what it all means:

1. Wikis could revolutionize the way companies document policies, processes, and procedures. HR policies, sales manuals, and supply chain management processes can be documented in living wikis that evolve over time from the input of in-house and external professionals. Why do we need to hire a consultant to tell us how to sell to our customers when we have countless in-house subject matter experts? There are lots of questions like this that can be at least partially answered in wikis—and let's not forget how wikis can be used for training.

2. Blogs can be used to vet ideas, strategies, projects, and programs. They can—along with wikis—be used for knowledge management. (Do we really need monster applications for knowledge management?) They can also be used as living suggestion boxes and chat rooms designed to allow employees to vent and contribute in attributable and anonymous ways.

3. Podcasts can be used for pre-meeting, in-meeting, and post-meeting documentation. Repositories of podcasts can contribute to institutional memory and together comprise a rich audit trail of corporate initiatives and decision making.

4. RSS filters can be used to fine-tune information flows of all kinds to employees, customers, suppliers, and partners. These custom news feeds can leverage information in almost effortless ways. I love the fact that we tell them what to do and they just do it. (Does anyone remember PointCast?)

5. Mashup technology makes it easier to develop applications that solve specific problems—if only temporarily. Put some end users in a room full of APIs and watch what happens. Suddenly it's possible to combine incompatible pieces into coherent wholes with the complements of companies that understand the value of sharing (for profit, of course).

6. Crowdsourcing can be used to extend the enterprise via the Web and leverage the expertise of lots of professionals on to corporate problems. If it's good enough for Procter & Gamble and DuPont, it should be good enough for everyone. Got some tough R&D problems? Post them on the Web. The crowdsourcing model will change corporate problem solving—once everyone gets over the fear of taking gifts from strangers.

7. Service-oriented architecture is the mother of Web 2.0 technologies. The whole notion of mix-and-match with help from strangers tethered to each other on the Web is a fundamental change in the way we think about software design, development, and delivery. SOA is actually a decentralizing force that will enable companies to solve computational and display problems much faster than they ever did in the past. What will it be like when we can point to glue and functionality and have them assemble themselves into solutions right before our eyes?

Look, I grew out of the hype culture a while ago, but I must admit that the things happening now clearly challenge the industry's fundamentals—at least the fundamentals that have been around for decades. The good news is that there are legions of Web 2.0 devotees who will accelerate the changes occurring now. The bad news is that for every two steps we take forward we'll take one backward because change always has as many enemies as it has champions. Ignore Web 1.0 Luddites and focus squarely on Web 3.0 while you happily exploit Web 2.0 tools, technologies, and perspectives. In less than a decade we'll look back on these days as the beginning of the next new thing, a time when collaboration redefined itself right in front of our screens.

Thinking about Web 2.0: The Right Questions for the Right Impact

Web 2.0 tools and technologies—like wikis, blogs, podcasts, mashups, folksonomies, RSS filters, social networks, virtual worlds, and crowdsourcing—offer new opportunities for corporate productivity and management. But how do you know which ones to pilot? How do you know what to assess? Here's a general-purpose R&D project plan that should help you navigate the Web 2.0 waters—and, most importantly, help you decide where to spend your Web 2.0 dollars.

The R&D Project

The challenge is to understand and measure the impact that wikis, blogs, podcasts, folksonomies, mashups, social networks, virtual worlds, RSS filters, and crowdsourcing have on corporate productivity and management. As global competition increases, and as innovation itself becomes increasingly decentralized, the mantra to "work smarter, not harder" is more relevant than ever. Web 2.0 technologies, if deployed properly, may well permit companies to cost-effectively increase their productivity and, ultimately, improve their competitive advantage—but there is very little known about the adoption patterns of Web 2.0 technologies or the impact these technologies can have on productivity and management.

The objectives of the R&D project are to:

■ Understand the *range* of Web 2.0 tools and techniques that might improve corporate productivity and management
■ Identify *how* Web 2.0 tools and techniques can be used to enhance corporate productivity and management
■ Measure the impact via the *collection* of data, interviews, and direct observation
■ Determine what *your Web 2.0 investment* should look like

The kinds of questions to be addressed include (see the full R&D matrix below):

- Can wikis, blogs, RSS filters, and folksonomies help companies with various forms of knowledge management?
- Can wikis be used to build quick "corporate encyclopedias," training manuals, and other forms of documentation?
- Can blogs be used to vet ideas about markets, customers, and strategies?
- Can podcasts be effectively used to document products?
- Can folksonomies be used to organize structured and unstructured content?
- Can RSS filters be used to create content streams to improve CRM?
- Can mashups be used for rapid application development (RAD)?
- Can crowdsourcing be used to stimulate innovation?

The research methods you might consider include:

- Profiling the range of Web 2.0 technologies available to you
- Defining "impact" across multiple dimensions of productivity
- Collecting data from designated participants in the pilot on the use of Web 2.0 technologies and the impact areas through a combination of surveys, interviews, and direct observation
- Developing a survey instrument
- Developing interview scripts
- Identifying business unit participants for interviewing
- Identifying business unit participants for direct observation
- Analyzing the data to identify usage patterns and impact
- Identifying correlations from the data among technologies and impact areas
- Measuring the relative impact of individual and groups of technologies on individual and groups of impact areas
- Integrating the interview and observational data into empirical analyses

Anticipated project results might include:

- An internal white paper on the impact that Web 2.0 technologies is having on productivity and management
- A plan to extend your Web 2.0 pilots and a comprehensive Web 2.0 investment strategy

The R&D project will determine which Web 2.0 technologies enhance which objectives. Hypotheses should not be developed for all the cells in the technologies/impact matrix (Figure 6.2), because some of the technologies will not map onto all the impact areas. But there will be a number of hypotheses that can be tested to measure just the right mix of technologies and impact.

Web 2.0 / Impact	Wikis	Blogs	RSS	Folks	Mashups	Crowds	Social	Podcasts	Virtual
Knowledge Management	✓	✓	✓	✓				✓	
Rapid Application Development				✓	✓	✓			
Customer Relationship Management	✓	✓	✓		✓	✓	✓	✓	✓
Collaboration/Communication	✓	✓	✓	✓			✓	✓	✓
Innovation	✓	✓	✓		✓	✓			
Training	✓	✓				✓		✓	

Figure 6.2 A Web 2.0 R&D matrix.

The Web 2.0 technologies to be defined and measured include:

- Wikis
- Blogs
- RSS Filters
- Folksonomies
- Mashups
- Podcasts
- Crowdsourcing
- Social networks
- Virtual worlds

The corporate productivity and management impact areas include:

- Knowledge management (KM)
- RAD
- CRM
- Collaboration and communication
- Innovation
- Training

Figure 6.2 summarizes the R&D plan.

The checks in the matrix indicate some initial thoughts about where impact will be most felt as you deploy more and more Web 2.0 technologies. These initial thoughts—customized to your organization—will guide your data collection and analysis but will not limit your data analysis. Ultimately, the research will permit generalizations about where Web 2.0 technologies will have the most impact and where you should invest to gain maximum impact.

The R&D Project Tasks

The following six tasks can be performed. You can modify them as you see fit, but the tasks should provide a good basis for the business case for your Web 2.0 pilot R&D project.

Task 1—Profile the Range of Available Web 2.0 Technologies

This task will involve the identification of the range of Web 2.0 technologies that have the potential to improve your corporate productivity and management. The initial list will include wikis, blogs, RSS filters, folksonomies, mashups, podcasts, crowdsourcing, social networks, and virtual worlds, but there could be additional technologies included in the research. The technologies will be profiled according to their maturity, their ease of integration into the mainstream computing and communications architecture, and their ability to adapt to your vertical industry. The identification and profiling of Web 2.0 technologies will permit the specification of the pilot's independent variables.

Task 2—Define "Impact" across Multiple Dimensions of Productivity and Management

This task will involve the identification of the range of corporate impact areas including KM, RAD, CRM, collaboration, communication, innovation, and training, among other related areas that you determine are meaningful to your company. The identification and profiling of the impact areas will permit the specification of the dependent variables in the proposed analysis. The impact areas will be identified according to their productivity and management efficacy to the overall performance of the organization.

Task 3—Collect Data on the Use of Web 2.0 Technologies and the Impact Areas through a Combination of Surveys, Interviews, and Direct Observation

This task will involve the collection of data designed to measure the impact that Web 2.0 technologies are having on your corporate productivity and management. Several forms of data will be collected. First, a survey instrument will be developed to measure the range of Web 2.0 applications that your company has adopted and the impact the technologies have had. Surveys will be e-mailed to managers and executives. Second, data will be collected from interviews with managers and executives. Business units will be identified that are willing to be early adopters of Web 2.0 technology. Finally, several business units will be targeted for direct observation, where specific Web 2.0 technologies will be analyzed in action.

Task 4—Analyze the Data to Identify Usage Patterns and Impact

This task will involve the identification of correlations from the survey data among the technologies and impact areas. The task will also involve the measurement of the relative impact of individual and groups of technologies on individual and groups of impact areas. Finally, the survey, interview, and observational data will be integrated.

Task 5—Report the Findings

This task will report the findings in several ways. First, an internal white paper will be written that describes the project and its results. Next, the company will consider developing some articles to be published in professional trade publications that showcase the project's results.

Task 6—Develop a Web 2.0 Investment Strategy

The final task is to develop a Web 2.0 investment strategy that identifies the Web 2.0 technologies that will receive additional investment, as well as those that will receive no additional funding. It should also include a project plan, a project champion (your company's "Web 2.0 Czar"?), and, of course, a budget, schedule, milestones, and the like.

Conclusion

Web 2.0 technologies have enormous potential—but how much is uncertain. The R&D pilot described here might help you better understand how and where Web 2.0 technologies might contribute to improved productivity and management. The primary message here is that new technologies—regardless of their origin, nature, or the amount of hype surrounding them—should be assessed for the contribution they might make to your organization before large-scale deployment occurs. Although Web 2.0 technologies definitely show promise, you need to better understand the depth of that promise before investing too heavily. The hope is that this short R&D proposal can help.

The Reality of New

Companies often talk a good game about innovation. Usually they talk better than they act. Has anyone ever heard anyone say that innovation was bad? Of course not. But the same people who pay lip service to the creative process are often the same ones who create financial and organizational disincentives to the process. It's sort of like what the federal government says—and does—about alternative energy; politicians talk a good game but haven't raised spending on the problem in years.

There's an important distinction among invention, innovation, and commercialization that we should acknowledge.

Invention occurs in garages and large corporate R&D shops: IBM and Microsoft will spend a combined $15+ billion on R&D in 2007. Venture capitalists invest billions of dollars every year in start-up businesses built on new digital technology. Invention requires risky investments—almost speculative investments—in technologies that may or may not mature enough to get them to the next innovation segment of the value chain.

Innovation builds on invention on its way to commercialization. It involves the development and construction of a product or a service. This segment includes prototyping and pilot applications. The purpose of innovation is to calibrate just how solid the inventive foundation on which the product or service is built really is. Real money is spent here to develop a product or service and prepare it for the marketplace. It's important to note that the invention-to-innovation process is not always owned or managed by the same company. In fact, this is where major interruptions in the value chain often occur. Some companies, like Microsoft, are as good (or better) at innovating as they are at inventing. Cisco *acquires* a lot of its inventions from which it innovates new products and services. Some companies are better at innovation than they are at invention—and vice versa. The skill sets are different and often distributed across several companies, consultants, and even intellectual property (IP) lawyers. Prototyping *is* fundamentally different from manufacturing.

Other skill sets are required to fully commercialize technology. The third segment of the value chain requires effective distribution, sales, and support. Some companies are better at packaging products than they are at innovating them, just as some companies are better at sales than they are at marketing. Commercialization should be the end result of successful innovation, and successful commercialization results in a solid ROI.

So where is your company on this invention → innovation → commercialization continuum? Put another way, what *do* you do well—and what *should* you do well?

Do companies usually know what they do well and poorly? Not as often as they should, that's for sure. The model I like the best is Cisco's acquisitive approach to "new." It buys new. Of course, it spends heavily on R&D, but it also plugs its technology holes with acquisition after acquisition. Microsoft continues to confuse me: it spends a ton on R&D and yet struggles to invent whole new computing models and technologies. IBM chugs along but concentrates its invention in a few hardware and software areas, like database technology.

Do you know where you excel—and where you need help? The toughest assessments are self-assessments. Think realistically about who you are, and if you have trouble figuring out what to do, think Cisco.

It's the Data, Stupid

It seems that after 30 years in this business, I still don't know how to listen when someone asks for something really simple, like actionable data. I'm not sure if it's a failing in me or my clients, but it seems that after all this time I still sometimes just don't get it. But I'm not the only one who doesn't get it. How many enterprise software vendors make it tough to get to the data that managers need? Yeah, that's right, all of them.

What am I talking about? I'm talking about our inability to translate breakfast, lunch, and dinner rants into interoperable technologies that provide decision makers with the right data at the right time for the right price. Why is this so hard?

Thirty years ago, I was told that data was king. It's taken me three decades to fully understand the importance of that simple statement and the importance attached to someone's need for information presented in the right way at the right time. Today, we think about all this as business intelligence (BI), which has become an enormous industry in and of itself. But it's more than that. It's the ability to answer questions about customers, growth, profitability, supply chains, inventories, pricing, and a whole lot more—instantly. Can we do this today? If the billions that companies are paying for BI vendors is any indication, we can't. BI today is a technology, not a business solution.

Just the other day it happened again. In a discussion about the development of a company's technology strategy, it became very clear that what the business wanted from the strategy was one thing: data. Did it care all that much about infrastructure, about the wonderfully reliable messaging platform, about the near-zero-latent network, about the upgrade to Vista? No. All it cared about was the ability to get data into its hands when it needs it to make decisions about only three things: how to make money, how to save money, how to improve service. If the "strategy" could help it do one or more of those things, it would be very happy. The rest, from its perspective, is boilerplate.

In many respects, this is the ultimate conclusion to the "IT doesn't matter" argument launched in 2003 by Nick Carr. I have said for years that Nick was half right—that operational technology has definitely commoditized but that strategic technology could still be a huge differentiator—when acquired, deployed and supported correctly. The business doesn't want to discuss how elegant, secure, reliable, or scalable the infrastructure is; it is obsessed with what technology can do for its ability to save money, make money, and improve service. Or, put another way, it is obsessed with its own performance and securing excellent employee reviews for itself and its teams. Technology's role is to make that happen, and in order to make that happen, we all need to focus—again—on data.

I used to draw cute distinctions between "data," "information," and "knowledge," you know, with information the extension of data and knowledge the end result of collective information interpreted by knowledge managers. Sure, the distinction was cute and even accurate—but no one really cares about how I—or anyone—slice up definitions of the same thing.

I actually feel a little stupid (I'm the "stupid" in the "it's the data, stupid"). I have been listening to the "data is king" and "friendly data" tunes for decades, but, unlike the Sade ("Your Love Is King") and James Taylor ("You've Got a Friend") songs that I can remember like it was "Yesterday" (another great song), I don't seem to understand what the words really mean.

So here's a simulated therapy session to help me through this conundrum:

Stupid (me): "So what does a CEO mean when he or she says: 'I want friendly data'?"

Data therapist: "What do you think he or she wants to say? What do you think he or she means by 'friendly'?"

Stupid: "You don't know"?

Data therapist: "How would I know? … I just facilitate things."

Stupid: "Do I get any lifelines"?

Data therapist: "Sure, it's your money."

Stupid: "Okay, let me call a C-level exec … C-level exec? Is that you? What do you need from me? What is 'friendly data,' anyway?"

C-level exec: "You really are stupid. It's so simple. Friendly data helps me make decisions. Friendly data is always there—accessible any way I want—via a Blackberry, an iPhone, or a PC. Friendly data is diagnostic—it helps me understand the current state and enables me to play what-if games. Friendly data is historical and anticipatory. Friendly data keeps me out of regulatory trouble. Friendly data helps me up-sell and cross-sell. Friendly data is a window into my products, services and—especially—my customers. Friendly data is dynamic and real-time. Friendly data never sleeps. What else do you want to know?"

Stupid: "We call that business intelligence. It's been around for years."

C-level exec: "Call it whatever you like. I really don't care."

Therapist: "This is going very well, but our time is up."

Stupid: "Same time next week?"

Therapist: "Sure."

Stupid: "Not you, stupid, I want to keep talking to the C-level exec. I need to become one. I need to feel the pain—and then make it go away. I might just be getting it. It really isn't about me at all. It's about C-level execs and what they need—and they need data."

C-level exec: "I'll work with you, of course, but you really have to get smarter about all this. I just saw something about on-demand BI that caught my eye. There's always someone who will listen. I'd love it to be you, but if you can't get by your data/metadata/information/knowledge/extraction/integration neuroses, I will move on."

Therapist: "I can cure him."

Stupid: "I can cure myself."

So let's agree to screen all our technology initiatives through a data filter. Let's agree to start with business processes and three business objectives. Let's quietly invest in data architecture and infrastructure without describing ad nauseum how wonderful our master data management is. Let's collaboratively build dashboards and marry them with mobile computing. Let's define the end game as real-time dynamic transaction processing. Let's pretend we're in a company cockpit and all we have are sensors, gauges, switches, and displays to fly the company. Let's stop being stupid.

They Know What We Like—And Where We Are!

Brace yourself for an annoying, though sometimes helpful, trend. Some think of it as "business intelligence," some as "personalization," and some just as 24/7 selling. As databases become more integrated, as shopping becomes more digital, and as "always-on" access devices become more pervasive, we can expect to be treated to all sorts of offers. It's another definition of "profiling"—and to some it feels like terrorism! If we allow them, companies will track us down like dogs and threaten us with offers we cannot refuse. We'll be slaughtered by our inability to just say no.

I already get e-mail (and snail mail) from companies that have profiled me. They've analyzed data about where I live, what I earn, and what I buy to determine what I like and what I'd pay for what they're selling. This is first-generation mass customization, child's play compared to what's coming down the information superhighway.

Built on much the same data that mass marketing assumes, mass customization infers beyond the simpler correlations—like age, wealth, time of year—to specific ideas about what you and I would really like to buy, based on inferences about us as part of a larger group *and* as individual consumers.

Contact can be "personalized" with customers, suppliers, partners, and employees through all varieties of messages including sales, marketing, service, and distribution. Over time—given how low digital transaction costs are compared to other ways companies touch the members of their value and supply chains, and how ubiquitous digital communication is becoming—companies will reassess their advertising and marketing budgets. They will go increasingly personal.

There's a great scene in the Tom Cruise/Steven Spielberg film, *Minority Report*. Cruise is walking in a city in 2054 and, as his eyes are (iris) scanned, he's immediately pitched a whole slate of personalized products and services. Imagine waiting for a plane or train and receiving countless messages about stuff you could buy that you already like and use all the time—but now its on sale 12 feet away? What if all employees, customers, suppliers, and partners could be pitched in ways that matched their interests, values, and personalities?

How will all this happen? It's all about the depth, location, and quality of customer data. It's also about the analyses performed on this data. Some companies have excellent behavioral scientists who run the data every which way in search of correlations that explain what customers value and why they buy what they do. Years ago in graduate school I wondered why I had to learn all about multiple regression equations. Now I understand how sales and marketing professionals could not possibly survive without solving all sorts of equations designed to explain which factors (independent variables) explain which outcomes (dependent variables). The power here is amazing. It's possible, for example, to determine:

- When to digitally (via browsers, cell phones, wireless PDAs, pagers) interrupt customers with a deal—and when not to interrupt them ...
- What size discounts need to be, by person, by season of the year, by customer location and time of day ...
- What combinations of products can be sold; what products don't mix with others ...
- What short-term and longer-term life events influence which purchases ...
- What forms and content of customer service each customer prefers ...

This is just a sampling of the kind of personalized and customized inferences that can be made; others are in the lab!

The trend is clear: customization and personalization will accelerate as the ability to integrate and correlate preference data—and instantly communicate with customers—increases. As inferential data and total access collide with location finders—like global positioning systems (GPS)—we'll never be safe again.

Is this a good thing or a bad thing? Here are three scenarios. You wake up in the morning in a bad mood. You tell your personal (digital software) agent that you will accept no offers from digital hucksters unless they double the discounts they usually offer—and if that's unacceptable you're going off the air. Or, you're in the middle of an important discussion and your cell phone beeps with an interesting offer—but only if you respond in the next ten minutes. Or, you're traveling on business in a strange city and it's close to dinner time. Your PDA buzzes with an idea: there's an Italian restaurant—it of course knows you like Italian food (what time it is and precisely where you are)—about a block from where you're standing with a table waiting for you and your colleagues. No reservation necessary; no phone call to confirm; just a quick digital reply on the device—which immediately displays the menu, the specials, and the wine list. As you walk toward the restaurant you and your associates discuss what goes best with what ...

Fortunately, or unfortunately, all this is inevitable. Get ready to be profiled—and attacked!

Back to the Future: Herding 3,000 Cats through a Worm Hole

I was recently struck by a solution recommended to a huge real estate company, a solution that I had a hand in crafting. I was also struck by how the old adage—"everything that goes around, comes around"—is still so true. While we don't talk that much anymore about "dumb terminals" or "green screens," we do talk about thin clients, server-based computing, and portals all the time. Here's a (true) story that demonstrates where "solutions" are going, that is, how solutions are dependent on the overall situation, the "users" of technology, the culture of a company, and the efficacy of a specific technology. As you read through the case, note how we used a relatively simple—but powerful and reliable—technology to solve a difficult problem—keeping cats (in this case, 3,000 real estate agents) happy. After I describe the case, we'll turn to some (old) lessons (re-)learned.

The Situation

Prudential Fox & Roach Realtors is an independently owned and operated member of Prudential Real Estate Affiliate, Inc. It's the fourth-largest provider of real estate services in the United States, with $15.5 billion in annual sales. The company operates 70 offices in the Pennsylvania, Delaware, and New Jersey area; there are 900 employees. Prudential Fox & Roach also contracts with more than 3,300 independent sales agents who work on commission—one of the key facts in this story.

The real estate "culture" has been relatively conservative in its exploitation of the Web and the online processes that Web-based applications enable. Companies like Lending Tree were actually established in the mid- to late-1990s, but their early revenues were slow to ramp—until the roll out of broadband communications accelerated well into the general population. Real estate consumers (buyers and sellers) were also slow to embrace the Web until it became relatively easy to list or find homes via the Web. Now it's common practice to surf the Web for homes and then contact agents for visits.

The agents at Prudential Fox & Roach/Trident (its mortgage partner) were also relatively slow to adopt new technology, but over the past few years the adoption rate has improved significantly. The challenge for the company was to make sure that its agents' use of the technology enhanced—not encumbered—real estate transaction processing. This is another key fact here: too much technology would swamp even the most willing technology adopters; too little would threaten agents' ability to compete.

Prudential Fox & Roach/Trident sought a better way to give its mobile sales agents and branch office employees access to the myriad applications, forms, and databases, such as multiple listing services, needed to list and sell a property. Specifically, the company wanted to deliver applications over the Internet, which offered wide availability and a familiar browser interface for agents, many of whom are not technologically sophisticated.

The agents are always on the move and frequently work evenings and weekends so they can accommodate the schedules of buyers and sellers; the company needed a way to give these agents simple, real-time information access from any location, such as a home office, so they could make the most of their time with clients—and if required, provide quotes or calculations on the spot. But because these Realtors are independent contractors and work on computers and network connections Prudential does not control (the third key fact), it was vital to provide security for the company's corporate applications and data. Stated somewhat differently, it would be impossible to control the applications if they were local to every agent's computer.

Prior to the implementation of the solution, the company attempted to deploy and support thousands of agents and office employees with a conventional hardware/software implementation model. Soon after the roll out of this solution, however, major problems began to arise.

Among the more troubling problems were:

- Inability to keep the applications that support the real estate transaction process current
- Inability to keep the process reliable or secure
- Inability to allow the process to rapidly scale
- Inability to keep ahead of the many "break and fix" requirements among computers that were "personal" or used for other than real estate business
- Inability to manage the process through distributed—but ungoverned—management policies and procedures

In short, the traditional acquire/deploy/support model did not satisfy the collaborative communications requirements of real estate brokers or agents, or mortgage brokers, and had to be replaced by one that facilitated the secure connection of professionals, offices, branches, and partners.

The Citrix Access Infrastructure Solutions for Remote Office Connectivity was selected as the platform to solve the access—and support—problems.* The technology enables organizations to securely deliver applications and information to remote offices and contact centers and maintain those applications and information from a central location.

Prudential Fox & Roach/Trident implemented Citrix MetaFrame Secure Access Manager to augment its existing MetaFrame Presentation Server environment with secure access to applications and information over the Internet. More than 3,000 independent agents and 900 employees now use a single point of access to multiple applications, databases, forms and documents, and tools such as Web search engines from any standard Web browser. Applications deployed via the solution range from older 16-bit software to "homegrown" solutions. They include "Neighborhood Locator," "School Report," and "PC Forms" that are required for house closings.

Stop for a moment and think about the approach. We needed to keep the agents away from the software applications. We wanted to minimize our contact with the machines. We wanted ubiquitous access to the applications. We wanted to control the applications. We wanted to present a predetermined, predefined suite of applications that defined the real estate transaction. We wanted their personal computers and laptops to behave like dumb terminals in a server-based computing environment. This sounds familiar on two levels. First, it sounds like the old days when we controlled everything with mainframe-based applications, but it also feels like the future where applications will increasingly be hosted (and rented) by software vendors and their partners—a truly back to the future approach.

The Solution

Supporting independent agents involves supporting many users logging in from devices that Prudential Fox & Roach does not own, over connections it does not control, which raises security concerns. The Citrix platform provides a number of security measures that helps the company protect corporate information. The approach delivers standards-based encryption of data over the network and allows Prudential Fox & Roach to provide access based on user roles, so it can control who sees which information. With three main groups of users—corporate employees, employees of a subsidiary that provides mortgage and title services, and independent agents—Prudential Fox & Roach can provide access tailored to each group's individual business needs.

One of the goals of the implementation was to simplify both the user experience and the technology administrator's job. Many of the agents are not technically savvy, so simplicity is critical; the approach offers a consistent and simple interface no matter where the agent is logging on. In addition, it provides data backup for agents. For administrators, the platform enables efficient, centralized deployment of applications and updates. Under its former acquire/deploy/support model, Prudential Fox & Roach required three times as many field technical support staff to keep applications and systems up to date than it needs after the Citrix implementation.

The whole approach—with impact—can be summarized:

- **Applications deployed**
  - Multiple Listing Service (MLS), a real estate database
  - "School Report" by Homestore
  - "PC Forms" by PCFORMATION
  - "Know the Neighborhood" by eNeighborhoods
  - "RealFA$T Forms"

- **Networking environment**
  - Citrix MetaFrame XP Presentation Server, Feature Release 3 running on seven HP DL380 servers
  - Citrix MetaFrame Secure Access Manager
  - Microsoft Windows 2000 Servers
  - Frame Relay WAN, Internet

- **Benefits**
  - Shortens the sales cycle with Web-based access
  - Provides data security for remote and mobile users
  - Reduces support requirements by 60 percent
  - Simplifies computing for nontechnical users

Back to the Future

The initial agent technology support solution involved caring for each and every desktop and laptop computer for well over 3,000 agents. This approach failed on several levels. First, it was impossible to keep up with the demand. Each time an agent or employee had a problem, the company dispatched a technician. The number of problems quickly outstripped the company's ability to respond. Agents and employees were left waiting in an increasingly longer support queue. Second, the cost to maintain the approach was astronomical. Not only was the company responsible for "break and fix" for more than 3,000 machines, it also had to keep all the software applications current on all the machines. It was impossible to control all the versions of all the applications on agent computers. Third, Prudential Fox & Roach/Trident wanted to begin to strategically leverage technology to support its agents, employees, and customers. The support model undermined this corporate objective.

The business technology strategy of the company was to help their agents without requiring much from them, without requiring them to become sophisticated technology users. The strategy called for shifting control of computing resources from users to the enterprise. Reliability, security, and scalability, among other objectives, were achieved by moving all the applications to servers accessible 24/7 by highly mobile agents.

These days everyone's worried about the future role that technology will play in business, especially given outsourcing trends, trends toward technology commoditization, and the growing perception that technology does not create competitive advantage. This case is interesting because it was initially driven by a desire to cut costs and improve service, but ended up enabling agents to do more deals faster and therefore generate more revenue for themselves and the real estate broker. Strategic impact? Absolutely. Operationally efficient? Without question. The solution also integrated an old idea—centralized applications control—with new delivery technology—the Internet. The whole movement toward distributed computing in the 1990s and the early twenty-first century is evolving toward 1980s concepts—but with a couple of important twists: mobility and ubiquity, both courtesy of the Web.

The business technology strategy here was driven by operational and strategic considerations, an objective assessment of the user population, the exploitation of reliable access technology, and a willingness to think a little outside the box, or at least a little like we used to think.

The Consumer's Internet: Thin Clients and Fat Hosts for Everyone

It's All There

As I said in Chapter 5, the World Wide Web is all-inclusive. There's not much one cannot find, analyze, or purchase on the Web. The past ten years has seen the evolution of the Web from a passive repository of information to a proactive pusher of content and a ubiquitous enabler of transactions. Educational curricula, music, films, surveys, customer service portals, travel planning, job placement boards, and even personal matchmaking services are all on the Web. For some, the Web is woven so deeply into the fabric of their lives that it's impossible for them to imagine a disconnected world.

Thin Access

This argues that the Internet is the ultimate virtual server and all that anyone needs to access its content and transaction capabilities is a very thin, throwaway client. The argument obviously is that we should focus much more on the virtual server than on the device used to access it. In fact, given communications technologies and trends, it makes sense to invest in the "host" much more than the "client." There's also the digital divide issue: the cheaper the access device, the more people can participate in the digital consumer revolution.

Let's look at several trends that point to why this approach makes sense.

First and foremost, network access is almost ubiquitous today: we use desktops, laptops, PDAs, thin clients, and a host of multifunctional converged devices—such as integrated pagers, cell phones, and PDAs—to access local area networks, wide area networks, virtual private networks, the Internet, and hosted applications on these networks, as well as applications that run locally on these devices. The networks work.

The cost to acquire, install, and support the devices, however, is out of control. Industry analysts, for example, report that the annual support cost for a single wireless PDA is nearly $4,500 per employee, per year.

Small, cheap, reliable devices that rely on always-on consumer networks make sense. Shifting computing power from desktops and laptops to professionally managed servers makes sense. Moving storage from local drives to remote storage area networks makes sense. Fat clients should lose some weight—as we bulk up our already able, underutilized servers. The TCO—not to mention the ROI—of skinny client/fat server architectures is compelling.

The Device

One way to approach this is to begin with what the ideal converged device might look like and then strip it down to make it as thin and cost-effective as possible—while still allowing it to be functional. Some of the characteristics that "fat clients" now deploy (and under development) include:

- Small (pocketable; about the size of a larger PDA on the market today) with as large a screen as possible within the given form factor
- Touch screen
- Expandable memory
- GSM or CDMA cellular phone service with broadband (EV-DO or EDGE)
- Address/phonebook
- Mp3 playback (via broadband or memory)
- Video playback (via broadband or memory)
- Web browsing with full Java support
- Popular OS allowing a wide range of programs (PalmOS or Win Mobile)
- Camera with video capabilities
- GPS with full mapping capabilities
- Bluetooth (file transfer, keyboard, headset, etc. compatibility)
- Wi-Fi

The likely initial cost for such devices is in the $500 to $700 range. Over time, we can certainly expect the costs to drop, but the ongoing maintenance and replacement costs for such powerful devices will remain substantial. There will also be "feature wars," which will result in high-end devices whose prices will always be initially set high.

But what if there was another way to exploit all that content and transaction processing capability? What if we could develop devices so thin and cheap that everyone could afford one? Here are some of the characteristics such devices might have:

- Even smaller form factor (comfortably pocketable; about the size of a non-flip mobile phone), as large a screen as possible in that form factor
- Touch screen
- GSM or CDMA mobile phone service with Internet, ideally with broadband
- Web browsing with full Java (or any open standard) support that makes e-mail client, word processor, audio/video playback, and the like available without installing applications, which can be accessed directly from the Web

Wide area wireless network technologies, such as WiMAX, have the potential to drastically reduce the price of such devices. With WiMAX, companies could blanket entire cities with WiFi-like broadband Internet service. This would not only enhance the always-on nature of thin Internet access devices, but potentially could render the entire mobile phone industry obsolete due to voice-over-IP (VoIP) services.

We estimate that over time the cost for ultrathin devices will be less than $100. We would expect that these thin Web clients would literally become throwaways, thus eliminating completely the break-and-fix/replacement cycle that plagues so many IT shops and frustrates so many not-so-technology-savvy consumers. The price point would also make the clients affordable to just about everyone.

The Business Model

There are several models here—the model of how the Web should work, the technology that powers it, and the business model that determines how people make money—the lifeblood of all consumer technology models.

The Internet is a passport to endless communications, content, and transactions. There's great appeal in stepping back from managing any aspect of the communications infrastructure or content management on fat devices that require their own substantial care and feeding. When the industry first started thinking about thin, everyone understood the network and transaction processing implications of thin client architecture. In those days, there was a lot of uncertainty about just how to power the transactions that a 24/7 network would deliver. But more recently, architectures have developed that suggest just how a thin client/fat host might work. New service-oriented architectures (SOAs) will make it possible for transaction power—and flexibility—to reside on distributed servers capable of communicating and fabricating transactions at a moment's notice. SOA combined with AJAX (asynchronous JavaScript and XML) will make it possible for consumers to use incredibly skinny devices to accomplish all sorts of Web-based activities. What this all means in practice is that our ability to extend distributed computing is growing dramatically and that new architectures will make it possible to imagine all sorts of seamless, instant communications from all sorts of devices—including ultrathin ones.

How will people make money in a thin client/fat host world?

Needless to say, money will be made building the devices and supercharging the browsers necessary to exploit new SOA and AJAX capabilities. But most of the money will be made by the utility model suggested by thin client/fat host Web computing. Users will pay for what they use, as they use it; they will not pay for subscriptions or the equivalent of enterprise licenses that may or may not be used enough to justify the initial and ongoing fees. The model suggested here is similar to the utility computing model that many companies believe will define how technology is acquired and deployed in the not-too-distant future. "Paying by the drink" is one of the mantras of the utility computing movement, a mantra that many believe will extend to the consumer market where there's already lots of precedents for its acceptance and success.

Fat hosts will blanket services over one another, like enabling a consumer to watch his or her cable television feed on their thin device (see www.slingmedia. com). Fat hosts that provide services as such have the potential to revolutionize the cable and satellite TV industry. These companies will eventually abandon their existing distribution models in favor of distributing their services through the Internet.

The proliferation of wide area wireless networks will also force the mobile phone companies to alter their distribution models. With a technology like WiMAX built into inexpensive thin clients, consumers will no longer need to be connected to anything besides the Internet as all other services become blanketed over it. If only one primary technology manifests itself, these companies will simply become wireless Internet service providers, with each a different means for users to connect to the same network.

Universal Web access can be facilitated by the use of the thinnest possible clients. As part of the utility computing model, these clients can distribute the Web's content to just about everyone. Many of the problems we've encountered deploying and supporting ever increasingly fat clients would literally disappear in this model. The pricey "feature wars" that now dominate the access device market would shift to software hosted on ever increasingly capable servers—not on the devices everyone is now expected to upgrade on a regular basis.

Commercializing Information Technology: A Four-Step Methodology

The methodology we've developed for assessing the commercial potential of specific technologies involves four steps to develop a plan for the exploitation of alternative technology opportunities. Each step has its own set of tasks and involves:

- Technology trends analysis
- Market identification and business case development
- Strategic planning
- Execution

Step 1: Technology Trends Analyses

Technology trends analysis serves as the first step in identifying high-potential commercializable technology. We conduct quarterly technology trends analyses through a proprietary forecasting methodology based on the quantitative analysis of published content. Scans of hundreds of sources yield insight into the trajectory and pace of trends in several areas:

- Enterprise software
- Communications
- Architectures
- Infrastructures
- Technology services

Patterns are then assessed against an existing database of trends developed over a longer period of time. The patterns and trends are then qualitatively validated via "real" analysts and practitioners including investment banking analysts, CIOs, and CTOs.

The trends analyses provide insight into technologies likely to be adopted over the next three to five years. Given the temporal lag between technology research and development and actual go-to-market timing, we—like everyone else—seek "anticipatory" opportunities.

Some of the technologies currently under analysis include:

- Mass customization and personalization
- Automated supply chain planning and management
- SOA-driven integration and interoperability
- Real-time business analytics
- Video-on-demand (VOD) and IPTV
- Smart content understanding and management

Technologies are added—or deleted—from our list several times a year.

Step 1 activities and products include:

- Technology trends analyses:
  - Identification and ranking of specific research and development opportunities

- Details of high potential commercialization opportunities in terms of vertical or horizontal market application, definition of business need, buyer motivations/catalysts
- Mapping of opportunities for corporate adoption

Step 2: Enumeration and Development

The primary objectives of this step include a profile of both the applicable markets and economic case, as well as a confirmation of the technology itself.

Applicable Markets Profile

This exercise involves a top-down approach to defining the potential market application(s) of the technology under development. The results will ultimately answer the question of "is there in fact a market need for this technology and what is the potential size?" Deliverables of the applicable markets profile include:

■ Qualitative and quantitative value proposition for each identified application
■ Definition of buyer motivations/catalysts with regard to individual applications
■ Definition of competitive advantage, uniqueness, differentiation, or unmet market need
■ Identification and top-down sizing of potential market applications
■ Identification of barriers to entry and competition/substitute technologies in each market application
■ Preliminary pricing analyses based on both cost of production and delivery and value to the customer

Economic Case

The development of an economic case for the technology will inevitably be the foundation for the economic and delivery model (license, sale, or business creation). This exercise furthers the business case for commercialization in the form of dollars and cents. Deliverables of the economic case include:

■ Definition of the business idea in terms of capital, profit and loss, and valuation
■ Assessment of probable commercialization forms—licensing, asset sale, or business creation

- Is this technology likely to be a feature, product, or business?
■ Overview of a feasible economic model including:
  - Temporal revenue estimate based on market penetration assumptions
  - Positioning and distribution methodology, and related impact on cost structure
  - Assessment of ongoing research and development costs
■ Development of intellectual property valuation model based on varied commercialization outcomes—licensing, asset sale, business creation

Technology Confirmation

This exercise is primarily meant to define, in terms of commercialization potential, the features of the technology, operational and performance expectations, and its delivery in the marketplace. Deliverables of the technology confirmation task include:

- Full definition of the technology, including functional and technical requirements and features, and product design specifications
- Defining characteristics/metrics of both technical and operational performance
- Methodologies of delivery and integration within the commercial environment (e.g., interoperability, open architecture, industry standards, etc.)
- Identification, review, and assessment of prior art, potentially competitive or substitute technologies
- Nomination of probable early-adopter customers/beta testers
- Development of plan for and pursuit of intellectual property protection (patentability and patent enforceability)

At this stage, we implement a filter based on 14 questions that must be satisfactorily answered by the completion of Step 2 activities:

1. Is the research and development initiative on the right technology/market trends trajectory?
2. Will the product have the right infrastructure story?
3. Will the product sell clearly into budget cycles and budget lines?
4. Can this technology's impact be measured quantitatively?
5. Is this a technology that does not require fundamental changes in how people behave or major changes in organizational or corporate culture?
6. Is this a technology that represents total, end-to-end "solutions"?
7. Does this technology have multiple market applications?
8. Does this technology serve a clear horizontal and vertical strategy?
9. Does this technology solve a problem that has high industry awareness or recognition?

10. Will this technology integrate into the right technology development, marketing, and channel alliances and partnerships?
11. Is this technology in the "political sweet spot" of target buyers?
12. Does the organization possess the required human capital and domain expertise to commercialize?
13. Does there exist a likely set of early adopters within at least one identified applicable market?
14. What is this technology's persuasive products/services message—is it compelling?

Step 3: Planning

The applicable markets profile from Step 2 is transitioned here into a comprehensive go-to-market strategy. The activities of this step are divided into strategic planning and market development planning. The product of these activities—effectively a go-to-market strategy—forms the foundation for launching revenue-producing activities—an executable plan, deep market intelligence, positioning, communication strategy, and the like. This step also ensures access to quality industry input.

Strategic Planning

The strategic planning process pulls together the preliminary market work performed in Step 2 with more in-depth research and diligence into the identified applicable markets. Wherever possible, we leverage our strategic relationships within the venture and technology communities to acquire expertise for domain knowledge or functional expertise. Deliverables for the strategic planning exercise include:

- Reaffirmation of the "commercialization mission" for the technology
- SWOT/situation analysis (internal and external considerations)
- Market segmentation and prioritization
- Market positioning
- "Whole product" planning:
  - Specific target markets, sizing and growth
  - Value proposition (qualitative and quantitative)
  - Functionality overview
  - Pricing
  - Channels
  - Partners
  - Competitors
  - Messaging and positioning
  - Awareness creation and demand generation activities

- Product demonstration
- Delivery methodology—partnerships, reselling, …
- Target licensees
■ Profile of ideal licensee
  - Licensee support
  - Economics
■ Revenue—typical deal size, components of deal (license, partner administered services, hardware, maintenance, etc.)
■ Expense—development, business development and marketing, partnerships, …
■ Capital plan—in the event of commercialization award or private capital made available
■ "Voice of the market"—in-depth primary research of licensees, prospects, integrators, complementary software/hardware vendors, competitors; and secondary sources such as industry and financial analysts
  - Identification of who in the organization will buy and who will make purchase decision
  - Buyer behavior and purchasing catalysts

Market Development Planning

The market development exercise translates the strategic plan into a cohesive set of programs, plans, and priorities for commercializing the technology under development.

■ Initial market launch/beta testing—targeted identification of an early-adopter industry participant to beta launch the technology in a commercial setting
■ Marketing programs—focus on taking desired messaging and positioning to the targeted markets and prioritized customers through an integrated set of awareness creation and demand generation initiatives. This plan will encompass initiatives for all key audiences:
  - Customers/prospects
  - Partners
  - Industry analysts
  - Press
  - Potential acquirers
■ Licensing programs—outline the complete licensing process and responsibilities and describe programs needed to enable success:
  - Commercial evaluation option agreement
  - Exclusive or nonexclusive license agreement
■ Partners and channels—detailed plan to execute supporting partner and channel strategy. Activities may range from identifying targets, establish-

ing third-party relationships, taking third-party relationships to market, and partner and channel support programs.

■ Human capital plan—details the appropriate resources required to execute market development plan:
  - Headcount requirements
  - Roles and responsibilities
  - Key processes
  - Budget
■ Milestones—establishment of objectives to measure and monitor success.

Step 4: Execution and Commercialization

Initial execution of the go-to-market strategy primarily involves introduction of the product to early-adopter beta users. Data is the initial focus of Step 4—activities that surround assessing initial performance of the technology in the marketplace, obtaining customer feedback, and monitoring marketplace reactions.

Technology Assessment

The initial assessment of the technology and its acceptance/performance in the marketplace on launch is a process critical to the future success of commercialization. Often substantive revisions or alterations are precipitated from this feedback loop, resulting in a product with improved specifications, performance, delivery, and so on. An open relationship with the technology's early adopter is important in enabling:

■ Collection of beta performance statistics and adherence to specifications
■ Development of final commercial product specifications
■ Implementation of design modifications
■ Identification of performance hurdles, including scale

Customer Feedback

Customer feedback over and above the technology assessment provides valuable information for future marketing of the technology—it serves as a genuine verification of the chosen positioning and marketing approach. Deliverables include:

■ Design and administration of customer survey
■ Analysis of customer feedback on:
  - Pricing
  - Design

- Function
- Positioning
- Delivery

Monitoring the Marketplace

While competitor responses to the launch of a beta technology are unlikely, the importance of monitoring the marketplace reaction to the technology's introduction will be important in designing competitive responses, modifying the market positioning of the product and related communications, and planning future expansion into additional applicable markets. Deliverables here include:

- ◼ Survey/interviews with industry analysts
- ◼ Identification of subsequent applicable markets

Conclusion

These steps comprise a methodology for assessing the commercialization potential of specific technologies. Most of the methodology is best applied at organizations that create or market (resell) technology, though some of it applies to internal assessments that CIOs and CTOs make about the overall desirability of technologies they are planning to deploy. If the steps are taken objectively, they will generate a solid assessment of a technology's commercial potential.

Business Intelligence in the Early Twenty-First Century: Models and Mining for Dynamic Real-Time Business Optimization

Introduction

Let's anticipate where we'll all be in ten years and then try to figure out how to get there. As more and more technology becomes increasingly commoditized, and as technology continues to deliver reliable, secure and "always-on" services, the role that technology plays in the early twenty-first century is going to continue to change dramatically: 20 years ago we said it was all going to be about the data; 20 years from now it's all going to be about information and knowledge—and the "intelligence" they enable.

Candidly, the promise of "business intelligence" (BI) has outstripped the delivery of meaningful performance. We'll still be cleaning up data, migrating data, trying to keep our data secure, and worrying about database platform compatibility. But things are changing. Master data management is now more than an art form, and database architectures are becoming increasingly open. But much more importantly, we're all beginning to think less about data logistics and more about analysis.

Figure 6.3 suggests that the real action is below the line where analysis departs from storage. But what does this really mean? Figure 6.3 represents the clash between commoditization and competitive advantage. Storage technology is a commodity; analysis—when done right—is strategic.

The whole emphasis on BI is predicated on the ability to analyze data that's stored in various ways and on alternative platforms. Storage technologies enable analytical ones, but how should we think about the analytical ones now and going forward?

BI today is more descriptive than prescriptive, in spite of what the major BI vendors tell us. It's more about organizing and sorting data than planning or decision making around what the data tells us. We all talk a good game about the distinctions among data, information, and knowledge, but even that discussion is more descriptive than anything else. In other words, we do a lot of talking about BI but take relatively little action to actually make decisions based on intelligent information processing—in spite of all the dashboards we build.

So Where Are We Now?

We are in the conceptual phase of true BI. Of course there are significant software applications that enable all sorts of data analysis of manufacturing, customer, product, and transaction processes. Of course, there are major database management vendors that provide embedded and reasonably integrated data analysis tools, and there are definitely companies that run their business from analytical portals that provide insight into their operations. But there are some major problems connected with achieving this nirvana. As suggested above, there are still huge issues around the quality and location of data. Consequently, companies have to invest heavily in

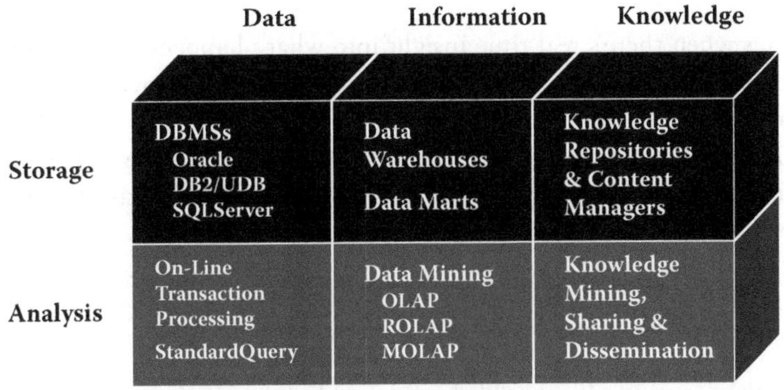

	Data	Information	Knowledge
Storage	DBMSs Oracle DB2/UDB SQLServer	Data Warehouses Data Marts	Knowledge Repositories & Content Managers
Analysis	On-Line Transaction Processing StandardQuery	Data Mining OLAP ROLAP MOLAP	Knowledge Mining, Sharing & Dissemination

Figure 6.3 Storage versus analysis.

their data infrastructure and architecture to exploit BI opportunities. This investment significantly reduces the return on BI investments and sometimes even challenges the overall cost/benefit of BI. When "benefits realization" gets muddled in the executive suite, technology investments become vulnerable. How many BI projects have failed over the past ten years? Like CRM applications, BI projects have often met with resistance, have frequently cost far more than expected, and have too frequently failed to generate any significant business impact. Is this because BI technology is bad? It's much more likely that the immaturity of our data environments is at the root of BI "failures" than the inherent weakness of either the BI concept or generally available BI tools.

Where Are We Going?

The real impact of BI is dependent on several maturing streams of innovation. Let's first describe what the perfect picture looks like in, say, 2010 or 2015. By that time business will be largely automated with a variety of if–then triggers throughout operations. Information will not be inspected by humans as much as it's assessed by software. Business rules will drive most business processes—rules that are manually changed but much more frequently triggered by the same if–then rules that will together automate key processes and transactions.

The more data, information, and knowledge brought to bear on operations and transaction processing, the closer we all get to real-time optimization, the ultimate objective of dynamic strategy and tactics. When companies know exactly what's happening with their customers, manufacturing processes, and suppliers in real time, when the same companies have elaborate rules engines in place, and when these companies automate the rules, then we'll have dynamic real-time optimization, the ultimate expression of BI.

The New BI

BI matures when there's real-time insight into what's happening, embedded judgments (rules) about what's good and bad about what's happening, and the automated and quasi-automated ability to do something about what's happening. Ultimately, all this is an optimization equation with descriptive data feeding explanatory data which, in turn, feeds prescriptive data. For BI to be truly effective this loop must be closed—and continuous.

Things to Do Now

The first thing companies should do today is build an introspective architecture capable of providing wide and deep insight into how they operate, how they make money, how they lose money, and the ability to ask what-if questions about the impact of alternative processes. There are a variety of approaches here. The emerging business process management (BPM) suites provide one mapping approach. The business rules management (BRM) crowd offers also insight into key processes. Even simpler process mapping tools—like those based on systems dynamics methods—can do the job. But the key investment principle is integration, so it makes sense to invest in one of the more robust mainstream process modeling suites rather than a one-off tool that may or may not be around in a few years.

The key here is to build an architecture that consists of objectives, methods, and tools that enables process mapping at all levels of the organization. So that we all keep the BI objective in mind, this investment is a prerequisite to real-time optimization through comprehensive "intelligence." But like all "architectures," the recommendation assumes that internal decision-making processes and the corporate culture actually want to dissect their business processes and models. The investment in process mapping is significant and if there's doubt about the value of such an undertaking, it cannot succeed—and will waste a lot of time, money, and effort in the process of its internal collapse. I mention this because like all enterprise initiatives—be they Y2K, security, privacy, CRM, ERP, or Six Sigma—the enterprise has to want to learn about itself and then change in response to what it learns.

The next thing companies should do is inspect their database platforms and architectures. If a company has multiple disparate data sets and nonstandardized database platforms, it is ill-positioned to exploit process mapping or the full range of existing or emerging BI tools. More importantly, its ability to achieve real-time optimization will be threatened. Given the consolidation in the database sector, it's also wise to stay mainstream with solutions in the Oracle, IBM, or Microsoft direction.

Third, companies should be modeling the descriptive and prescriptive questions and answers they'd like their BI environment to handle. Such Q&A exercises constitute BI requirements gathering and should position companies to think about BI today and BI tomorrow when BI will aspire to real-time optimization of business processes and overall business models. The models should yield a set of rules about what-should-happen-when, rules that represent optimal corporate performance. Today, these rules are captured in rules engines that are usually integrated only in a limited way, but tomorrow will be fully integrated and dynamic. The key to modeling today is to apply white board thinking to what optimization is as opposed to thinking constrained by what we know the current capabilities look like.

Fourth, companies should be piloting existing BI tools for their ability to support descriptive and prescriptive questions and answers. Huge investments are probably not advisable at this point for most companies, especially if they are still struggling with platform standardization and larger data quality, security, or access issues. But as these issues disappear, companies should strive to identify the processes, methods, and tools most likely to satisfy their expected BI requirements, which, again, will all tilt toward real-time optimization.

Finally, companies should try to influence the major BI vendors. Although this is tough for smaller companies to accomplish, the larger enterprises—especially if they band together—can have considerable influence on the features and connectivity of next-generation BI tools. More importantly, large enterprises can influence the way BI vendors think about real-time optimization, which results from synergy among BI tools, BPM tools, rules engines, and the processes necessary to support the ongoing search for optimal performance. Most BI vendors think in terms of evolutionary changes to their functional repertoires—not whole new symphonies. It may be that the larger enterprises should play the role of maestro in the quest for real-time optimization.

Master Data Management for Business Intelligence and Customer Analytics

This section consists of three parts on data management and analysis. We'll look first at master data management (MDM), then turn to BI, and wrap up with customer analytics. The order of these parts is important. MDM is the analytical infrastructure to which we paid too little attention for years. BI is the general approach we should take to data and information utilization and optimization, and customer analytics is a special instance of BI enabled by MDM.

Master Data Management (and Data Warehousing)

Wikipedia describes MDM:

> *Master Data Management* (*MDM*), also known as Reference Data Management, is a discipline in information technology (IT) that focuses on the management of reference or master data that is shared by several disparate IT systems and groups. MDM is required to warrant consistent computing between diverse system architectures and business functions.

> Large companies often have IT systems that are used by diverse business functions (e.g., finance, sales, R&D, etc.) and span across multiple countries. These diverse systems usually need to share key data that is relevant to the parent company (e.g., products, customers, and suppliers). It is critical for the company to consistently use these shared data elements through various IT systems.

> MDM also becomes important when two or more companies want to share data across corporate boundaries. In this case, MDM becomes

an industry issue such as is the case with the finance industry and the required STP (Straight Through Processing) or T+1.

In the Y computing model, MDM is one of three computing types: OLTP transactional computing (typically ERP), DSS (Decision Support Systems), and MDM. These types range from operational reporting to EIS (Executive Information Systems). Master data management is not only required to coordinate different ERP systems, but also necessary to supply metadata for aggregating and integrating transactional data.

The same source describes data warehousing (DW):

A data warehouse is the main repository of the organization's historical data, its corporate memory. For example, an organization would use the information that's stored in its data warehouse to find out what day of the week they sold the most widgets in May 1992, or how employee sick leave the week before Christmas differed between California and Quebec from 2001–2005. In other words, the data warehouse contains the raw material for management's decision support system. The critical factor leading to the use of a data warehouse is that a data analyst can perform complex queries and analysis (such as data mining) on the information without slowing down the operational systems.

While operational systems are optimized for simplicity and speed of modification (online transaction processing, or OLTP) through heavy use of database normalization and an entity-relationship model, the data warehouse is optimized for reporting and analysis (online analytical processing, or OLAP). Frequently data-in-data warehouses is heavily denormalized, summarized or stored in a dimension-based model, but this is not always required to achieve acceptable query response times.

MDM and DW are siblings separated by a decade or two. The requirement was always there—even more so in the middle years of computing and databases. Why "middle years"? In the early days of computing, data and applications were integrated. Then we moved to large database management platforms, mostly from companies like Sybase, Informix, IBM, and Oracle. When distributed computing hit the industry in the late 1980s, we started to decentralize data and applications across suites of vertical software applications that were increasingly nonstandardized. Data warehouses and data marts began to appear during this time as a way to integrate, deliver, and standardize data in the enterprise.

Fast forward a decade or so and we now find ourselves in the world of increasing applications standardization and data consolidation as more and more legacy applications are retired. MDM is emerging as the industry's newest data/information/knowledge discipline inside and outside of the firewall. MDM is now strategic, not just operational. If companies want to expand their supply chains, for example, they need to invest in shared master data.

MDM Approaches

Consistency is the ultimate objective of MDM. In some organizations, there are multiple sources of data that have to be integrated to enable analyses and decision making. The data itself speaks to customers, suppliers, employees, and other corporate partners. It may be tied to specific applications or spread across existing data warehouses and data marts.

For years we have focused on data and applications integration. Many of the approaches we've used to achieve integration persist today, like enterprise application integration (EAI), extraction, transformation, and loading (ETL), and, more recently, Web services and SOA technologies that allow data to be wrapped in quasi-standardized interfaces. MDM (and its supporting technologies) usually involve some form of data consolidation where data from multiple sources ends up in a single place; the propagation of data that facilitates data movement; and the federation of data that enables one view of all the data and information that an organization needs to integrate and analyze.

Most companies use multiple techniques to achieve MDM. In other words, there are a variety of tools and techniques that companies use to identify, integrate, manage, and "open" their data stores for analysis and decision making. The key is to settle on a set of methods, tools, and techniques that work for your company and then standardize on the overall MDM process. Some of these tools, techniques, and methods—ETL, EAI, and even content management (CM)—are sometimes grown in-house, but most often are commercial tools, techniques, and methods that have been used for some time in an organization. Some of the more sophisticated approaches require synchronization with source data so that updates flow in both directions. Others are more passive, where data is extracted and then analyzed, but there's no change in the source data stores.

MDM Governance

As with all important business technology initiatives, MDM requires discipline that occurs within a larger governance framework. The governance around MDM should be defined, discussed, and documented. What are the objectives? What tools will be used? Who owns the data stores? How will integrated data be maintained? What is the approach to federation and propagation? The answers to these kinds of questions will define an MDM governance strategy. But in addition to methods, tools, and techniques, MDM governance should embody the overall philosophy around data integration.

MDM and Business Intelligence

Wikipedia describes business intelligence:

> *Business intelligence (BI)* refers to applications and technologies that are used to gather, provide access to, and analyze data and information about their company operations. Business intelligence systems can help companies have a more comprehensive knowledge of the factors affecting their business, such as metrics on sales, production, and internal operations; and they can help companies to make better business decisions.
>
> Business intelligence applications and technologies can help companies analyze changing trends in market share, changes in customer behavior and spending patterns, customers' preferences, company capabilities, and market conditions. Business intelligence can be used to help analysts and managers determine which adjustments are most likely to respond to changing trends.
>
> In the competitive customer-service sector, companies need to have accurate, up-to-date information on customer preferences, so that the company can quickly adapt to their changing demands. Business intelligence enables companies to gather information on the trends in the marketplace and come up with innovative products or services in anticipation of customer's changing demands. Business intelligence applications can also help managers to be better informed about actions that a company's competitors are taking. As well, BI can help companies share selected strategic information with business partners. For example, some businesses use BI systems to share information with their suppliers (e.g., inventory levels, performance metrics, and other supply chain data).

BI—like MDM—is part technology, part governance, and part philosophy. It cannot be emphasized more how important philosophy is to the exploitation of MDM, BI, and customer analytics. We should no longer have to learn that process investments should precede technology investments, but many companies still ignore this lesson. Investments need to be made in both process and technology for BI to be effective. There needs to be a commitment to making data accessible and therefore to investments that will ready the data and information infrastructure for analysis. Commitments to MDM and BI are often shallow; companies that want to upgrade their BI capabilities must invest in MDM, BI, governance, infrastructure, and architecture. There are no shortcuts here.

Why BI? Ultimately, BI fuels analysis and monitoring. Analysis includes insight into internal and external operations and transactions. BI tools and techniques enable a variety of tactical and operational analyses including—among others:

- The analysis of large and small quantities of data
- The ability to slice and dice data like sales, customer service, production, and distribution
- The ability to analyze and present data across vertical industries

The internal and external distinction, and the distinction between operational and strategic applications, is important to BI planning and execution—as Figure 6.4 suggests.

BI should be an all-encompassing strategy. Internal/operational foci include research and development, network efficiency, security, applications management, and overall operational performance of the infrastructure. Internal/strategic foci include business process management, business activity monitoring, process reengineering, strategic performance management, and even competitor intelligence. External/operational foci include supply chain planning and management, distribution, sales channel effectiveness, and sales and production alliance performance.

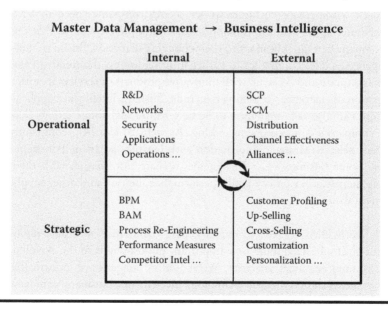

Figure 6.4   Internal/external/operational/strategic BI built on MDM.

External/strategic foci include customer profiling, up-selling and cross-selling performance, customization, and personalization. There are all sorts of methods, tools, and techniques out there to help you achieve these BI objectives, but remember—again—that BI is as much a philosophy-to-process as it is a technology. Without a commitment to analytical processes, BI investments will not return very much.

The ultimate impact of BI is dependent on several maturing streams of innovation. So let's describe what the perfect picture looks like in, say, 2010 or 2015. By that time, business will be largely automated with a variety of if–then triggers throughout operations. Information will not be inspected by humans as much as it's assessed by software. Business rules will drive most business processes—rules that are manually changed but much more frequently triggered by the same if–then rules that will together automate key processes and transactions. The more data, information, and knowledge are brought to bear on operations and transaction processing, the closer we all get to real-time optimization, the ultimate objective of dynamic strategy and tactics. When companies know exactly what's happening with their customers, manufacturing processes and suppliers in real time, when the same companies have elaborate rules engines in place, and when these companies automate the rules, then we'll have dynamic real-time optimization, the ultimate expression of BI.

BI matures when there's real-time insight into what's happening, embedded judgments (rules) about what's good and bad about what's happening, and the automated and quasi-automated ability to do something about what's happening. Ultimately, all this is an optimization equation with descriptive data feeding explanatory data that, in turn, feeds prescriptive data. For BI to be truly effective, the loop in Figure 6.4 must be closed—and continuous.

"BI 2.0" is the trajectory of the end game—though the end game may well require BI 3.0 for its actualization. The industry is galvanizing around BI 2.0 as the ultimate BI vision. What this means is that BI has finally gotten some major league buzz—which is not to say that its capabilities have developed dramatically from where they were last year or the year before.

MDM for Business Intelligence to Customer Analytics

As we turn our attention to customer analytics (Figure 6.5), BI receives an important mission—perhaps its most important mission. BI-for-customer-analytics means several things. It assumes that the explicit goal of the BI investment is wider and deeper information on customers defined in terms of their contributions to the business. This means identifying customers that are profitable, unprofitable, easy to deal with, hard to deal with, positioned to up-sell, positioned to cross-sell, part of the larger supply chain, not part of the supply chain, eBusiness customers, prospective eBusiness customers, customers unlikely to conduct eBusiness, and customers whose life cycle can be projected and optimized. It also means that

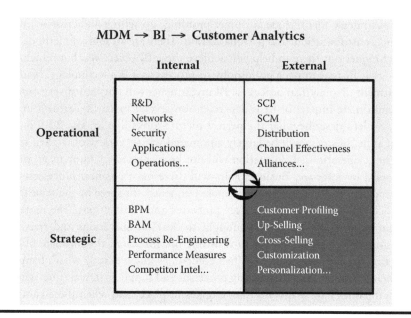

MDM → BI → Customer Analytics

	Internal	**External**
Operational	R&D Networks Security Applications Operations...	SCP SCM Distribution Channel Effectiveness Alliances...
Strategic	BPM BAM Process Re-Engineering Performance Measures Competitor Intel...	Customer Profiling Up-Selling Cross-Selling Customization Personalization...

Figure 6.5   BI built on MDM focused on CA.

additional customers can be found through inferential modeling of what makes customers buy your products and services. It also assumes that investments will be made in MDM and BI to permit robust customer analytics.

MDM + BI = Customer Analytics

Wikipedia describes customer analytics (CA) and CRM along these lines:

Active: A centralized database for storing data, which can be used to automate business processes and common tasks.

Operational: The automation or support of customer processes involving sales or service representatives.

Collaborative: Direct communication with customers not involving sales or service representatives ("self service").

Analytical: The analysis of customer data for a broad range of purposes.

Operational (analytics) provides support to "front office" business processes, including sales, marketing and service. Each interaction with a customer is generally added to a customer's contact history, and staff can retrieve information on customers from the database as necessary.

Focus on customers value is key to a successful CRM strategy. Different customers have to be treated differently. Variables like customers ranking, actual value, and potential value are strategy drivers.

Collaborative (analytics) covers the direct interaction with customers. This can include a variety of channels, such as Internet, e-mail, automated phone/interactive voice response (IVR). It can generally be equated with "self service." The objectives can be broad, including cost reduction and service improvements. Many organizations are searching for new ways to use customer intimacy to gain and retain a competitive advantage. Collaborative (analytics) provides a comprehensive view of the customer, with various departments pooling customer data from different sales and communication channels. Collaborative (analytics) also includes Partner Relationship Management (PRM), which enables organizations to manage their relationships with partners (consultants, resellers, and distributors), and potentially the customers of those partners.

Analytical (customer analytics) inspects customer data for a variety of purposes including: design and execution of targeted marketing campaigns to optimize marketing effectiveness; design and execution of specific customer campaigns, including customer acquisition, cross-selling, up-selling, retention; analysis of customer behavior to aid product and service decision making (e.g., pricing, new product development, etc.); management decisions, e.g., financial forecasting and customer profitability analysis; risk assessment and fraud detector for credit card transactions. Analytical CRM generally makes heavy use of predictive analytics.

Several commercial software packages are available that vary in their approach to (what is generally known as) CRM. However, CRM is not just a technology, but rather a holistic approach to an organization's philosophy in dealing with its customers. This includes policies and processes, front-of-house customer service, employee training, marketing, and systems and information management. CRM therefore also needs to consider broader organizational requirements.

All these investments in MDM, BI, CA, and CRM should be purposeful. In fact, investments in MDM and BI should be made after a CA/CRM strategy is developed. Once this strategy is developed, then a MDM/BI investment map should be developed.

This kind of reverse applications engineering should drive investments in data and analysis. The list of CA/CRM strategic and operational objectives should include the ability to:

- Identify and integrate customer data across applications and lines of business
- Securely store master and redundant copies of all customer data
- Profile customer behavior over time with patterns and trends
- Cross-sell across business units and products and services
- Up-sell existing customers with additional and more profitable products and services
- Develop customer acquisition and retention campaigns
- "Touch" customers physically and digitally based on analysis and receipt of preferences
- Build whole customer management and customer life cycles that can be monetized over time
- Customize and personalize products and services
- Develop financial models of individual and classes of customers that yield specific cash flow forecasts, cost management strategies, and overall revenue/profitability pictures for each customer and class of customer

These objectives suggest the kind of data necessary to optimize customer monetization.

What else?

- Empirical metrics for each of these objectives should be developed to provide evidence for effectiveness, trends, profiling, and the like. It's essential to understand what's accurate and inaccurate and what's working and what's failing.
- Alternative analytical methodologies should be leveraged on to the data. For example, there are several ways to forecast customer behavior based on techniques like multiple regression analysis all the way to the use of Bayes theorem of conditional probabilities. It's important to note the different forecasts that different methods generate and understand the differences among them. Much more importantly, alternative methods should be used to answer key questions and to provide some normalizing of the results.
- Reporting should be easy, flexible, and in the right form. While "content" is great, "form" is just as important to decision makers who must decide what to do—and not do—with their customers. Dashboards and similar easy-to-use, customized views of customer data and activity are absolutely essential to effective MDM/BI/CA/CRM. The data also needs to be queryable supporting real-time "what-if" analyses. This is another capability that should be reverse-engineered back to MDM and BI investments.

Conclusion

Serious CA/CRM capabilities are enabled by the right investments in MDM and BI. The overall message here is to pursue a holistic data/analysis strategy that begins with strategic and operational objectives that enable specific customer planning, servicing, and optimization. Investments in MDM and BI should be driven by these objectives—which should not include only CA/CRM. Other data/analysis objectives should be included as well, such as supply chain, cost management, manufacturing, distribution, and even finance objectives. In other words, all of us should develop overarching data/analysis strategies that should drive our MDM and BI investments not just from time to time but continuously. As our technology infrastructures become more and more sophisticated it should become challenged to solve real problems at the strategic and operational edge of corporate decision making.

Strategies and Tactics around "New": Time for a Reality Check

It's safe to say that our invention → innovation → commercialization process is far from perfect. In fact, there are too many examples of how the invention/innovation/commercialization value chain has betrayed those who have invented new digital technology, examples of how the values of those inventions were actually diluted across the segments of the value chain. What comes to mind? How about the many technology inventions that came from Xerox's Palo Alto Research Center (PARC) that were commercialized by others? How about the Defense Advanced Research Projects Agency's (DARPA) inventions in artificial intelligence, simulators, and communications standards (like TCP/IP) that were commercialized by U.S. and non-U.S. companies?

Some U.S. companies like Procter & Gamble (P&G) have made innovation and implementation core competencies, though here too we see companies distributing both the innovation and implementation processes globally through the outsourcing of R&D, manufacturing, distribution, and sales. U.S. government investment in innovation is also declining, exacerbating the U.S. ability to exploit all phases of the technology value chain.

The Invention/Innovation/Commercialization Value Chain

There are major distinctions among invention, innovation, and commercialization and the investments necessary to generate a return on those investments. There are opportunities on both ends of the value chain.

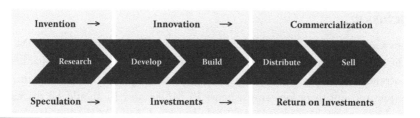

Figure 6.6   The value chain.

Figure 6.6 suggests that there are three distinct segments of the value chain comprising invention, innovation, and commercialization.

Innovation builds on invention on its way to commercialization. It involves the development and construction of a product or a service. This segment includes prototyping and pilot applications. The purpose of innovation is to calibrate just how solid the inventive foundation on which the product or service is built really is. Real money is spent here to develop a product or service and prepare it for the marketplace. It's important to note that the invention-to-innovation process is not always owned or managed by the same company. In fact, this is where major interruptions in the value chain often occur. Some companies, arguably like Microsoft, are as good (or better) at innovating as they are at inventing. Cisco *acquires* a lot of its inventions from which it innovates new products and services. Some companies are better at innovation than they are at invention—and vice versa. The skill sets are different and often distributed across several companies, consultants, and even IP lawyers. Prototyping *is* fundamentally different from manufacturing.

Other skill sets are required to fully commercialize technology. The third segment of the value chain requires effective distribution, sales, and support. Some companies are better at packaging products than they are at innovating them, just as some companies are better at sales than they are at marketing. Commercialization should be the end result of successful innovation, and successful commercialization results in a solid ROI.

Best Practice Reality Check

We know that some companies are good at invention but relatively poor at commercialization. We know that some companies are able to monetize most of the value chain. What do the most successful companies do? What don't they do? How have best practices changed over time? What should they look like in the early twenty-first century in an increasingly competitive global marketplace? How does your company optimize the invention → innovation → commercialization process? Are you good at this, or do you struggle? Where is your expertise, your core competency?

What are the processes and organizational structures that optimize the value chain from invention to commercialization? What are the processes that support research, development, manufacturing, distribution, and sales? What has worked well for you in the past and how has the process has changed over time? For example, offshore R&D outsourcing was almost nonexistent in the 1980s, but has grown considerably since then. Is this the way you should seed invention? What about innovation? Has your company perfected "fail fast/fail cheap" prototyping? Are you relying more and more on offshore innovation? The overall objective of your reality check is to determine how the value chain best serves—or undermines—your organization.

Your primary objective here is to outline a series of steps that can be taken in the invention/innovation/commercialization process that will result in significant ROI. Cost, risk, and impact should all be considered. For example, one of the reasons U.S. companies have outsourced some if not all of their R&D is because labor rates for PhD-level technologists are significantly lower offshore. Another reason is the lack of skills (due to confused government policies around student visas and educational support of science and technology curricula) available to companies that need specific technological expertise. Here are three steps you might take to determine where your expertise lies today (and should lie tomorrow):

1. **Describe, Profile, and Measure Invention:** Collect some data about invention methods and processes that have dominated the U.S. invention process. Assess your invention quotient. Determine if it's where it should be and how—if you determine you need a higher quotient—you can improve the situation.

2. **Describe, Profile, and Measure Innovation:** Collect data about the innovation methods and processes that have dominated the U.S. innovation process. Assess your innovation quotient. Determine if it's where it should be and how—if you determine you need a higher quotient—you can improve the situation.

3. **Describe, Profile, and Measure Commercialization:** Collect data about commercialization methods and processes that have dominated the U.S. commercialization process. Assess your commercialization quotient. Determine if it's where it should be and how—if you determine you need a higher quotient—you can improve the situation.

Steps 1, 2, and 3 will reveal the output shown in Figure 6.7.

These steps will reveal the extent to which the value chain is broken, revealing trends and examples that will help us understand the importance of holistic invention/innovation/commercialization. Figure 6.8 suggests that our perspective here will be on the entire invention/innovation/commercialization value chain and how the value chain has—or has not—yielded adequate ROI.

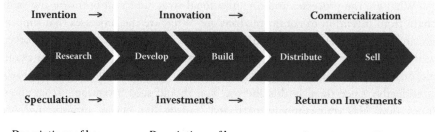

Descriptions of how successful & unsuccessful companies inventnew digital technologies & Services; profiling o finvention methods, tools & techniques; mapping of themethods, tools & techniques over time; internal assessments about your company's capabilities...	Descriptions of how successful & unsuccessful companies innovate new digital products & services; profiling of innovation methods, tools & techniques; mapping of the methods, tools & techniques over time; internal assessments about your company's capabilities...	Descriptions of how successful & unsuccessful companies commercialize new digital products & services; profilingof commercialization methods, tools & techniques; mapping of the methods, tools & techniques over time; internal assessments about your company's capabilities...

Figure 6.7   Output from Steps 1, 2, and 3.

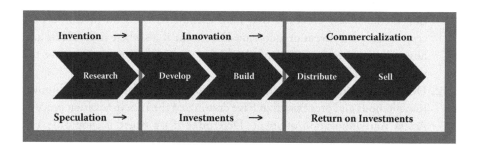

Descriptions of how companies optimize the value chain from invention to innovation to commercialization; profiling of the best practices for full optimization of the value chain; internal assessments about your company's capabilities ...

Figure 6.8   Step 4.

Conclusion

The pressure to invent, innovate, and commercialize technology has never been greater. Because a huge amount of IT has become commoditized, there's renewed emphasis on "new." Thinking about "new" through the three lenses of invention, innovation, and commercialization might help identify your core competencies today and get you to think about what they should be tomorrow. Once they're identified, then you can go about the business of organizing and funding the process.

It's also important to appreciate the importance of invention, innovation, and commercialization as a source of national wealth creation. The U.S. government has recently made funding decisions that do not support the invention and innovation process in digital technology. Funding has been cut in some of the most productive agencies due to political biases, not national interests. Especially disconcerting is the development of physical R&D centers outside of the United States by U.S. companies that could otherwise fund U.S.-based invention and innovation. Although labor rates have certainly contributed to the desire to outsource R&D, there are other motivations as well. Some U.S. companies are committed to developing footholds across the globe as a way of hedging their manufacturing and distribution bets. Others believe that creativity may in fact be regional; still others think that given the long-term decline in computer science, electrical engineering, and management information systems majors in U.S. colleges and universities, they better invest where the number of professionals in the technical fields is increasing. Whatever the reasoning, too many U.S. companies are hedging too many invention/innovation bets.

Other countries have, perhaps in response to U.S. invention/innovation lethargy and miscalculations, increased their support of digital technology R&D. They have also encouraged students to major in digital technology of one kind or another.

The decisions that nations make about technology invention and innovation are as important—sometimes much more so—as the decisions that companies make. Given the importance of government support, it might make sense to check into what your government is really doing to fuel the invention and innovation process.

Profiling Your Strategic Technology Alliances

This section suggests you take a hard look at your strategic technology alliances. How many do you have? Are they productive? How do you decide which ones to pursue—and which ones to terminate? Some of the alliances you may have include:

- Channel alliances to sell your hardware, software, or services
- Manufacturing alliances to produce hardware components and finished products
- Outsourcing alliances to develop, test, and support software and your infrastructure
- Outsourcing alliances to support your infrastructure
- Marketing alliances to advertise, sell, and cross-sell your products and services

■ R&D alliances to offset some of your internal research costs …

There are hundreds of possibilities. The key is to understand them in the context of your core competencies, profitability, and growth. Is it time to step back and assess your alliances? Let's start with some definitions.

Definitions

Wikipedia describes a strategic alliance as:

> A formal relationship formed between two or more parties to pursue a set of agreed upon goals or to meet a critical business need while remaining independent organizations. Partners may provide the strategic alliance with resources such as products, distribution channels, manufacturing capability, project funding, capital equipment, knowledge, expertise, or intellectual property. The alliance is a cooperation or collaboration which aims for a synergy where each partner hopes that the benefits from the alliance will be greater than those from individual efforts. The alliance often involves technology transfer (access to knowledge and expertise), economic specialization, shared expenses and shared risk.

Benefits of Strategic Alliances

Strategic alliances often bring partners the following benefits:

1. Access to their partner's distribution channels and international market presence
2. Access to their partner's products, technology, and intellectual property
3. Access to partner's capital
4. New markets for their products and services or new products for their customers
5. Increased brand awareness through partner's channels
6. Reduced product development time and faster-to-market products
7. Reduced R&D costs and risks
8. Rapidly achieve scale, critical mass and momentum (Economies of Scale—bigger is better)
9. Establish technological standards for the industry and early products that meet the standards
10. By-product utilization
11. Management skills

Types of Strategic Alliances

Various terms have been used to describe forms of strategic partnering. These include "international coalitions," "strategic networks" and, most commonly, "strategic alliances." Definitions are equally varied. An alliance may be seen as the "joining of forces and resources, for a specified or indefinite period, to achieve a common objective."

Stages of Alliance Formation

A typical strategic alliance formation process involves these steps:

1. **Strategy Development**: Strategy development involves studying the alliance's feasibility, objectives and rationale, focusing on the major issues and challenges and development of resource strategies for production, technology, and people. It requires aligning alliance objectives with the overall corporate strategy.
2. **Partner Assessment**: Partner assessment involves analyzing a potential partner's strengths and weaknesses, creating strategies for accommodating all partners' management styles, preparing appropriate partner selection criteria, understanding a partner's motives for joining the alliance, and addressing resource capability gaps that may exist for a partner.
3. **Contract Negotiation**: Contract negotiation involves determining whether all parties have realistic objectives, forming high calibre negotiating teams, defining each partner's contributions and rewards as well as protect any proprietary information, addressing termination clauses, penalties for poor performance, and highlighting the degree to which arbitration procedures are clearly stated and understood.
4. **Alliance Operation**: Alliance operation involves addressing senior management's commitment, finding the caliber of resources devoted to the alliance, linking of budgets and resources with strategic priorities, measuring and rewarding alliance performance, and assessing the performance and results of the alliance.
5. **Alliance Termination**: Alliance termination involves winding down the alliance, for instance when its objectives have been met or cannot be met, or when a partner adjusts priorities or reallocates resources elsewhere.

Risks of Strategic Alliances

Strategic alliances can lead to competition rather than cooperation, to loss of competitive knowledge, to conflicts resulting from incompatible cultures and objectives, and to reduced management control. A study of almost 900 joint ventures found that less than half were mutually agreed to have been successful by all parties.

An alliance can fail for many reasons:

1. Failure to understand and adapt to a new style of management
2. Failure to learn and understand cultural differences between the organizations
3. Lack of commitment to succeed
4. Strategic goal divergence
5. Insufficient trust

These definitions of benefits, types, stages, and risks of alliances set the stage for an analysis of your strategic alliances and especially the performance of these alliances over time.

Analysis

What does your alliance landscape look like? How many alliances do you have? A useful assessment is about profiling your relationship methodology, history, and performance over time. Are you good at alliance formulation, management, and termination? Do you have preferred forms, like joint ventures? Do you know?

You should look at the types of strategic alliances you have, their relative benefits, their risks, and how you should form, manage, and terminate alliances. You should also explore some of the more notable and controversial alliances to better understand the general alliance milieu, such as the complicated manufacturing alliances that Mattel has with China, the on-again/off-again Daimler-Chrysler alliance/merger/alliance, and the extremely-productive-then-ill-fated Dell/HP alliance, among others from the business headlines. We should analyze alliances that our companies have developed and exploited (or failed to exploit) and perhaps learn from the analysis of global alliances and the alliances that your company seeks, manages, and exits.

The proposed profiling exercise might be organized around the graphic in Figure 6.9. Note that the forms and phases of alliances should be discussed in the context of risk management and through the analysis of multiple competitor case studies. This is a practical exercise. Its purpose is to address the strengths and weaknesses of your alliances, to illustrate through case study analysis "good" and "bad"

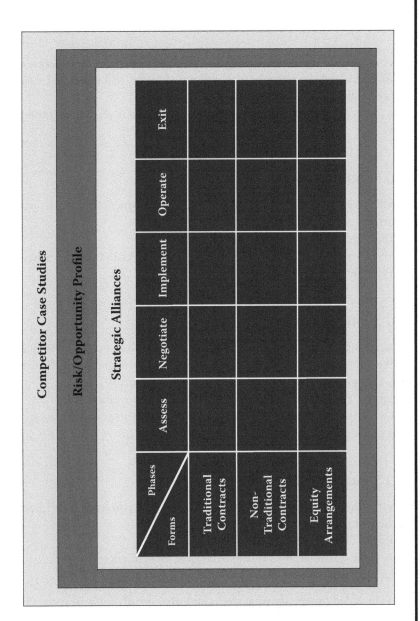

Figure 6.9 The strategic technology alliance matrix.

alliances, and, ultimately, to enable you to implement a due diligence template for optimal alliance outcomes.

Results

When you've completed the exercise, you will take away the following in terms of new ways of thinking about alliances, some things that you will know and some things you'll be able to do.

The list of ten takeaways is distributed across this "think/know/do" continuum:

What You Should **Think** …

1. That alliances are complex but potentially extremely beneficial to participating partners …
2. That there are several phases and forms of alliances …
3. That there are risks associated with every alliance, risks that must be managed throughout the entire alliance life cycle …

What You Should **Know** …

4. The overall life cycle of alliance agreements and the phases of that life cycle as well as the various formal, informal, contractual, noncontractual, equity-based, and non-equity-based forms that alliances can take …
5. The range of risk factors that surround all alliance arrangements …
6. The illustrative and exceptional cases that demonstrate the best and worst of alliance organization, management, and termination …

What You Should Be Able to **Do** …

7. Profile the best and worst alliance phases and forms you have experienced over the past ten years …
8. Identify the best alliance partners over the past decade …
9. Calculate the quantitative costs and benefits of each alliance
10. Develop a refined alliance strategy …

All this is intended to identify what works and what doesn't for your company. Strategic alliances are critically important to most companies, but many companies don't know enough about their own alliance experience. Assessing your actual performance is about making decisions as to what to initiate, continue, and terminate. As always, there will be lots of complications around these decisions, especially "political" complications, but the more empirical data brought to bear on the assessment, the better.

The world is also constantly changing. A seven-year-old alliance may or may not still make sense. Your competitors may have initiated a whole host of new creative alliances. Companies should strategize about which forms of alliances will fuel the most profitable growth in five years. The big questions about alliances are all performance based. Take a hard look at your existing alliances and dream about—and then pursue—the ones you'd really like to have.

Epilogue

The discussions we've just had were organized into six chapters:

- Perspectives
- Organization
- People
- Acquisition and measurement
- Operational effectiveness
- Strategic effectiveness

As suggested in the Preface, best practices are often confusing, redundant, and subject to all varieties of interpretation; and yet, they're often extremely useful—and practical.

Practical is the key word here. But integration must accompany best practices. As Figure 7.1 suggests, the five focus areas are all interrelated and interdependent. They work together or not at all. Some companies are great infrastructure service providers while others are better at strategic technology. Some have their organizations finely tuned while others are chaotic. Some optimize their sourcing and performance measurement process and some are hopelessly ineffective acquiring, deploying, or supporting technology. The best of the best are reasonably good in all five areas. The great ones get them all right.

The objective I suppose is excellence across the board. But it's nearly impossible to get everything right all the time.

A more detailed look at the five areas appears in Figure 7.2. The idea here is to once again show the interrelationships and interdependencies but also show some details about the big issues in each of the areas. Just like the field of business technology management, Figure 7.2 is a little optically challenged—but it tries to orient us simultaneously to the simplicity and complexity of the world in which we live.

Making matters worse is the field's volatility. Yes, business technology management is a moving target. Today's best practices are always evolving. Remember when outsourcing was the exception rather than the rule? When data centers (also known as "glass houses") ruled the world? Now we have to contend with increas-

Figure 7.1 The integrated five pieces of business technology optimization.

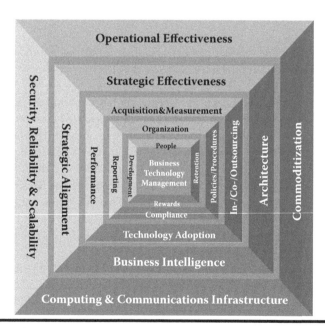

Figure 7.2 The integrated five pieces of business technology optimization.

ingly decentralized global organizations and technologies that make the standard-ization best practice harder and harder to implement. In fact, the whole notion of standardization is morphing into its own new best practice where managers must standardize technologies inside and outside the corporate firewall.

But let's not forget the objective of business technology management. Ulti-mately, all of this is about helping the business grow profitably through a mix of cost management and revenue generation best practices. Once we master these best practices, we become seamless contributors to our company's success. There's no better outcome for the twenty-first century technology professional.

Index

T - #0090 - 101024 - C0 - 234/156/20 [22] - CB - 9781420063332 - Gloss Lamination